# The Politics of Legislation
*The Rent Act 1957*

# The Politics of Legislation

The Rent Act 1957

## Malcolm Joel Barnett

Assistant Professor of Political Science at the
University of Wisconsin, Milwaukee

London School of Economics and Political Science

Weidenfeld and Nicolson 5 Winsley Street W 1

SBN 297 17834 2

Printed in Great Britain by
C. Tinling & Co. Ltd., Prescot and London

To My Parents

# Contents

# List of Tables

A*

# Foreword

In the last few years the British have been asking increasingly persistent and critical questions about the structure and powers of their government. But it is still very difficult to find out how the most powerful and venerated parts of our constitution actually work. Dr Barnett has gone to the heart of this system to ask how an Act of Parliament is made. How was a major change in policy formulated and passed into law? What parts did parliament, ministers, civil servants, local government, pressure groups and the press play in the story? He does not claim to have got the whole story, but he gives us more of it than we have had for any other recent change in domestic policy.

This book is more than a scholarly contribution to our understanding of British government. It was possible to write it because the actors in the story were prepared to talk about the workings of government with almost American frankness. It took an American to get them to do that. But the help they gave Dr Barnett offers hope that debate about the power structure in this country can become more open, more realistic and ultimately more productive.

The Rent Act of 1957 was only one piece of legislation, and unlikely to be typical of the legislative process. But it was the most heatedly and lengthily debated act of the parliament which passed it, and there have been few which provoked a more passionate desire for public and parliamentary participation in their making.

The opportunity for action was given by the political climate of the day, represented in the ministers chosen to preside over this branch of the administration. The action proposed and the motive power which drove it to a conclusion, despite rough political weather and changes of minister, came from the civil service – and particularly from one principal in the Ministry of Housing and Local Government. Weeks of parliamentary debate made little impact on the original proposals. Pressures applied by interested groups and outside experts also achieved little. Academic research workers had, at this time, no help to offer. The one pressure group which exerted a major influence was directed by an able man, recently recruited from the civil service where he had been a colleague of the officials responsible for the measure.

The civil service did its work with devotion and high technical skill. But the ideas enshrined in the Act were old ones, quite inadequate to the needs of the times; the assumptions and the information which formed the basis for the whole discussion were flimsy, or wrong; and the results proved disastrous.

It would be tempting to conclude that we need more open government in which experts play a more effective part. Dr Barnett shows that such a conclusion fails to penetrate to the central dilemmas of the system. It is because British parliaments do attempt to shape the legislation passed in their name – unlike the parliaments of some other countries whose practices we are exhorted to adopt – that the legislative process is inextricably political and largely private.

The Fulton Committee has recently urged the civil service to develop and distinguish the skills of economic and of social administration. Dr Barnett shows that higher standards of competence were needed in both these fields. But the regulation of rents, like most of the responsibilities of government, poses questions which are both economic and social – questions which cannot be wisely answered if one aspect is stressed to the exclusion of the other.

The reader must form his own conclusions about the best ways of resolving these dilemmas. But this book will show him that social reform calls for accurate and widespread knowledge of the problems to be tackled, that such knowledge must be contributed partly by people who are independent of government, and that knowledge will not be put to effective use unless government is sufficiently concerned about the human needs at stake.

Many are now asking how we can improve our administrative and legislative processes. Their answers will not help us much unless they can also find ways of ensuring that we know more, and care more, about the problems and the people these processes deal with.

D. V. DONNISON

London School of Economics
and Political Science

# Preface

This book is a modified version of my doctoral thesis, accepted by the University of London in June 1967. My study in Britain was made possible by a Leverhulme Graduate Entrance Studentship at the London School of Economics and Political Science and a Bursary from the University of London. The London School of Economics and the University of Kansas have lent facilities to enable me to transform thesis to book.

I owe a special debt to my tutors, Mr A. J. Beattie and Professor D. V. Donnison. They have given of their time, effort and resources far beyond that which any student has a right to expect. They taught, guided, assisted and encouraged me in the study of politics and the preparation both of thesis and of book.

My thanks to Professor J. A. G. Griffith, Professor Wallace Sayre and Mr D. E. Regan, who commented upon some pieces of the thesis, especially those concerned with the Ministry of Housing and Local Government. I am also grateful for the suggestions of Professor Bernard Crick, Mr R. J. Ranger and Mr M. G. Daly and for the assistance of F. Vahdat.

To my mother, my colleagues, my students and my friends, my sincere thanks for their assistance.

MALCOLM JOEL BARNETT

Passfield Hall
London, August 1968

# Acknowledgements

The author is indebted to the librarians of the British Library of Political and Economic Science, the British Museum and the House of Commons for their assistance.

The following allowed me to use their libraries and to quote from documents contained therein: the British Institute of Public Opinion; the Chartered Auctioneers' and Estate Agents' Institute; the Citizens' Advice Bureau; the Conservative Research Department; the Conservative and Unionist Central Office; the Labour Party; the London Labour Party; the Ministry of Housing and Local Government; the National Federation of Property Owners; the Royal Institution of Chartered Surveyors.

The following authors and publishers allowed me to quote from their books: Staples Press, MacGibbon and Kee Ltd and Lionel Needleman, *The Economics of Housing*; Cambridge University Press and Sir W. Ivor Jennings, *Cabinet Government*; Faber and Faber Ltd and C. H. Sisson, *The Spirit of British Administration*; Methuen and Co. Ltd and Sir Alan Herbert, *Independent Member*; Penguin Books Ltd and D. V. Donnison, *The Government of Housing*; Routledge and Kegan Paul Ltd and J. B. Cullingworth, *Housing Needs and Planning Policy*; Tavistock Publications Ltd and Sir Geoffrey Vickers, *Value Systems and Social Process*; G. Bell and Sons, Occasional Papers in Social Administration; also from *The Times*, *The Guardian* and *The Economist*.

The author acknowledges the assistance of the above with thanks.

# Abbreviations

The following abbreviations have been used in this book:

| | |
|---|---|
| Association of Land and Property Owners: | A L P |
| Association of Municipal Corporations: | A M C |
| British Institute of Public Opinion: | B I P O |
| Cambridge University Press: | C U P |
| Chartered Auctioneers' and Estate Agents' Institute: | C A E A I |
| Conservative Political Centre: | C P C |
| Conservative Research Department: | C R D |
| Conservative and Unionist Central Office: | C U C O |
| Gross Rateable Value | G R V |
| London County Council: | L C C |
| London Labour Party | L L P |
| London Trades Council: | L T C |
| Manuscripts Collection: | M S S |
| Ministry of Housing and Local Government: | M H L G |
| National Federation of Property Owners: | N F P O |
| Occasional Papers in Social Administration: | O P S A |
| Oxford University Press: | O U P |
| Parliamentary Debates: Commons: | H C Deb.5s |
| Parliamentary Debates: Lords: | H L Deb.5s |
| House of Commons, Standing Committee A, 1956–7: | 1956–7 H C S C Deb.I |
| Parliamentary Labour Party: | P L P |
| Royal Institution of Chartered Surveyors: | R I C S |
| Trade Union Congress: | T U C |

# Chronology

| | |
|---|---|
| *1953–4* | Housing Repairs and Rents Act<br>Landlord and Tenant Act (1954)<br>Achieved construction of 300,000 houses per year |
| *1955*<br>February | Mr H. Symon retired as under-secretary of Local Government Division and Mr S. Wilkinson retired as under-secretary of Housing Division at the Ministry |
| December | Mr Sandys announces to House of Commons that the government will introduce new legislation on Rent Restriction<br>Drafting had begun |
| *1956*<br>March–April | Statistical investigations by the Ministry |
| Summer | Decision of the Future Legislation Committee to allot time and Parliamentary Counsel |
| October | Mr Sandys announces proposals in a speech to the Conservative Party Conference |
| 7 November | First reading of the Bill in the Commons<br>Debate on Housing and Rents in Debate on the Address (Commons) |
| 21–2 November | Second Reading in the Commons |
| 6 December–<br>15 March 1957 | Consideration in Standing Committee A (Commons) |
| *1957*<br>January 13 | Mr Brooke becomes minister and Mr Bevins becomes parliamentary secretary of the Ministry of Housing and Local Government |

| | |
|---|---|
| 4 February | Allocation of Time (Guillotine) Resolution in the Commons |
| 26–7 March | Consideration on Report in the Commons |
| 28 March | Third Reading in the Commons |
| 16 April | Second Reading in the Lords |
| 14 May | Consideration in Committee in the Lords |
| 21 May | Consideration on Report in the Lords |
| 28 May | Third Reading in the Lords |
| 5 June | Consideration of Lords' Amendments in the Commons |
| 17 July | Royal Assent |

*Note:* The following have made changes in their name or title subsequent to the events of this book: Mr Henry Brooke is now Baron Brooke of Cumnor; Sir Anthony Eden is now Earl of Avon; Mr George Lindgren is now Baron Lindgren of Welwyn Garden City; Mr Gilbert Mitchison is now Baron Mitchison; and Dame Evelyn Sharp is now Baroness Sharp of Hornsey

# 1

# The Politics of Legislation

The importance of communication to political regulation increases with the number of participants in the system being regulated and the number in the decision-making process.* The legislative process which produced the Rent Act (1957), the case studied here, may not delineate definitive answers to the role of legislature, pressure groups, parties and government (including the government as a collectivity, ministers and civil servants). But it does reveal a breakdown in the application of knowledge to policy making. The evidence speaks for itself.

The evidence about the Rent Act takes two forms: what was and what might have been. To ask why information relevant to decision-making was lacking, why important questions of policy and application never became the focus for debate, why parties chose the paths they took, why pressure groups were effective or ineffective does not in itself suggest a remedy. But the answers reinforce the arguments made by others as to the course in which change should be directed: broadly speaking towards improved communication.

All thinking about rent restriction was conducted within a set of intellectual parameters which defied constructive thought. Housing policy and rent control in particular were considered temporary measures. All the participants thought in terms of improvisations which they proposed to carry out in ignorance of the nature and working of the housing market (the supply side); in ignorance of the character of housing demand and the economic and social changes it reflected (the demand side); and in political symbolism in which myths about landlords and tenants defied rational discussion. All rent restriction in the twentieth century had been shaped in similar constraints, but bad precedent could not aid the legislative process.

Parliament is the most thoroughly analysed section of the parts of the legislative process. The tradition from Bagehot through Jennings

* This is developed in the appendix on the legislative process. Communication is taken to mean the process or interaction by which ideas and information are made available, evaluated, and translated into policy.

and Professor Crick, with evidence on contemporary practice added by Mr Ronald Butt and the pamphleteers, provides endless suggestions for the sort of change that would make Parliament more effective. The chapter on Combat is an effort to connect what theory suggests is the purpose of Parliament with what actually occurs. What should be happening? What is happening?

Pressure groups are supposed to push their special interest, professional or venal, and to inform political participants so as to influence decisions. Yet as is shown in the chapter on Pressure Groups they had relatively little impact. A communications gap prevented effective communication by all of the groups to the parts of the legislative process where decisions were being taken. Information and ideas developed by the groups often did not reach the civil servants in the Ministry (with one exception, a group whose secretary had been a senior civil servant in the Ministry). Without a clear notion of the rationale behind the Bill, the groups were often hampered in their assistance to parliamentarians. Again, the theory of helpful or at least informative pressure group activity differed from the realities.

The theory of British party politics is rightly eschewed by the amateur, as those two collosi, Beer and McKenzie, together with their disciples, dispute. In the chapters on the Conservative and Labour parties in this study, the question is not the general nature of party but simply what party was doing in this instance. Certainly the two parties had developed distinctive policies as regards rent control. But these were often the product of circumstances and tradition rather than careful research and debate. Not even the backbench parliamentary committees were, in the end, able to exert much influence on the legislative process.*

Neither careful planning nor insight determined priorities, policies and decisions on rent restriction. Personnel changes and consequent shifts in responsibility hampered the Housing and Local Government divisions of the Ministry. The confusion as to whether rent control policy was to be shaped by Housing or Local Government divisions

---

* Mr Ronald Butt in *Power of Parliament*, Constable, London, 1967, argues quite persuasively that Parliament no longer has a meaningful role in the legislative process other than to set its scope and limits. But he insists that MPs still do have a role. One of his instances is backbench pressure, in party and standing committees, on the minister during the committee stage of the Rent Bill. Though this book treats the same evidence, the conclusion seems to be that backbench activity was not very important. In the end it is simply a question of balance.

was resolved only at the last moment. The Ministry was further hampered by the inadequacy of its research organisation and the total inability to provide relevant data in sufficient quantities and with sufficient authority. Was this inevitable?

Whether this lack of communication between civil servants, between civil servants and ministers, between Ministry and outsiders (both parliamentary and pressure groups) was inevitable leads to the attitudes outlined in the Report of the Fulton Committee on the civil service. How great was the need for professionals? Was greater openness in both executive and parliamentary consultations necessary? Should not politician and public have been better informed? Should disputes about fact and about policy have been carried out in the open? Could change strengthen the decision-making process?*

The people involved in the decisions on the Rent Bill, ministers or civil servants, parliamentary figures or publicists, were also politicians. None could avoid the purely political considerations: the response of party, Parliament and perhaps public. It is in recognition of this political essence that civil servants have remained 'amateurs'. Could professional economists or social administrators have coped better? As Professor D. V. Donnison has pointed out in his pamphlets and in *Government of Housing*, none could have handled the collection and assimilation of data worse than those involved. Evidence in this book reinforces his conclusions. Certainly in the departments dealing with social problems there is need for more awareness of the problems both in depth (e.g. greater familiarity with rent restriction forms and the complications in using them) and in scope, a greater awareness of the human problems with which government must work.

Yet it is difficult to define what specialists might have been used in drafting rent restriction legislation, for the choice is political. Was the problem economic, social or political? In the case of the Rent Act the failure was in part due to the inability of economists and social administrators to think together about the operation of the working-class housing market. Which kind of expertise should have been used at each point in the decision-making process? Given perfect communication all could have been employed. But given the necessary restriction at the time, how much communication was possible?

* The facts of the case are laid out in the chapters on the Ministry and the drafting and modification processes. These questions are raised in the Report of the Committee, *The Civil Service*, Cmnd 3638, 1968, paras. 44-7, 273-8.

In one respect anything would have been better. The minister had some conception, however limited, of what he wanted: reduction in control, more houses to let in the private sector, reduced need for council housing. Specialised civil servants might have made proposals and devised legislation that would better fulfil the minister's purpose. Or they might have pointed out more clearly the difficulties involved and urged him to think again.

The real problem, as William Plowden has pointed out in his *New Society* article,[1] is the context in which decision-making takes place. Every decision by the government is political. This is in part the consequence of Opposition, and even government backbench demands for satisfaction from the 'responsible minister', at the least hint of error. These demands may even include the minister's resignation. Ministers are naturally unwilling to allow outsiders to acquire information that may not merely force a change in a particular decision but destroy a political career. For the same reason they cannot afford, amateur as the political system forces them to be, to enter into public disputes on policy with 'expert' civil servants. Openness requires a certain tolerance by the Opposition.

Another requirement for greater openness is the elimination not merely of ministerial responsibility but civil service responsibility as well. The civil servant would have to be established – in the French fashion – free from challenge so long as he properly performs his duties. Yet the elimination of responsibility would be unacceptable to Parliament. MPs may not turn out a minister who has made a wrong decision, or had one taken in his name, but the threat is sufficient to keep both minister and civil servant alert to possible political repercussions. This hold, the very last vestige of Parliament's claim to participation in the traditional model, is the very hold that must be surrendered if Parliament is to participate effectively.

Some ministerial business is so political that it could never safely be opened to public view. This is the business of turning ideas into legislation and gaining public acceptance. The civil service recognises the special problems of 'legislation' when it brings together people of experience in legislating on a particular problem to help with each effort and provides one civil servant with what amounts to political instinct (though with minister's rather than party's survival at heart) for each team. Though thinking about policy and planning may well be crucial, the tasks of preparing a bill from a list of ideas and shepherding the bill through Parliament and public occupy a great deal of time. The other great problem for civil servants is the mass of Parliamentary questions they must deal with. These very political problems could be turned over to a parliamentary division staffed by experts in politics and public relations as well as technical experts on the problems which concerned the Ministry. 'Experts' might be given the opportunity to see this side of the Ministry's business without becoming overburdened by it.

Those civil servants outside the parliamentary division could not merely toss up ideas, as they do at present, they could stop to consider the ideas, and utilise the many resources of contemporary sciences (social and economic). They could take the time to work out all the implications and possibilities surrounding new notions.

These divisional civil servants could not escape from politics. Ideas, policy proposals, plans, even research data, are as political as the clauses of a bill. They may direct action or force action along a particular line. This was clearly recognised by the civil servants in charge of the 1957 Rent Act, who carefully did little research and did it as secretly as possible. They wanted supporting evidence for decisions taken rather than evidence that might raise new and unwanted problems. Only in a transformed political climate would greater openness be possible.

Would Parliament and public benefit? Members of Parliament, as much as the general public, are isolated from the core of the legislative process which takes place within the ministries. The clerk of the House of Commons (Sir Barnett Cocks), Professor Crick and others, in their pleas for better staff, specialist committees and better working quarters, have emphasised the difficulty which outsiders have in finding out what the administration means to do. A parliamentary division that properly prepares legislation so that time in debate can be devoted to essentials and that provides answers no less informative than those now given would be of benefit to Parliament. But the real benefit might come from greater openness between the non-parliamentary divisions and Parliament.

The Fulton Committee suggested that civil servants might be more open with the research work done preparatory to decision-making. Such research may have political consequences. Recent royal commissions have indicated that researchers can be directed to produce evidence for debate rather than for a rational consideration of alternatives. As research becomes widespread, and its results more available within the Ministry, leakage is inevitable. The leakage on rent restriction after 1957 taught the Ministry that the particular strategies on rent control should not be tried again, and that if they were to do research in the future this might better be issued under the political control of the Ministry. This cannot hurt Parliament.

As communication within the Ministry improves – it must if government is to continue effective – the views of particular civil servants concerned with problems are bound to become known. This is especially so as long as the Ministries remain dependent upon pressure groups for all sorts of information and advice. As communications improve, the argument that the civil servant cannot reveal divergency with the minister becomes less cogent.

In the discussions of the 1957 Rent Act a real advantage was held by those outsiders – especially pressure groups – who knew the lines of argument within the Ministry, whom to approach on particular topics and had the opportunity for consultation in advance of public presentation. Others were at a disadvantage as were the decision-makers who were not given the opportunity to hear alternate views. A civil service functionally organised, as Fulton suggests, and with sufficient time to listen, might well have avoided some of the blunders made on the Rent Act. The Ministry would have benefited (as it did in 1965*) from greater consultation, and the public could have been better prepared for the decisions finally taken. This could happen only if there were sufficient openness so that outsiders know where to go on each problem.

If the rules of politics could be transformed, then it would be possible to ask for presentation to Parliament and public of the facts upon which decisions are taken, and a great deal of Ministry discussion prior to the final decision. It is unlikely in the absence of changes that the politicians, amateurs by nature, will enter public debates or that civil servants would willingly participate. If changes were to take place in the political ground rules – more restraint by those outside government in criticising mistakes, release of the minister from responsibility for his civil servants, assurance to civil servants of their political independence – then the fruits of a division between parliamentary and other business might well be open to Parliament as well as government. Parliament and public, given some knowledge of the issues, could be aware of and have an opportunity to discuss and communicate with the executive about decisions while they are being made.

* On the 1965 Rent Act discussions.

The difficulty in 1956–7 was that those outside the Ministry were asked to comment in the absence of adequate information, and even in the absence of such little information as the Ministry itself possessed, upon decisions that had already been taken. And yet the forms of the legislative process required that Parliament seem to attempt to alter those decisions – an effort no longer possible in the present state of parliamentary government. By allowing Parliament (and public) to participate in these preliminary debates, MPs would be given a chance to be constructive without destroying the ultimate initiative of the government or the responsibility and propaganda opportunities of the parties in Parliament.

Taken together, the separation of parliamentary and public relations business within each Ministry, and the reforms in the career patterns of civil servants and increased openness between civil servants and outsiders (which often includes their political masters), form the basis for a strengthened legislative process. While improving the capacity of the executive, the reform would also improve the capacity of Parliament and public to assist and to judge the executive in the performance of its duties. The need for facts, a range of views on issues, and theoretical frames of reference for responsible decision-making is too obviously advantageous to be overlooked as a road to reform.

In the absence of reform, the 1957 Rent Act, as a bill, represented an amalgam rather than a synthesis of the policy requirements of the civil servants and politicians. Due to a change of ministers in midstream, a new group with somewhat different priorities and in different political circumstances had to carry the Bill through most of its parliamentary career. Further amalgamations and even less synthesis were inevitable. In this process, pressure groups, the press and communications media, indeed Parliament itself, played a relatively minor role.

The consequence of poor research, the absence of communication within the Ministry and between the Ministry and its audience, both parliamentary and public, was legislation that raised more problems than it solved. As an economic and social measure the 1957 Rent Act failed to achieve the purposes of the government or to respond to the economic and social changes still in progress. Despite all the shouting, in the end the Bill left contemporary politics unaltered.

The legislative process must be judged by its failures. Its performance on rent restriction is particularly gloomy. Without a well developed system of communications, the facts, a full appraisal of views, or an accurate analysis of the political implications, never made their way into the decision-making process. Parliament, pressure groups and parties were restricted in their impact upon legislation. The civil service, bogged down with routine parliamentary business, was unable to devote sufficient time to thinking about the needs and possible solutions for the rented housing problem. Whether, given the attitudes of the civil service towards expertise and research, it could have done so had the opportunity presented itself, is also open to question. Both internal and external communications mandated failure. The separation of preparation of bills from the substance of policy-making might induce a climate within the Ministries where more viable decisions would be taken. In a changed political climate of more openness by civil servants and by government there would be hope that Britain might escape from the ecological trap into which the legislative process on the Rent Act (1957) indicates regulation of political problems has fallen.

NOTE

1 William Plowden, 'The Failure of Peacemeal Reform', *New Society*, No. 303 (18 July 1968), pp. 82 ff.

# 2
# The Background

The Rent Act was drafted and debated in a changing and ever more complex contemporary political scene. Of particular importance was the changing context within which national policies had to be formulated, the place and composition of the cabinet and the international problems with which it had to deal. Of course, decisions were made by people. But the character and relationships between the principals significantly affected the decision-making process. To distinguish between the effect of external events and the decision-makers should help to explain the decisions in the 1957 Rent Act debates.

The British cabinet, like the president of the United States, moulds the character of politics on any given issue, at any given time. In Britain not all members of the cabinet were equally significant. The changes in the composition of the cabinet immediately preceding and during the Rent Act debates were relevant to the outcome.

The position of the cabinet, and the prime minister, depended much upon the probability of the prime minister remaining dominant. In foreign affairs Sir Anthony Eden's position was not in doubt. Mr Hugh Thomas has recounted that 'Eden dominated the cabinet more than Churchill had ever done'. One senior member of the cabinet recalled that in foreign affairs Sir Anthony's word was law. 'Thus in the unfolding crisis of Suez each decision taken by Britain was peculiarly Eden's'.[1] But this position in foreign affairs arose as much from Sir Anthony's acknowledged experience as from his position. Certainly, his general position as prime minister was not secure. He was in poor health. This is dangerous for any prime minister whose power, in part at least, depends upon the knowledge that he will be able to continue to hold office and dispense or withhold patronage. The knowledge that 'Already Eden was taking many pills' could not add to his authority.[2] Nor was his position with the party good: in January 1955 he had been criticised for 'Wanting the smack of firm government'. Mr Butler's illness and general lassitude made Sir

Anthony's position even more difficult; he had to assume, at least temporarily, general responsibility for home affairs at a time when Suez was the dominant concern. It is no part of this thesis to explain in detail the reasons for the changes Mr Macmillan made in the formation of his first cabinet. It is essential only to point out that these changes were not caused by the Rent Bill.

The period leading up to the autumn of 1956–7 began on 5 April 1955 with the resignation of Sir Winston Churchill as prime minister. The election which Sir Anthony Eden won during that month, with a majority of sixty, was devoted in large part to the rearmament debate, especially the production of nuclear weapons. With the Bevan dispute only hastily patched up, that Labour did so well was surprising. Sir Anthony was helped by the budget of Mr Butler, strictly an election budget. In the autumn it had to be supplemented by a variety of measures, such as increases in purchase taxes, cuts in housing subsidies, and checks on local authority loans. That autumn the Burgess and Maclean scandal was the chief national political issue.

But aside from the autumn budget most of the political news was made by Labour. At the start of the new Parliament Mr Hugh Dalton announced that he would not stand for membership of the parliamentary committee and urged others of similar age to do likewise. Mr Attlee and Mr Morrison retained the leadership posts. But on 7 December they resigned, and after a struggle Mr Hugh Gaitskell became leader of the parliamentary party. This internal struggle meant that the TUC carried the attack on the autumn budget. Cabinet changes were made on 20 December, just as the Cyprus struggles began to look ominous. The new year opened with both Labour and Conservatives in disarray.

During this time activity on what was to become the Rent Bill was already occupying the Housing Division of the Ministry of Housing and Local Government. In October 1955 the cabinet approved in principle the introduction of a bill to decontrol rents. But the Ministry staff was in unusual turmoil. Two leading under-secretaries, either one of whom might have been expected to take charge of the proposed bill, and both of whom were knowledgeable on the question, left the Ministry. The under-secretary for Housing left to go into private enterprise away from his own field. The under-secretary for Local Government (Mr H. Symon) became the chief executive officer of a landlord's pressure group. Of him, more will be said later. Certainly a departmental committee was sitting at this period (at least, persons no longer associated with the civil service recall minutes drafted for such a committee). In December 1955 a section of the Housing Division had already got the outline of a Bill well in hand. Many basic decisions remained to be taken. But the most important event affecting the future of the Bill had nothing, directly, to do with it. The permanent secretary of the Ministry retired, to be succeeded by his deputy, Dame Evelyn Sharp. If there had been any doubt, it was soon evident that she would cast her shadow into every corner of the Ministry. Certainly, the Ministry which entered 1956, both as a Ministry and as an organisation to deal with rent control, was far different from that of the previous year.

In early 1956 such organisations as the Middle Class Alliance and the People's League for the Defence of Freedom were causing some concern in the Conservative Central Office on account of their militancy. The press were conducting a campaign against the government. Even the normally loyal *Daily Telegraph* was disappointed. But these pressures were not unusual and the scene was generally quiet.* The major issue of the period was the abolition of the death penalty, which was carried in February by a vote of 292 to 262 in the Commons only to be defeated in the Lords. This necessitated a government Bill which satisfied no one. Premium Bonds were introduced against fierce nonconformist protest. The bank rate rose from $4\frac{1}{2}$ to $5\frac{1}{2}$ per cent, and a whole series of subsidies were cut, ranging from bread and milk to the imposition of prescription charges. Ghana and Malaya became independent. MPs gave themselves an increase in salary. Perhaps the major event of foreign interest was the visit of Mr Khruschev and Mr Bulganin in April. The political events which were most noticed were the series of by-elections at which Labour's fortunes seemed to revive markedly. With the reconciliation of Mr Bevan and his election as treasurer, a Labour victory seemed almost possible.

During the first six months of 1956 most of the decisions about the Rent Bill were taken by the Ministry. Information was collected and evaluated. The heads of the Bill were drawn up. All this would have been completed by July, when the Future Legislation Committee

* *The Times*, 28 and 29 June 1956, p. 6. The People's League for the Defence of Freedom was a petit bourgeois organisation concerned with the evils of bureaucracy, unions, and government.

would allocate parliamentary counsel for drafting and priority for parliamentary time.*

The succeeding six months, from 19 July until 11 January, were dominated by Suez. On 19 July the United States and Britain withdrew support for the Aswan High Dam project and on 26 July the Suez Canal was nationalised. From that day onwards the prime minister, together with a cabinet committee and some other members of the cabinet, were concerned first and foremost with the nature of the British response. An additional international crisis intruded. On 23 October, following the success of the Polish transformations, the Hungarian revolution began. By 3–4 November, when Russian troops occupied Budapest, this ceased to be a matter for policy concern. On 29 October, in what has been recognised as part of a combined Anglo-French-Israeli operation,[3] Israel launched an attack on Egypt in the Sinai peninsula. The international and domestic response to the British-French operations that followed, not to mention the activity of those forces, occupied the full time of the government. On 6 November a ceasefire was declared. On 3 December, after renewed United Nations appeals, Britain announced that her forces would be withdrawn from Suez. Withdrawal was completed on 22 December. Sir Anthony rested in Majorca between 23 November and 14 December. In the meantime a substantial American loan was given to Britain. Sir Anthony returned to face a debate on Suez. On 10 January he resigned, for reasons of health. The next day Mr Macmillan became prime minister. These events were bound to have some effect on the Rent Act, as would any political activity of the time.

The table opposite may help to clarify the changes in cabinet that had taken place since April 1955.

The changes within the cabinet revealed a turbulent domestic political scene, and the Conservative Party in a disarray equalled only in 1963 and thereafter. The Labour Party achieved a unity which it had not had for years, and would not have for many more. The moral issue which Suez posed found Mr Bevan and Mr Gaitskell, for once, on the same side. Many of the great Socialist principles were offended by Suez: internationalism, and pacific settlement of disputes – that is, support for the United Nations. That Mr Gaitskell succeeded in

* Information on the pattern of cabinet considerations during the middle 1950s was obtained in an interview with the Rt. Hon. Sir Edward Boyle, MP, and from an explanatory letter of 23 November 1966.

TABLE 1

*Principal Members of Cabinet: 7 April 1955–13 January 1957*

| | 7 April 1955 | 20 December 1955 | 13 January 1957 |
|---|---|---|---|
| *Prime Minister* | Eden | | Macmillan |
| *Chancellor of Exchequer* | Butler | Macmillan | Thorneycroft |
| *Lord President* | Salisbury | | |
| *Foreign Secretary* | Macmillan | Selwyn Lloyd | |
| *Home Office* | G. Lloyd-George | | Butler |
| *Commonwealth Relations* | Home | | |
| *Board of Trade* | Thorneycroft | | Eccles |
| *Lord Chancellor* | Kilmuir | | |
| *Health* | Macleod | | |
| *Agriculture* | Heathcoat-Amory | | |
| *Education* | Eccles | | Hailsham |
| *Lord Privy Seal* | | Butler | |
| *Defence* | Selwyn Lloyd | Moncton | Sandys |
| *Housing* | Sandys | | Brooke |

earning 'the special enmity reserved by Conservatives for traitors to their class and its traditions'[4] no doubt helped unite a party in which such divisions often assumed a symbolic importance. Conservatives, however, found themselves divided into three camps. A few, Epstein puts them at fifty to sixty, opposed the government's policy. Only ten became publicly recognised, Nicholson, Medlicott, Nutting, Banks, Boyle, Astor, Boothby, Yates, Spearman and Kirk. On the other hand a group of 'Pro-Suez Extremists' thought that Britain should not withdraw in response to world pressure. About twenty members could be counted in this group; most of the remainder were content to support the government whether or not they particularly agreed with the policy (and most did agree).[5] These divisions were serious enough of themselves. But more important were the indications and implications of cabinet disagreements. Unlike the American situation the cabinet could not survive with a combination of both 'Hawks' and 'Doves'. Resignations were inevitable.

From all of this the Ministry of Housing and its Rent Bill seemed removed. Mr Sandys has never been shown to be a member of the inner cabinet group which was concerned with Suez planning. Nor was this an issue of moment to his parliamentary secretary, Mr J. Enoch Powell. The Ministry had no business which was affected by Suez – except the inevitable fiscal restrictions that would follow. During the period from July through November 1956 the Housing Division was concerned mainly with drafting the Bill, with the

B

assistance of the parliamentary counsel, and the preparation of a White Paper. The second reading took place on 21–2 November. The committee stage began on 6 December. Though these events suffered, necessarily, from the concern which Suez produced, there seemed to be no indication that international events had any great impact. But to assess this, other details, especially the change of ministers – with the appointment of 13 January of Mr Brooke as minister and Mr R. Bevins as parliamentary secretary – should be considered.

The domestic consequences of the Suez operation were of vital concern to the new government, as was the re-establishment of Britain's international credit. In addition it had also to restore the badly damaged credit of the Conservative Party in the country. The leadership seemed discredited. The new leader was an unknown quantity and his past political behaviour suspect. The disarray of the party was made evident by the Lewisham North and Carmarthen* by-elections and the constituency party disputes with Suez rebels. All of these problems left the new government with more than sufficient concerns.

At this same time the Rent Bill was going through its crucial phases. Through January, February and March 1957 the standing committee worked on the Bill, hastened by a guillotine imposed on 4 February. On 26–7 March the Bill was taken in the full House on Report. It received its third reading the following day, 28 March. From 16 April until 28 May the Bill was considered in Lords. Having received Commons' consent to Lords' amendments, the Bill received the Royal Assent on 17 July. The public stages had lasted seven months.

While these political events formed a framework within which the Rent Bill proceeded, of considerable influence was the character of the participants in the decision-making process. These people – civil servants, ministers, politicians, pressure group officials – were both part of the background within which any Bill had to be drafted and active participants in the decision-making process.

No longer, as evidence to the Fulton Commission has indicated, are civil servants anonymous. Although Mr Anthony Howard complained that he was unable to report Whitehall affairs 'from the inside', the anonymity of civil servants and the policies they propose has diminished.[6] Despite the restraints of the Official Secrets Act and

* See below page 241.

ministerial discretion, there were many sources which reported, or confirmed, the activities of the principal civil servants concerned with the Bill. Mr S. W. C. Phillips, under-secretary, was head of the Housing Division. The departmental solicitor had primary responsibility for legal matters. But the main responsibility rested upon a principal in the division. Both the traditions of the service and his masters confirm that he was a most influential figure in the outcome of discussions. He had had previous experience with rent control, both practical and legislative. He is a respected scholar on many subjects. He was very much a 'principal with prospects' as his later career demonstrated.[7]

Certainly none had greater prospects than Mr Duncan Sandys, in 1956 the Minister of Housing and Local Government. His birth (the son of Captain George Sandys), his education (Eton and Magdalen College, Oxford), and his marriage to Sir Winston Churchill's daughter, were no hindrance to his political career.[8] As Minister of Supply in the Churchill government, he won the right to a seat in the cabinet. He became Minister of Housing and Local Government in October 1954. Of him *The Economist* has said in more recent times:

This is the man at his best: dogged and hard-working. But those Tories who find his present posture attractive should remember his limitations: lack of imagination and an almost total inability to delegate responsibility. His pedantic insistence on personally screwing in every nut and bolt of every departmental issue, large or small, is still remembered with a shudder in Whitehall. Nor should the Tories overrate his political judgment.[9]

How and why policy decisions were taken by this man, we must ask hereafter.

If Mr Sandys lacked imagination he could turn to his parliamentary secretary for a more than adequate store. Mr J. Enoch Powell, himself a former Professor of Classics, was one of the few Tory politicians with an inquiring mind and a scholar's personality, with both its weaknesses as well as its strengths. His politics have been hard to document. How could one explain, with references, a politician who so often asserted that he should be judged by what he said, not by what he did? Already Mr Powell had started to develop the political conceptions that have today given his followers a distinctive flavour.

The ministers who succeeded Mr Sandys and Mr Powell, when the cabinet was shuffled following the resignation of Sir Anthony Eden, were of quite different character. The new minister, Mr Henry Brooke, a former head of the Minority in the London County Council, served from 1954–7 as financial secretary to the Treasury, where he dealt mainly with taxation and revenue problems. He had been a school friend of Mr Butler and a Balliol man – both good qualifications for cabinet rank.[10] Of Mr Brooke, Mr Sampson remarked: 'a dedicated administrator. . . . He has a passion for detail, and he personifies the old Treasury attitude of austere and dogged resolve'.[11] To others he may have seemed 'priggish', and his firmness construed as obstinacy. Mr Bevins praised Mr Brooke for his capacity to take decisions on merit, without reference to the political consequences. Only his most violent critics and his radical colleagues questioned this. Mr Brooke's fate, however, was marked by the Rent Act. Nothing he has touched since has had any popularity or brought him political credit.

A man similarly fated was Mr Reginald Bevins, parliamentary secretary under Mr Brooke. Already in 1957 this self-made man was claiming that ill-luck and prejudice pursued him. For, having slighted Mr Macmillan, he had to accept a parliamentary secretaryship when a Ministry was his due. He complained that his background and his manner made success within the Tory Party impossible.[12] As a parliamentary performer he was totally unsuccessful. Like Mr Brooke, his subsequent posts were to add to his political stature but not to his credit with the public. His best characteristic, according to many, was his loyalty to former colleagues. In an otherwise spiteful book, he had high praise for Mr Brooke and Dame Evelyn Sharp, the permanent secretary.

The dominant figure by far at the Ministry of Housing between 1955–66 was Dame Evelyn Sharp. Her name and that of the Ministry were virtually synonymous. Professional to the core, she was like the abbesses of the Middle Ages, except that her commitment was not to God but to political power. Her intellectual brilliance acute, her experience enormous, she had seen the inside of every Ministry and most parts of the British government in her career. She dominated most of the men with whom she dealt. Was her strength merely due to her intellectual superiority? Perhaps it was also the Briton's amazement at the success and toughness which he attributes to men alone. The American will recognise in her the power evinced by the senior woman's college president or the corporate executive.[13] But of all the ministers, only Mr Sandys was not captivated by her spell.

All others who have dealt with her tell 'Dame Evelyn' stories in the manner usually reserved for 'Churchill stories'.

The politicians who took part in the debates were of varied origins and interests. But only their parliamentary careers are relevant to the eventual outcome. The leader of the Opposition on the Bill was Mr Gilbert Mitchison, a member of the parliamentary committee of the Parliamentary Labour Party. There was a certain irony in the coincidence that Mr Mitchison, who in 1945 defeated Mr John Profumo at Kettering, was to lead the Opposition on a Bill which was to be discredited in part as a consequence of Mr Profumo's activities. Mr Mitchison's deputy was Mr George Lindgren, who had been a parliamentary secretary to Dalton in the last days of the Ministry of Town and Country Planning. The third principal in the Labour ranks was Mr James MacColl, chairman of the Housing and Local Government subject group. On the Tory side were the officers of the Tory Housing Committee, Mr John Hay (who also served a landlord pressure group), Mr Graeme Finlay and Sir Ian Horobin (the vice-chairmen), and Mr Graham Page, the secretary. In addition there were landlords' representatives such as Sir Eric Errington and London M Ps with constituency problems such as Mr Henry Price and Mr Robert Jenkins. To these men, the job of 'scrutiny' was mainly intrusted – or assumed.

To replace Bagehot's monarch, pressure groups now stood in the wings seeking to be consulted, to advise, and to cajole. The professional associations, the Royal Institute of Chartered Surveyors and the Chartered Auctioneers' and Estate Agents' Institute represented the 'administrators' of the properties in question. The landlords were represented by two main groups, the Association of Land and Property Owners and the National Federation of Property Owners. The former had as its secretary Mr H. Symon, a former under-secretary of the Ministry of Housing and Local Government. Mr Reginald Sizen, a former journalist, was secretary of N F P O. All these organisations, professional and interest, had participated in the Ministry's policy formulation on rent control from the time the Conservatives returned to power, and before. On the tenants' side, trade unions, the Communist Party and *ad hoc* tenants' committees formed a politically and organisationally nondescript group. But all these were noticeably active in the legislative process on this Bill.

The events of Suez and its aftermath, as well as these various individuals and groups, form part of the background to the Rent

Bill. Taken together the history of rent control legislation, the contemporary political aspirations of individuals and party groups, and the economic, social and political requirements in national as well as electoral interests formed the background to the Rent Act, 1957.

## NOTES

1 *The Sunday Times*, 4 September 1966, p. 21.
2 *Ibid.*
3 *The Sunday Times*, 4 September 1966, p. 21.
4 Leon D. Epstein, *British Politics in the Suez Crisis*, Pall Mall, London, 1964, p. 77.
5 *Ibid.*, chapter 6.
6 *The New York Times Magazine*, 23 October 1966.
7 Richard E. Neustadt, 'White House and Whitehall' (Mimeographed: 'Prepared for Delivery at the 1965 Annual Meeting of the American Political Science Association . . .').
8 A. Sampson, *Anatomy of Britain*, Hodder and Stoughton, London, 1962, p. 87.
9 *The Economist*, 20 August 1966, p. 716.
10 A. Sampson, *Anatomy of Britain*, p. 138.
11 *Ibid.*, p. 288.
12 R. Bevins, *The Greasy Pole*, Hodder and Stoughton, London, 1965.
13 *Ibid.*, p. 51.

# 3
# The Context

## The History of Control

Like the Passenger Acts,[1] legislation on rent control was conducted within the framework of precedent. Almost every major clause in the 1957 Rent Act had its antecedent in one or more of the previous acts. Even the arguments of the debates in 1956–7 may be found in the records on previous acts in the 1920s and 1930s. This corpus of legislation and debate will be surveyed in this section.

To the lawyer rent control started in 1920 and proceeded through 1923, 1924, 1933, 1938, 1939, 1946, 1954, 1957 and 1965. Yet none forgot that rent control, until 1965, was regarded as an emergency measure and that its major impetus was the necessity of war. A Report in 1915 pointed out that the great influx of munition workers to Clyde Bank and the rise in interest rates and maintenance costs (which landlords put at 10 per cent) had caused a rise in rents. These averaged 6 per cent, but many rises of the order of 15–25 per cent were reported. The requirements of war also meant that rates (in Scotland paid in part by the landlord) also rose.[2] One consequence was the Glasgow riots. Protests were inflamed by the assertion that the wives and children of servicemen were being thrown into the streets while the servicemen were abroad in defence of democracy, and landlords. The minister admitted in debate that he would have opposed action in peacetime.[3] But the emergency had to be dealt with. There was a rumour that he came to this conclusion on the advice of Sir Ian McTaggart, a leading Scots property owner. A proposal to apply control by order-in-council to the particular areas where it was necessary was abandoned in favour of national control. This was done at the insistence of Conservatives in Parliament. The potential advantages of regional control were to remain unacceptable until 1965.[4] The upper limits, i.e. the limits above which control regulations would not apply were set at £35 net rateable value in London, £30 in Scotland, and £26 in the rest of England and Wales. But the 1915 Act was to be a temporary measure, ending six months after the end of the war.

Just as the war was coming to an end the Hunter Report was submitted.[5] This pointed to the demands of the mortgagees to increase interest rates and of owners to have extra funds to meet higher repair costs and compensate for the inability to sell.[6] Tenants argued that while some increases might be necessary these should go only to good landlords, not to those who failed to maintain their houses to standard.[7] Some, including Mr Sidney Webb, argued that increases should be granted for the provision of adequate housing, not simply to make capital invested in housing similar to other forms of investment.[8] The majority concluded that it would be impossible to remove control at present.[9] For that reason it recommended an increase of 35 per cent in rents and 1 per cent in mortgage rates, during the period 1920–3.[10] But it did believe that rent control had to end,[11] as only thus would private enterprise provide the necessary houses to let. Already the lines of battle on control were drawn. A minority of the committee, Neville and Ryder (Labour members), declared there could be no ultimate end to control as long as there was still an acute shortage of accommodation. They insisted that rent increases should be granted only for repairs, not for capital return. At about the same time the limits of control were raised to £70 net rateable value in London, £60 in Scotland, and £52 in the rest of England and Wales. But it was not until 1920 that the Hunter Report was acted upon and modern rent control history began.

In 1920 the Salisbury Committee[12] reported in favour of the continuation of rent control along the lines suggested by the Labour minority in the Hunter Report. The committee urged that the limits be raised to £105 in London, £78 elsewhere in England and Wales and £90 in Scotland. This was done in the 1920 Act.[13] The committee did urge that some relief be given to landlords to allow for repairs. They urged a 25 per cent increase, with the proviso that the tenant could move to get payment suspended or revoked during the period in which the repairs were not made.[14] The Act of 1920 provided for an increase of 6 per cent for repairs carried out before the Act and 8 per cent thereafter.[15] The committee further urged increases totalling 40 per cent over two years. The Act awarded a flat increase of 15 per cent plus increases of 25 per cent if the landlord was responsible for all repairs, and subject to agreement if he were responsible for less.[16] The committee objected to the practice of key money[17] and this was sustained in the prohibition of premiums contained in the 1920 Act.[18] The county courts were given power to suspend the increases in rent if the accommodation was 'not in all respects fit for human habitation or . . . not in a reasonable state of repair'.[19] This Act marked the start of the 'liberal' period of rent control legislation.

Though condemned by Labour at the time, the 1923 Onslow Report and the Act of the same year could hardly be said to reverse this liberal trend towards extending the protection awarded to the tenant. The committee was concerned that there would be unrest if control were removed and there would be no new construction to let so long as control remained.[20] They concluded that controls should be removed, but not yet,[21] and that the present economic condition (a sharp recession) made any increase in rents undesirable. But they did propose a withdrawal of the lowest rated houses by allowing control to lapse when the landlord regained possession. They argued that the requirements under which the courts would grant the landlord possession were impossibly restrictive and should be modified.[22] But they did urge that tenants should not have to pay increases for repairs which were not made.[23] Again, the Labour members dissented.

The essential provision of the 1923 Rent and Mortgage Interest Restrictions Act[24] excluded dwellings from the operation of the Act when the landlord gained possession of a dwelling, or if he granted a lease on it in excess of one year.[25] This provision for 'decontrol on vacant possession' was to be a significant precedent in the preparation of future legislation. In addition the 1923 Act provided for certificates of disrepair and further defined practices which might be regarded as demanding premiums for tenancy.[26] This Act needed some additional strength to protect tenants. This was provided in 1924 by the 'Prevention of Eviction Act'.[27]

But minor as the Acts of 1923 and 1924 were in the changes imposed, they had disastrous effects, due largely to bad timing. The coincidence of a sudden recession led to strife. The Constable Committee majority reported[28] that tenants were using all sorts of devices to avoid paying the increases. The certificates of disrepair were effective checks against any increases.[29] The committee pointed out that overcrowding and unsanitary housing not only had an effect on the health and morale of the population but also 'accentuates discontent with the situation'.[30] At the same time the committee pointed out that Scots landlords were getting a lesser return than the English and Welsh.[31] P. J. Dollan in a minority report argued that 'the principal problem is not one of rent but of poverty'. Most, he claimed,

B*

would willingly pay their rent if they could afford to do so and if the standards were minimal. Rent increases became trivial in the subsequent temporary period of prosperity.

The 1931 Marley Committee Report marked a change in direction.[32] This Report emphasised the shortage of working-class housing which, since the war, had been mitigated solely by the activities of the local authorities. The solution proposed was decontrol,[33] not of all accommodation but certainly of the higher rated houses. It was, however, urged that some of the houses decontrolled by vacant possession should be recontrolled. Several proposals such as the use of rent tribunals were rejected. But also rejected was the notion that control had any substantial effect on private enterprise.[34] At the same time the Report made clear that tenants were not using their rights. Tenants were urged to show more courage in using the disrepair procedure.[35] For the minority Willie Graham argued that working-class housing should be recontrolled, rents further restricted, repairs control better enforced and rent courts used. He rejected the slice decontrol proposed by the committee. This decontrol, adopted by the 1933 Act, can be summarised as follows:

TABLE 2

*Decontrol Adopted by the 1933 Rent Act*

|  | London | Rest of England and Wales | Scotland |
|---|---|---|---|
|  | *N R V* | *N R V* | *N R V* |
| Class A (to be decontrolled immediately) | £45 | £35 | £45 |
| Class B (to be decontrolled soon) | £20–£45 | £13–£35 | £26·5–£45 |
| Class C (retained in control) | less than £20 | £13 | £26·5 |

In fact, the 1933 Rent and Mortgage Interest Restrictions (Amendment) Act[36] provided for immediate decontrol of A, decontrol of B on vacant possession and no decontrol of C. To prevent injustices the condition of suitable alternative accommodation was modified so that the courts now had discretion to determine whether they thought an order for possession 'reasonable'.[37] The debate on this occasion should be followed closely for the insight it offered into future thinking on rent control.

In many respects the 1932–3 debate was preliminary to the debates on policy which were to be held in 1956–7. For that reason the positions taken on the various issues raised, not merely the debate on the Bill itself, should be examined. The minister in charge, Sir Hilton Young (Minister of Health), argued that 'when natural forces have their free play, they can be left to their free play, but when you are restraining and confining them by laws, you have constantly to exercise vigilance to see that the laws are adapted to the changing circumstances which they have to meet'.[38] 'It is recognised by all of us that we are working towards the goal of being able to get rid of the system altogether'.[39] Control, he argued, frustrated the movement of tenants to better or more suitable accommodation.[40] Indeed, some Tories argued that you could only get more C class houses by decontrolling them.[41] Attacking this doctrine Mr Anthony Greenwood said, 'They [the landlords] demand to have perfect right to do what they like with their own. That is an early Victorian theory which is not applicable today'.[42] Maxton went even further and demanded why, when every other sector had been asked to make some sacrifice, none was asked of the landlord.[43] During the amending stages the two principal questions were the postponement of the operation of the Bill and the recontrol of class C houses already decontrolled. Both were rejected by the government and the House. Of the government's concession, Buchanan of the I L P commented, 'He has given us nothing but he has done it very civilly'.[44] Class rhetoric having been uttered, the process of decontrol was begun.

Already, however, the focus of concern was being shifted. Increasingly, the problem of maintenance was being viewed as the dominant problem to which public policy ought to be addressed. In a Report dated 1933 under the chairmanship of Mr Moyne, a committee argued that though sufficient statutory powers to compel proper maintenance existed, the various government departments had been negligent in their use.[45] Deteriorating property, it was argued, should be taken into public ownership to be administered by the local authorities[46] to be financed through the Public Works Loan Board.[47] The matter was not to be pursued until 1954.

If repairs were for a while a dominant problem, the problem of control, *per se*, soon re-emerged. In the first Ridley Committee Report[48] the problems of slum clearance were discussed at length. But the main policy conclusions were those relating to decontrol. The committee proposed that regional decontrol be used to combat the regional difficulties which made overall decontrol undesirable.[49] This, they argued, would simplify the early decontrol of as much as possible.

The minority attacked these conclusions and argued that the committee had underemphasised the extent to which inadequate provision for working-class housing was still a factor in the market. But even some of the majority had doubts about immediate decontrol. These doubts were ignored. The pronouncement in favour of decontrol was made in a White Paper of 1938 which preceded the Bill itself.[50]

The process of decontrol started by the 1933 Act was extended by the Increase of Rent and Mortgage Interest (Restrictions) Act, 1938.[51] It never came into force because of emergency measures taken in September 1939 at the outbreak of the second world war. The principal provision of the 1938 Act was to lower decontrol to £35 upper limit in London and Scotland and £20 in the rest of England and Wales. This halved the limit of Group B houses.[52] Again the minister asserted that 'we do not believe that control is a desirable permanent measure, and the ultimate object of the government is to bring control to an end as soon as it is no longer needed. . . .'[53] Already, it was argued, there was sufficient excess accommodation.[54] Already they could point to examples of practices which at a later date would be known as Rachmanism.[55] But with the coming of war the limits of control were raised to £100 in London, £90 in Scotland and £75 in England and Wales (outside of London). The original cause of rent control once again thwarted its abolition.

Thoughts on rent control persisted during the war. In 1945 Lord Ridley again chaired a committee to report on postwar policy. Rent control, they agreed, would have to continue indefinitely because of the wartime situation. They recommended that rent tribunals be used to deal with matters currently in court jurisdictions. Increases were recognised as necessary if modern facilities were to be developed, even though new construction had never been controlled; and they strongly recommended that decontrol by vacant possession be abandoned because of the harm it did.[56] In a minority report Buchanan and Key urged that local authority houses ought also to be subject to control. But a Labour government came to power.

Not until 1946 did Aneurin Bevan (as Minister of Health) act on the rent control problem as far as unfurnished accommodation was concerned. In the Landlord and Tenant (Rent Control) Act, 1946,[57] no change was made in the limits of control set in 1939. The primary modification was the introduction of tribunals to fix standard rents, as had already been done in 1946 for furnished accommodation. These were to fix rents on a 'reasonable' basis.[58] The Conservatives' attack was not very effective as they were divided on what was wrong. Generally, they disliked the tribunals.[59] The Act further strengthened the prohibition of premiums.[60] In sum, this Act did not basically alter the rent control system.

Some have interpreted the successive Acts of 1954 and 1957 as an attempt to restore the *status quo ante* of 1938. Certainly the effect of these Acts in increasing rents and reducing the scope of control lend plausibility to such a thesis. The details of the 1954–7 period are traced in later chapters. But the new feature of that period, and of those Acts, ought to be noted. The White Paper, and subsequent debate, of 1953 onwards focused upon the repair problem, largely ignored since 1933. Certainly, however, the provisions for percentage increases, slice decontrol, and decontrol of vacant possession were old friends recalled to their role – the termination of rent control. The principal innovation was the use of rateable value as a basis for calculating rents (i.e. as a standard of 'reasonableness'). The net effect of the 1954 and 1957 Acts was to provide a special repairs increase and subsequently a general recalculation of standard rents. In addition control was ended on all dwellings with net rateable value (i.e. valuation for rating purposes, as distinguished from the gross rateable value or estimated rental income which was the basis for calculating controlled rents under the 1957 Act) of £40 in London and Scotland and £30 elsewhere. Though the Act came into effect in fits and starts due to amendments in the Commons and in a 1958 amending Act, the Act was fully operative by 1960.

The Housing Repairs and Rents Act, 1954[61] was concerned in equal measure with slum clearance and repairs. Part I of the Act dealt with slum clearance and encouraged local authorities to take activities to further the abolition of slums. Part II dealt with controlled housing. This provided for an increase based upon the Inland Revenue's allowance for repairs in computing rating. All new dwellings or those converted and let were excluded from the operation of the rent restriction acts.

The principal effort at decontrol was the 1957 Rent Act.[62] This provided for a general increase in controlled rents to what was considered a fair level. This was thought to be about twice the gross rateable value. Some houses were released from control altogether. These were all dwellings with net rateable value above £40 in London and Scotland and £30 in the rest of England and Wales. In addition, dwellings were to be decontrolled when the landlord obtained vacant possession. Premiums were again prohibited and fines imposed for their acceptance. A minimum of four weeks' notice to quit on both sides was specified, replacing the traditional one week, or minimum tenure provisions then customary. The provisions on repairs were reversed. Instead of the system obtaining up to 1957, when the burden of proving good repair had rested on the landlord, the burden of proving bad repair now rested upon the tenant. This was to discourage the use of disrepair procedure which had traditionally hampered rent increases.

By 1963 many difficulties in the operation of the Rent Act (1957) both physical and political had emerged. The Milner Holland Committee was appointed to investigate the problem of housing in Greater London, which was the cause of great public scandal and concern. The committee pointed out that contrary to the usual suppositions the shortage of housing in London was acute, and likely to remain so. The supply of privately rented accommodation was decreasing, not increasing – the converse of the expectations of those responsible for the 1957 Rent Act. Rent control was a short-term solution and a most unsatisfactory one. Investors could not be expected to put money into houses to let if there was no profit. But control of some sort was needed to protect tenants. There were factors outside control which might explain the inability of landlords to make a profit. Though landlords were certainly not all Rachmans, the abuse of the vacant possession clause and the general harassment of tenants needed to be dealt with. The committee insisted that it was time for rent control to be considered within the general context of housing policy rather than as a party-political football.[63]

But Labour had a commitment to deal with the problems of the 1957 Act (or those associated in the public mind with it). After a stopgap measure – the Protection from Eviction Act, 1964, this was accomplished in the Rent Act, 1965, which incorporated some of the Milner Holland suggestions. A form of control called 'regulation' was introduced for all dwellings up to the value of £400 in London, £200 elsewhere. This was to cover dwellings decontrolled in 1954 and 1957. Rent officers were appointed in every county, county borough, and the London boroughs to determine 'fair rents', 'having regard to all the circumstances and, in particular, to the age, character and locality of the premises'. In particular, the circumstances of landlord and tenant and scarcity were to be ignored.[64] Landlord or tenant were allowed to object to these decisions, in which case the rent would be fixed by a Rent Assessment Committee of three – a lawyer, a surveyor and a layman – picked from a panel responsible for dealing with such appeals within a large area. Decontrol, or ending of regulation, on a regional basis was provided for. Clauses protecting tenants from harassment were included to meet the public outcry about Rachmanism.

The 1965 Rent Act and the Milner Holland Committee Report which preceded it confirmed those who had faith in the cyclical pattern of change. For once again the limits of control were raised, the 'reasonable rent' standard restored (albeit in a different guise), decontrol on vacant possession ended, and the various restraints which had favoured the landlord were replaced by old friends of the tenant, especially the tribunal. But the 1965 Act also included many innovations. Rules about security of tenure, harassment, eviction procedure, which were to apply to all tenancies, public and private, controlled and decontrolled, marked a major innovation. If the new Act is really operated, including section II, it will raise far more rents than it will lower. The Act has created a bias to legal proceedings that favours landlords who can afford lawyers.

But however one might view the cyclical theory, the role of precedent should not be ignored. Whether precedent became a dominating motive in drafting is a separate question. Certainly the form of rent control legislation lent weight to the *a priori* assumption that precedent was critical. But the broader question which must be answered is whether any legislation 'with a past' can ever be free of history's constraints. It remains to see what form these constraints assumed.

## The Political Past and Ideology

Other factors shaped politicians' decisions. One was the recollection of the importance of rent control and housing in general as electoral issues. Another was the 'ideology' prevalent in 1957. The political precedents merit description. And an outline of the meanings of ideology in the context of this thesis will be provided. For the past and ideology formed, with precedent and economic considerations, the context in which decisions were taken.

The provision of housing first became a major political issue with

---

* The Acts which deal with rent control have been codified in the Rent Act (1968). This Act, a product of the Law Commission, makes no fundamental changes in the law.

the passage of the Housing and Town Planning Act of 1919, usually known as the Addison Act. The consequences of this measure were the massive entry of the government into the provision of housing, the emergence of the Ministry of Health as a major ministry, and the growth of the planned estates.[65] This took place without any awareness, by Conservatives or Labour, of the implications for government activity.[66] Never again were housing and rent control to be treated with so much unanimity.

But there were very few instances in which housing and rent control played key roles in the political world. Only one politician before 1957 had clearly lost an election due to his activity on rent control. Mr Griffith-Boscawen, the Minister of Health, lost his seat in a by-election in the normally safe constituency of Mitcham, due to the outcry against the 1920 Act and some of its unfortunate consequences.[67] Two other ministers also lost by-elections at that time. Mr A. J. P. Taylor claims, without evidence, that East Fulham was affected by housing.[68] But this was a rather broader issue than rent control, even if true.

Certainly, in the second world war years housing was an important debating issue. 'Homes fit for heroes' had been a major slogan in 1918.[69] The success of the Addison and Wheatley and Chamberlain Acts was viewed as politically significant at the time. Indeed, Mr Taylor argues that the voters in 1935 '. . . cared only for their own future: first housing, and then full employment and social security'.[70] But, as will be shown in chapter 5, there was no evidence that housing, and certainly not rent control, played an important part in the general elections following the war, at least until 1959.

But this did not eliminate housing as an issue which politicians saw as significant. For with firm disregard of facts which, as will be shown, tended to characterise politicians' views of housing issues in the 1950s, politicians no doubt considered the possibility, however remote, that decisions on rent control would have electoral consequences.

But electoral consequences are not, of themselves, a sufficient basis for decisions. Politicians need some means for structuring their decisions. 'Ideology' is one such means. But this term had many senses. I propose to distinguish which senses were appropriate to the debates of the mid-1950s and which can be ignored.

There were two senses of the meaning of 'ideology' which were clearly not applicable to the British political world of 1957, or at least the non-Communist parts of it. There was no ideology of class hostility, at least so far as politicians were concerned. There was no sense of ideology based upon the ultimate domination and 'class victory' for the workers or the middle class or whatever. Nor was there an ideology which might have been known in older times as a 'philosophy'. There was no self-validating system of some complexity offering an explanation of all phenomena.

But there were two senses in which an 'ideology' might be discerned on the British scene. The parties each had a crude (in the case of the Conservatives) or sophisticated (in the case of Labour) prescription or causal belief which they applied indiscriminately to all areas of political experience. The other sense in which there was an ideology relevant to the Rent Act was the general feeling of the civil service, shared often by their political masters, that decisions ought to be taken without any of the cautions imposed by a 'rational' process such as the quest for all possible information. This assumed that the necessity for taking a decision justified quick judgments. The role of these two forms of ideology will be developed in the relevant chapters of the thesis.

It was important to make clear the minimal role of housing and rent control as electoral issues and the special meanings and forms of ideology to fill out the context within which the legislative process on the 1957 Rent Act was conducted.

## The Economics of Housing

The housing situation, and the place of rented housing, have not, until quite recently, been the subject of much study. Old truths were accepted fact. Thus, much of the information in this section was not available to legislators in 1957. But many of the statistics, especially the human statistics, ought to have been part of their consciousness while drafting and debating the Rent Act. The purpose of this section is to provide the physical setting within which rent control policy might have been more realistically shaped, had it been understood.

In this section, five problems will be treated. First, the housing in the market, especially the privately rented housing, requires description – not only quantitatively but also qualitatively. This will help to show the needs and shortages which the Rent Act was intended to overcome. Coupled with this must be a description of the people who occupy each sector of the market. Third, the transformations in the market, its sectors, and the people who live in or seek to obtain housing in each sector, must be outlined. The reasons for these changes, the extent to which they were a consequence of the Rent Act or of slum clearance, subsidised building, tax effects, etc. will be outlined. Finally, something will be said about the state of the debate on housing and rent control to show the policy alternatives available to the government.

The distribution of housing, and its quality, was strongly influenced by tenure patterns. The distribution in the last twenty years was outlined by Professor Donnison as follows:

TABLE 3

*Estimates of the Tenure of Households, 1947–64*[71]

| Tenure | Households (per cent) | | | |
|---|---|---|---|---|
| | 1947 | 1958 | 1962 | 1964 |
| | (Great Britain) | (England) | (England) | (England and Wales) |
| Owner-Occupiers | 26 | 39 | 43 | 46 |
| Council Tenants | 13 | 20 | 21 | 26 |
| Other* | 61 | 40 | 36 | 28 |

* Most of these would be private renters.

Source: D. V. Donnison *The Government of Housing.*

The table opposite was drawn by Professor Donnison to show the distribution of amenities among various types of accommodation.

The significant points in this table were, as Professor Donnison has pointed out, the relatively poor quality of privately rented housing, both absolutely and in relation to other forms of accommodation. Half of privately rented accommodation had no baths, two-fifths had no hot water, one-fifth had no flush toilet, and half were terraced houses.[73] These houses had low rateable value: one-third had values of £10 or less.[74] Yet privately rented housing formed an important part of the market precisely for this reason. Their rents were, on the whole, lower than those of council houses. And while they could be more expensive than owner-occupier dwellings, they provided cheap housing with poor amenities for those families which could afford no better.[75]

Though the state of housing in each sector of the market was significant, even more significant was the nature and income of the households in the various sectors. The profile of tenants by the type

TABLE 4

*Tenure and Housing Equipment, 1958* (expressed in percentages)[72]

| | | total households | owner-occupiers | council tenants | other tenants un-furnished | furnished | rent-free, etc. |
|---|---|---|---|---|---|---|---|
| *no. of householders* | | | | | | | |
| *interviewed:* | | 3,137 | 1,225 | 641 | 1,102 | 74 | 95 |
| *Households having or not having:* | | | | | | | |
| kitchen | U: | 94 | 97 | 97 | 90 | 61 | 93 |
| | S: | 3 | 1 | 2 | 5 | 28 | 3 |
| | N: | 3 | 1 | 1 | 5 | 11 | 4 |
| cooker | U: | 94 | 97 | 95 | 92 | 68 | 91 |
| with oven | S: | 3 | 1 | 2 | 4 | 27 | 3 |
| | N: | 2 | 1 | 2 | 3 | 5 | 6 |
| kitchen sink | U: | 94 | 98 | 97 | 90 | 59 | 89 |
| | S: | 4 | 2 | 2 | 5 | 30 | 4 |
| | N: | 3 | 1 | 1 | 5 | 11 | 6 |
| fixed bath | U: | 65 | 80 | 92 | 37 | 34 | 43 |
| | S: | 6 | 4 | 2 | 7 | 49 | 3 |
| | N: | 29 | 16 | 5 | 56 | 18 | 54 |
| flush toilet | U: | 84 | 90 | 95 | 75 | 45 | 75 |
| | S: | 10 | 4 | 3 | 16 | 54 | 12 |
| | N: | 6 | 6 | 2 | 8 | 1 | 14 |
| hot water | U or S: | 72 | 86 | 88 | 47 | 69 | 73 |
| supply | N: | 28 | 14 | 12 | 53 | 31 | 27 |
| garden | U: | 68 | 81 | 84 | 48 | 18 | 66 |
| | S: | 7 | 4 | — | 12 | 51 | 5 |
| | N: | 25 | 15 | 16 | 41 | 31 | 28 |

(Symbols: U = unshared, S = shared, N = none)
Source: Donnison *et al.*, *Housing Since the Rent Act.*

of accommodation they occupied was presented as shown on page 32 by Professor Donnison:

The occupiers of privately rented accommodation tended to be the poorly paid,[77] the very young and the very old. As important sectors of the community these needed accommodation. Any government was bound to be concerned about the decline in supply of such accommodation. It was these patterns of change which formed the basis of government activity during the middle 1950s.

But for a considerable time the extent and nature of the shortage was not apparent. Professor Donnison pointed out that the 1951 estimate of the number of households in 1961 was 14,022 million.

TABLE 5

*Tenure and Occupation of Head of Household, 1958*[76]

| occupation | total households | owner-occupiers | council tenants | other tenants un-furnished | furnished | rent-free, etc. |
|---|---|---|---|---|---|---|
| administrative, professional and managerial | 12 | 21 | 3 | 7 | 20 | 18 |
| farmers, shop-keepers and small employers | 6 | 8 | 2 | 5 | 1 | 9 |
| clerical workers and shop assistants | 7 | 9 | 5 | 7 | 11 | 2 |
| foremen and skilled workers | 31 | 26 | 43 | 32 | 35 | 8 |
| other manual workers and personal service | 20 | 11 | 29 | 25 | 20 | 38 |
| retired and unoccupied | 23 | 24 | 17 | 24 | 12 | 23 |
| unclassified | * | * | * | * | nil | 1 |

(* = less than 0·5 per cent)

Source: Donnison *et al.*, *Housing Since the Rent Act.*

The 1961 Report indicated that there were 14,890 million. This meant that there were 6 per cent more households than demographic experts had expected.[78] For a considerable time the postwar shortage of housing was so visibly acute that mass building was seen as the only answer.[79] But changes in the population were to become important. Increasingly, as the 1950s progressed, it became apparent that the household configuration of society was altering. There were an increasing proportion of elderly households, often comprising one or two persons. At the same time the proportion of young households, single persons or young married couples, also rose sharply (though this was of greater significance in large connurbations than in the country as a whole).[80] The consequence was, as Professor Donnison pointed out, that there were not merely shortages due to the altered age structure and number of households, but also because of the unequal distribution of the existing stock of housing.[81]

This could be accounted for in part by the changing purpose to which accommodation was put and its division into sectors. Before the second world war the majority of people lived in privately let dwellings. But increasingly in the years following the war there was a movement, of all classes, towards owner-occupation or council house tenancy. This movement could be seen in the first table of this section (p. 30).[82] At the same time the reduction in average size of household-dwelling units meant that accommodation built to house the rather large Victorian household was no longer suitable, or economic. In London and other major cities these Victorian houses were transformed, as rapidly as their owners could obtain possession, into multiple dwellings – boarding houses, flatlets, etc.[83] Thus there were increasing shortages in the total supply of complete houses or dwellings to let.

Part of this decrease in the supply of dwellings to let was attributable to the altered standards of accommodation. A substantial proportion of British housing was, and still is, quite old, though perhaps not more so than other European countries. But certainly Britain had replacement problems rather different from those of, say, Western Germany. As Professor Donnison said:

> West Germany's big city slums were eliminated by the housing policies of the R.A.F. and U.S.A.A.F. . . . Most of the slums in this country stand in the cities, where they will not be automatically and painlessly replaced in the normal course of economic development and migration.[84]

From 1954 onwards, with the partial satisfaction of the most immediate housing shortages, attention, both public and governmental, was turned to the standard of accommodation. The 1954 Housing Repairs and Rents Act aimed in its first part to increase the rate of slum clearance. This was essential since the community would no longer inhabit dwellings which had formerly been considered adequate.[85] Since little or no private accommodation to let had been built since the first world war, it was this sector which was hardest hit by the changes, and hence lost a greater proportion of its stock.

The key to the shortage of accommodation to let lay in the diminishing stock. Why were no houses to let built after the first world war? Why did owners who gained vacant possession prefer to sell rather than let? Many different explanations have been offered. Professor Wendt argued that the fear and uncertainty, not to mention the restriction on income imposed by the Rent Restriction Acts discouraged new private construction to let.[86] A. A. Nevitt argued that it was not specific housing or rents policies but rather the structure of taxation, coupled with subsidised competition from council housing and building societies, that forced the change, which she placed partially on the supply and partly on the demand side. She argued that the private landlord was never able to obtain a sufficient return to make his property desirable, in part because, especially for the poorer landlords, taxation upon income left insufficient rental income to repair their houses on an economic basis or allow for depreciation. That is, though landlords might have sufficient income to do repairs, they did not get a fair return on the repairs they did.[87] At the same time, she contended, the landlord could not charge a rent competitive with the 'rent' paid by owner-occupiers. These, once they had paid their deposit and obtained a mortgage, had considerable tax concession – in fact a form of concealed subsidy. The consequence was that increasingly the working classes for whom rental had formerly been a *sine qua non* could, and did, purchase their own homes. Since it was in the owner-occupation sector that demand was greatest, it was for this, not for the rental market, that builders were prepared to invest their capital. This was particularly so because unlike the situation which obtained in the nineteenth century houses were no longer the most desirable form of investment for the capital of outside investors.[88] The other factor in the decline of privately let houses was the increased competition from the state-subsidised council dwellings, which of course were not subject to the economic tests that made an increase in the private sector difficult.

The council house became a necessity in post-first world war Britain when the cost of construction temporarily made the provision of housing to let for the working classes and returned servicemen economically impossible. Eight hundred thousand houses were needed immediately. Public service was the only answer.[89] Later (after 1930), local authorities were urged to use council house construction as part of a programme of slum clearance. As the years wore on, and within the limits of central government policy and local authority initiative, the provision of council housing came to be regarded as an important and necessary public service. Such new housing was expensive. Even with subsidies out of the general rates, council house rents needed to be much higher than similar sized privately rented (and controlled) accommodation if the statutory requirements for balancing the housing account were to be fulfilled.[90] But tenants proved willing to pay these higher rents because of the superior amenities, and despite the inconvenience both social and physical imposed by council estate life. Certainly in post-second world war Britain, thanks in part to the dominance of council house construction in the period of Labour rule, prior to 1951, council housing became increasingly significant as a source of accommodation to let.

But the primary factor in the reduction of available private accommodation to let, some argued, was the operation of the Rent Restriction Acts. The details of the operation of these Acts are summarised in chapter 4. But the consequences attributed to the operation of the Acts had little connection with the specified details. The restriction on rents, some contended, not merely discouraged landlords by restricting their freedom of action, it prevented landlords from behaving in an economic fashion. In the absence of rent control repairs might have been made. Control had meant that in the years following the second world war (though not before then) funds for repairs were non-existence. In any case, the landlord did not make enough profit from rents to encourage his interest in the property as an investment worth preserving. Low rents, below the 'market' level, formed a concealed subsidy from landlord to tenant. Under these circumstances, it was contended, there was every reason why the landlord should want to contract out. The essence of the thesis was that the landlord would serve the national interest if given the opportunity.

This was contested by Mr John Greve. He pointed out that most landlords were over sixty-one years of age. A substantial fraction were widows or widowers. Many had no other source of income. 41 per cent of the individual landlords owned only one house to let, 8 per cent owned less than five. Many of these individual landlords wanted to get out. Only 23 per cent of those sampled, mostly large landlords with diverse assets, thought the business outlook was favourable even when decontrol seemed inevitable. It was clear that the largest potential suppliers were the least willing.[91] Professor Donnison pointed out that since the war building controls had been relaxed, rent restrictions altered, and generous improvement grants offered. Yet this had not increased the supply of houses to let. 'How many of their successors [the landlords] would recognise a free market if they saw one, and how many are capable of responding to the incentives it offers?' Professor Donnison asked.[92] Rent control, Professor Donnison and Mr Greve contended, had only kept an otherwise irresponsible landlord group from exploiting the shortages of the mid-1950s.[93]

The debate about rent control was really part of a larger debate about the role of the government in housing. All agreed that housing was to some extent a social service. But during the middle 1950s the general feeling was that it was not the duty of government to provide good housing for everyone. It was the duty of government to clear slums and to rehouse those unable to house themselves, or to protect those unable to defend themselves in a free market. The dislocation of the market, the misuse of accommodation, the failure to provide enough private housing to let of good quality, were all seen as the consequence of the regulated market. Given a free hand, the landlord and tenant would, jointly, put the situation right. The landlord would provide accommodation and maintain it because it was in his economic interest to do so. The tenant would seek accommodation appropriate to his needs because the anomalies and privileges of rent control would be ended. But towards the end of the 1950s arguments for government intervention increased. Some of the scarcities which had accompanied rent control were seen as long term, not short term as rent control had always assumed. Government already had a large role in housing – through subsidies, taxation policies, and the increased role of local authority housing. The market could never be freed. What was needed was rational regulation. This battle was fought at each housing debate. It was part of the context of the 1957 Rent Act debates.

## NOTES

1 Oliver MacDonagh, *A Pattern of Government Growth, 1800–60*, MacGibbon & Kee, London, 1961. (Hunter, ch.)

2 Scotland, Departmental Committee Report, 1914–16, Cd 8111 *Parliamentary Papers*, xxv, I.

3 76 H C Deb. 5s, col. 720.

4 *Ibid.*, col. 1,427.

5 Committee Report, Rent and Mortgage Interest (War Restrictions) Act, 1918, Cd 9235, *Parliamentary Papers*, xiii, 73.

6 *Ibid.*, para. 13.

7 *Ibid.*, para. 20.

8 *Ibid.*, para. 21.

9 *Ibid.*, para. 25.

10 *Ibid.*, para. 4.

11 *Ibid.*, para. 30.
12 Committee Report, Rent and Mortgage Interest (War Restrictions) Acts, 1920, Cmd 658, *Parliamentary Papers*, xviii, 315. (Lord Salisbury, ch.)
13 *Ibid.*, para. 11.
14 *Ibid.*, para. 5.
15 1920 Act, clause 2 (1–2).
16 *Ibid.*, clause 2 (1).
17 1920, Cmd 658, para. 24.
18 1920 Act, clause 8.
19 *Ibid.*, clause 2 (2).
20 Departmental Committee Report. Increase of Rent and Mortgage Interest (Restrictions) Act, 1920, 1923, Cmd 1803, xii, *Parliamentary Papers*, part II, 517, para 6. (Lord Onslow, ch.)
21 *Ibid.*, para. 7.
22 *Ibid.*, para. 10.
23 *Ibid.*, para. 13.
24 13 and 14 Geo. V, c. 18.
25 *Ibid.*, c. 2.
26 *Ibid.*, c. 5, 9.
27 14 and 15 Geo. V, c. 18.
28 Committee Report, Rent Restriction Acts, 1924–25, Cmd 2434, *Parliamentary Papers*, xv, 517. (Constable, ch.)
29 *Ibid.*, para. 35.
30 *Ibid.*, para. 64.
31 *Ibid.*, para. 67.
32 Ministry of Health Interdepartmental Committee Report, Rent Restriction Acts, 1930–31, Cmd 3911, *Parliamentary Papers*, xvii, 281. (Lord Morley, ch.)
33 *Ibid.*, para. 26.
34 *Ibid.*, para. 111.
35 *Ibid.*, para. 100.
36 23 and 24 Geo. V, c. 32.
37 *Ibid.*, c. 3.
38 273 H C Deb. 5s, col. 48.
39 *Ibid.*, col. 48.
40 *Ibid.*, col. 53.
41 *Ibid.*, col. 248.
42 *Ibid.*, col. 76.
43 *Ibid.*, col. 222.
44 278 H C Deb. 5s, col. 237.
45 Moyne Committee, 1932–3, Cmd 4397, *Parliamentary Papers*, xiii, I, para. 17.
46 *Ibid.*, paras 21, 33.
47 *Ibid.*, para. 63.
48 Inter-Departmental Committee Report, Rent Restriction Acts, 1937–8, Cmd 5621, *Parliamentary Papers*, xv, 217. (Lord Ridley, ch.)
49 *Ibid.*, para. 53.
50 Government Policy on Rent Restriction, 1937–8, Cmd 5667, *Parliamentary Papers*, xxi, 1017.
51 1 and 2 Geo. VI, c. 26.

52 *Ibid.*, c. 1.
53 332 H C Deb. 5s, cols 1135–6.
54 *Ibid.*, col. 1160.
55 *Ibid.*, col. 1225.
56 Inter-Departmental Committee Report, Rent Control, 1944–5, Cmd 6621, *Parliamentary Papers*, v, 499. (Lord Ridley, ch.)
57 12 and 13 Geo. VI, c. 40.
58 460 H C Deb. 5s, col. 575.
59 *Ibid.*, col. 639.
60 12 and 13 Geo. VI, c. 40, clause 2.
61 2 and 3 Eliz. 2, ch. 53.
62 5 and 6 Eliz. 2, ch. 25.
63 Committee Report, *Report of Committee on Housing in Greater London*, 1965, Cmd 2605. (Sir Milner Holland, ch.)
64 5 and 6 Eliz. 2, ch. 25, section 27.
65 C. L. Mowat, *Britain Between the Wars*, Methuen, London, 1955, p. 44.
66 *Ibid.*, p. 43.
67 *Ibid.*, p. 165.
68 A. J. P. Taylor, *English History, 1914–1945*, Oxford University Press, London, 1966, p. 210.
69 Mowat, p. 4.
70 Taylor, *English History, 1914–1915*, p. 210.
71 D. V. Donnison, *The Government of Housing*, Penguin, London, 1967, table 10, p. 186.
72 D. V. Donnison, C. Cockburn and T. Corlett, *Housing Since the Rent Act*, 'Occasional Papers in Social Administration' no. 3, Condicote Press, Welwyn, 1961, table 4, p. 16.
73 Donnison, *Government of Housing*, p. 189.
74 J. B. Cullingworth, *English Housing Trends*, 'Occasional Papers in Social Administration' no. 13, G. Bell, London, 1965, p. 22.
75 *Ibid.*, p. 49.
76 Donnison, *Housing Since the Rent Act*, table 10, p. 24.
77 Cullingworth, *English Housing Trends*, p. 26.
78 Donnison, *Government of Housing*, table 8, p. 154.
79 P. F. Wendt, *Housing Policy – The Search for Solutions*, University of California Press, Berkeley, 1963, pp. 23 ff.
80 See Cullingworth, *English Housing Trends*, pp. 24 ff., tables 4 and 5; Donnison, *Government of Housing*, p. 158.
81 Donnison, *Government of Housing*, p. 160.
82 See *Ibid.*, p. 194.
83 J. Rex and R. Moore, *Race Community and Conflict*, Oxford University Press, London, 1967.
84 Donnison, *Government of Housing*, p. 157.
85 Cullingworth, *English Housing Trends*, p. 79.
86 Wendt, *Housing Policy*, pp. 27 ff., 61 ff.
87 A. A. Nevitt, *Housing Taxation and Subsidies*, Nelson, London, 1966, p. 44.
88 *Ibid.*, pp. 36 ff.
89 C. L. Mowat, *Britain Between the Wars*, p. 454.

90 See Cullingworth, *English Housing Trends*, pp. 46–8.

91 J. Greve, *Private Landlords in England*, 'Occasional Papers in Social Administration' no. 16, G. Bell, London, 1965, pp. 25–7.

92 D. V. Donnison, *Housing Policy Since the War*, 'Occasional Papers in Social Administration' no. 1, Condicote Press, Welwyn, 1960, p. 32.

93 Donnison, *Government of Housing*, p. 172.

# 4
# The Quest for Policy

The preceding chapters were intended to show the background of
rent restriction. But it is to the context of the 1950s that the 1957 Act
must be connected. The 1957 Act owed a particular debt of parentage
to the 1954 Housing Repairs and Rents Act. Much may be attributed to
the 'state of the Ministry' which determined the priorities established.
The administrative structure in the Ministry, the relationship between
politicians and civil servants, and the state of the research organisation could be seen, both together and separately, to have had considerable impact not only in the quest for policy but in the legislative
process within government. In the final analysis, ideas could be trans-
posed into legislation only with regard to the contemporary scene as
the Ministry perceived it. What the Ministry saw and why are the
subjects of this chapter.

## The Housing Repairs and Rents Act (1954)

The White Paper which preceded the 1954 Act was relevant not
merely to the policy and legislative origins of that Act but to the 1957
Act as well. In this section, the issues of priority and policy before the
government in 1953 will be outlined: to what extent did the legislation have the effect desired and anticipated?

The Ministry of Housing, after 1951, had many complex problems
which required solution. Even the single issue of rent control was
multidimensional. Three main issues (the maintenance of the stock of
houses in good repair, security of tenure, and the future of rent
control as such) presented themselves. Alternatives on these issues
were being suggested even while the Ministry was occupied with the
more immediate problem in the housing field – the provision of
sufficient accommodation.

Policy discussions were characterised by a remarkable degree of
consensus. The debate on the state of the nation's stock of houses
started in May 1951 with the publication of the Royal Institution of
Chartered Surveyors' *A Memorandum on Rent Restrictions and*

*Repairs Problem.* The purpose of this report was twofold: it focused attention on the repairs problem and suggested new means of determining 'fair rent'.[1]

The Report pointed out that 'for every house that becomes unfit for habitation another has to be provided by the local authority', which could do so only with the assistance of an Exchequer subsidy. The cost of keeping the existing stock in 'proper repair' would be less than the subsidy required to build a new dwelling.[2]

A rent increase was suggested as a means to provide landlords with funds to keep their houses in repair. But to use a percentage increase, the traditional technique, would simply increase the anomalies of rent control which the second Ridley Committee proposed should be eliminated, and such an increase in rent would not be tied to the repairs actually required.[3] But some increase in rent was required as the surpluses which landlords might have been expected to accumulate during the war to do repairs either never existed or were quite inadequate in the face of rising repair costs.[4]

An alternative to the flat rate increase was found in the legal fiction which stated that the difference between gross and net value for rating purposes represented the cost of making improvements. Gross value was the Inland Revenue surveyor's estimate of the market rent for the unit in a given base year. Net value was the surveyor's estimate of the market rent less an amount sufficient to keep the unit in good repair. The current difference between these two, the R I C S argued, represented the actual cost of making repairs in 1939. The R I C S proposed that the cost of making repairs in 1952 could be ascertained as a multiple of the repairs deduction, by multiplying the repairs deduction by a sum equal to the rising cost of repairs. This amount only should be given to the landlord in the form of a rent increase.[5]

Similar proposals were made by the Chartered Auctioneers' and Estate Agents' Institute in their *Memorandum on the Amendment of the Rent Restriction Acts* of 1952. The Institute proposed that as an added check upon abuse of the proposed rent increase, a system of certificates of disrepair be introduced. This scheme, originally proposed by the second Ridley Committee, was based upon provision in the 1920 Act.[6]

The C A E A I also made proposals to deal with a variety of leasehold problems which were beginning to emerge. There was a general problem in south Wales, but the national problem was with business leases. The Institute proposed that mixed business and residential premises be under seven year lease which, if the parties themselves could not agree on a price, might be set by a tribunal.[7]

The C A E A I made clear in their memorandum that the acceptance of their proposals, and those of the R I C S would have consequences for the future of rent control. They pointed out that once having accepted rateable value as a base, all rents might, in the future, be fixed by reference to this base.[8] They pointed out that once repairs became of prime importance, the retention of control in new housing would become anomalous.[9] All this was taken into account by the government in determining policy.

This long debate on issues was made possible because the rent control problem was not a first priority of the Conservative government. Mr Macmillan had first to satisfy the party's pledge to build three hundred thousand houses per year. To this all his and the Ministry's efforts were turned. In 1953 the goal would be achieved. Time for thought and action on problems of rent control became possible.

The government announced its policy conclusions in a White Paper, *Houses: The Next Step.*[10] Some suggested that the Paper reflected the departmental view more than it reflected the politicians' conclusions. But there was no real evidence one way or another. The White Paper was drafted on the basis of a 1 per cent sample collected in the 1951 census. The government yearned to disengage as much as possible from the provision of housing. But this could not be accomplished in the short run. Instead, the government proposed to alter the forms of participation in the provision of housing.

The government made clear that its basic commitment would no longer be the general increase in the total stock. Now it would take primary interest in slum clearance. At the same time, the onus for increased taxation and specific responsibility for new construction would go to the local authorities.[11] By 'slum' the government meant property actually unfit for habitation. They proposed to exclude from this category dwellings which merely lacked basic amenities. This severely limited the commitment,[12] though it did not alter the legal definition of the term.

The provision of new housing, 'whether for let or sale', was to become a matter, primarily, of private rather than public enterprise. Thus it was hoped to further reduce the government's subsidy commitments.[13]

All this withdrawal by the government would be possible only if the existing stock of housing was brought up to and maintained in a good standard of repair. It was politically and philosophically impossible to abandon rent control, however distasteful the control.[14] But part of the landlord's funds would be provided by the rent increases due to revaluation.[15] To keep houses in the market, a sufficient rent increase to allow ongoing repairs had to be provided.[16]

Like the professional bodies, the government rejected the percentage increase.[17] Rent tribunals, the government said, would be equally ineffective. There was no standard upon which tribunals could make determinations.[18] The government therefore accepted the rateable value basis. With the report of the Girdwood Committee on the cost of repairs, the government presented cogent evidence to justify an increase equal to twice the statutory deduction.[19] The government contended that stringent controls on the increase would prevent a mere landlord's windfall.[20] The government accepted the professional bodies' view of the problem, and proposed to make a start in dealing with them subject only to political restraints.

Responsibility for preparing the draft White Paper and the subsequent Bills rested with the civil servants. But there is no certainty as to who actually did the work. It is said that both Mr Harold Symon, then under-secretary of the Local Government Division, and Mr S. P. W. Wilkinson, then under-secretary of the Housing Division, can claim the rather dubious credit. Of Mr Wilkinson it is claimed that the 1954 and 1957 Acts were stages along a policy path that he outlined for the incoming Conservative government in 1951. There is no evidence of this. Mr Symon's claim to have been the principal architect of the White Paper and Bill has often been accepted. But there is evidence to the contrary.

The responsible ministers were Mr Harold Macmillan and Mr Ernest Marples. Mr Macmillan was well liked by the Ministry. He is said to have run the Ministry the way he had run his publishing house. He held regular meetings of 'the board', in this case the under-secretaries of the relevant divisions. His enemies have suggested that he was over-cautious. It has been rumoured that the multiplier for the rent increase was cut from the 2·5 originally proposed to 2. This was due, it was said, to Mr Macmillan's Stockton memories. Indeed, *The Economist* contended that the increase was insubstantial and would not provide sufficient funds to encourage the necessary repairs. The checks provided in the Bill would not be sufficient to force landlords to do repairs. The R I C S came to the same conclusion.[21] Mr Marples is said to have taken little part in the work. Indeed, Mr Macmillan's frequent interventions to explicate errors made by Mr Marples in debate are attributed to Mr Marples' ignorance of the subject. The imprecise nature of civil service and ministerial responsibility was reflected in the Bill that resulted.

The Bill as it was introduced broadly proposed to transform the White Paper into legislation. Whether the restrictions were harmful, politically inspired, additions could not be known. On Report the decontrol of all converted dwellings and the exclusion from control of new dwellings was added. Though this was implicit in the White Paper this provision was added on Report to avoid inciting the Opposition too soon.[22] Despite his reputation, Mr Macmillan did not give way to amendments from any quarter and the Bill as drafted became law.

Mr Macmillan was helped in his obstinacy by the leader of the Opposition on the Bill, Mr Bevan. The Opposition had considerable sympathy for the Bill. The problems were acknowledged and only details of the Bill were questioned. The Opposition presented no alternative strategy. The Bill may have received scrutiny, but no real attack.

The Bill as passed has been adjudged a failure. The restrictions hedging the increases gave rise to endless litigation, as the various property journals' pages indicated. The considerable initial capital investment in repairs which had to be made within a limited period to qualify the property discouraged many landlords. The disrepair provisions proved a similar discouragement. Rents did not rise. Repairs were not made. No substantial new construction of private housing to let was undertaken.

But the Bill did have two lasting consequences: it introduced a variety of new techniques for dealing with rent control; it 'demonstrated' that rent control was not too politically explosive. The civil servants and politicians were ready to try again.

## Priorities

The drive towards three hundred thousand houses and the first attacks on rent restriction were soon over. Faced with the problem of what to do in the field of housing and local government, the government determined that its priorities needed re-examination.

Three aspects of the Ministry's work competed for attention. One constant source of concern was the state of local government, especially that of Greater London. Proposals for dealing with this would mature later. Planning, returned to the Ministry after a brief interlude of independence under Hugh Dalton, was a constant interest. With Mr Sandys's primary interest in planning* and the dynamic qualities of the deputy secretary in charge of the planning side of the Ministry's work, Dame Evelyn Sharp, it was not surprising that planning took pride of place. This was all the more likely as the then permanent secretary did not dominate his Ministry in the way Dame Evelyn was to do. The third aspect of Ministry work, housing, with which rents tended to be lumped, was dependent to a great extent on the activity as regarded the other sectors.

The toughest problem was London. The system of boroughs and functional responsibility in London was no longer reasonable. This problem occupied a considerable amount of Ministry attention, though the problem was not to be dealt with until 1957–8.[23] It was of special significance to the Conservatives, who were angered by the long-standing power of the London Labour Party. In this instance both policy and politics dictated its place.

Though the Ministry abandoned the sort of general planning practiced by Hugh Dalton's Ministry, aesthetic planning persisted, of necessity. This redirection was reflected in the Clean Air Act, Green Belt circulars, and new town development. What little research continued during the middle 1950s was done to aid this effort.

Two problems, rating and housing subsidies, affected all three of the major divisions of the Ministry. The decisions taken on these were necessary preliminaries to planning and the structure of local government responsibility for housing.

The rating system, which affected local government revenues most immediately and would have an impact on rents legislation, was hopelessly out of date. Reform had been postponed through war and crisis. The 1956 Valuation Act did nothing more than overhaul a long outdated procedure. But the question of what the base year should be, and similar questions, made this not a simple piece of legislation. How to reconcile the needs of the future with the demands of the precedents was not really resolved. But this revaluation was a necessary preliminary to rents legislation based upon rateable value.

The other necessary preliminary was a determination of the extent

* Note Mr Sandys' role in the Civic Trust and similar bodies.

c

of public, especially local government, responsibility for the provision of accommodation to let. The pledges made in *Houses: The Next Step* were fulfilled by the Housing Subsidies Act (1956). In this, the government withdrew from the construction of new houses on anything other than a welfare principle, except in the new towns programme, rationalised as a form of slum clearance. Thereafter further building of public housing was to be used mainly for slum clearance – to replace unfit housing and to rehouse those who could not obtain housing otherwise. Principal responsibility for new building was transferred from the public to the private sector. This was delayed by the 1955 general election which found the Bill still in the process of consideration by Parliament, and hence had to be reintroduced in the new Parliament.

The decisions on these two aspects of policy made rent control a possible but not a necessary subject for legislative consideration. Two other considerations gave rent control a claim. Any legislation of a regulatory nature, and especially rent control legislation, requires constant attention to 'patching up' and to revision in the light of new or unforeseen problems. This was naturally of great concern to the civil servants. Perhaps more influential on ministers and the government were political considerations. There are advantages in dealing with controversial matters in the first two years of a Parliament. The two or three succeeding years allow any political repercussions to die away.

Further factors motivating action were the assurances offered by the contemporary 'liberal' economists. The economy, it was contended, could stand tinkering without strain. Further, a liberal economy dedicated to free enterprise had to reduce public expenditure in such areas as housing.

It was within the requirements of the past and the contemporary priorities that legislation was shaped. The 1953–4 White Paper and Act contributed to later decisions. Other contemporary factors, internal to the Ministry, helped round out the decision-making structure.

## Governmental Structure

The activity of the Ministry of Housing and Local Government was shaped by the commitment to work through local authorities. Consequently, the Ministry could not assume an 'over-riding responsibility for ensuring the execution of national policy'.[24] Nor could the Ministry under these conditions make long-term plans safe in the assurance of their fulfilment, subject only to conflicting claims upon national resources. The addition of planning to the traditional concerns reflected as much the need to ration scarce resources as to inspire the socialist utopia. The diffuse nature of responsibility could be seen in the structure and authority of the Ministry.

The principal functions of the Ministry were reflected by large divisions: Local Government, Housing, New Towns, Water, Planning (London and the Home Counties; the Provinces), Minerals. There were also Local Government Finance, Engineering, Establishment and Organisation Divisions. Supplementing these were a variety of smaller units, some technical, some regulatory, some administrative. These were the Architect's Staff, Technical Planning Staff, Inspectors of Alkali, Estates Staff, Housing and Planning Inspectorate, Accountant General's Department, Legal and Parliamentary Staff. Coordination between the activities of 'Whitehall' and the local authority was achieved by a customer-oriented geographic arrangement of ten regional offices in England and a separate Welsh Office. These were intended to be the eyes of the Ministry and channels of communication between local authority and central direction. To these regional offices were attached the District Auditor's staff.[25] All this reflected the Ministry's origins in utilitarian concerns, and the continued dominance of the Ministry by the utilitarian spirit.

Like the Board of Trade, the Ministry of Housing and Local Government was only an administrative entity which coordinated a variety of public health and welfare functions. Traditionally, these were the responsibility of local authorities subject to the supervision of the type provided by the Poor Law Board. Many of the Ministry's other functions came from the Ministry of Health. Health itself was 'hived off' because of the dominant need to provide supervision for the National Health Service, and to prevent one minister holding responsibility for so many aspects of public concern. It is in this diverse setting that housing was directed.

Only a small part of the Ministry was directly concerned with housing. This Division consisted of an under-secretary and assorted administrative and other grade staff. For most of its activities, the division operated, consistent with the pattern set for the Ministry as a whole, through the regional offices to which they were only indirectly related. Local authorities often planned activities independently of the Ministry's Division on Housing. Consequently, the Ministry was not only unable to ensure that 'houses are built where they are certainly needed', it was equally unable to 'achieve a comprehensive assessment of relative need'.[26] Only the grossest controls were available to encourage or discourage construction: the obviously limited one of exhortation on the local authorities and the more effective limits imposed by use of financial powers. These limitations upon housing policy were partially inspired by the feelings of some that the health of local government ought to be encouraged through increased local responsibility even if this prevented effective policy. Professor Griffith comments extensively on the alternative relationships between central and local government.[27] It was within this administrative setting that housing policy, such as it was, could be formulated.

The implementation of the Housing Subsidies Act was the principal task of the Housing Division in 1956. Circular 29/56 encouraged the development of a Differential Rents policy by local authorities. This mean that tenants were to be charged different rents for similar accommodation according to the capacity of the tenants to pay. But the Division could do no more than urge. Under the Act, subsidies for 'general needs' construction were virtually eliminated. Publication of a White Paper reinforced the emphasis to be placed in the future on slum clearance.[28] But the actual impact was not and was not expected, at least by politicians, to be very great in monetary terms. For the new policy could be only as effective as the local authorities allowed. A big authority, like the London County Council, could operate in the open financial market. Smaller authorities found that despite incentives they could not implement the new policy for lack of funds. Another circular, which encouraged the provision of more housing for the aged, remained an equally pious hope.[29] If direct control was eschewed, indirect fiscal controls remained, at least theoretically, possible.

But this was not really possible in Britain. Housing construction was financed initially by the builders themselves. Demand for housing was created with the assistance of the building societies. But even to raise the interest rate, and so the cost of a mortgage, would not control the demand for new construction, for Public Health construction by local authorities was separate from this. No end could be foreseen. Nor could public construction be regulated in tandem with private construction. The anomalous situation arose in which control of a fiscal nature did no more to encourage private construction than physical control, by encouraging a shift towards owner-occupation.

One explanation for the failure to devise an effective policy for housing to let in the private sector was the absence of long-term responsibility within the Ministry. Indeed to this day precise responsibility for rent control policy during the 1950s remains a mystery. There is no doubt that in 1946 and 1955 responsibility for rent control lay with the Housing Division. The Acts of 1946 and 1957 were known to be the responsibility of officials in the Housing Division. Observers today are amazed that two officials have been rumoured responsible for the 1954 Housing Repairs and Rents Act, which, they believe, these officials ought to disown. The rivals are Mr Wilkinson, in the period to 1955 head of the Housing Division, and Mr H. Symon, in the same period head of the Local Government Division. Mr Wilkinson, it is claimed, had charge of rent control, which he directed in line with the overall Ministry policy on housing. Of Mr Symon it is claimed that ever since his work in 1933 he had been connected with rent control. It is suggested that responsibility for the topic followed him from division to division. There is conflicting testimony by contemporary observers. The most logical explanation seems to be that while Mr Wilkinson may well have had general responsibility for rent control as part of housing, many of the details of rent control policy and legislation were shaped by Mr Symon. Whether he had direct responsibility or not, his knowledge would give him a special place in any minister's counsels. In 1955 responsibility seems to have settled in the Housing Division.

But in 1955 the Ministry was in administrative turmoil. The permanent secretary, who had made no great personal impact upon the Ministry, retired. Dame Evelyn Sharp, the deputy secretary in charge of planning, succeeded as permanent secretary. The selection was made despite considerable doubts about women as permanent secretaries, Dame Evelyn's political views, and her past political attitudes.* No one questioned her toughness as a considerable asset for the role of permanent secretary. At the same time, the heads of both the Housing and Local Government Divisions (Wilkinson and Symon) left the Ministry for private affairs, the start of a trend of which the service had previously had little experience.[30] It was something of a shock. It was also disorganising. Succeeding Mr Wilkinson

---

* Especially her role in the ILP; see R. E. Dowse, *Left in the Centre*, Longmans, London, 1966, p. 83.

at Housing was Mr S. W. C. Phillips, who had been under-secretary in charge of Planning (London and Home Counties). Mr Phillips was particularly suitable since the principal rents and housing problems always arose in London. At least in part, future housing scarcities were the consequence of decisions about Green Belts and general planning with which he was familiar.

Though rent control arose as a consequence of war-born shortages, other policies necessitated its continuation in peace. Some of these new causes were the aesthetic plans drawn up by postwar governments, especially the Green Belt policy which had the effect of limiting new construction in London and requiring more intense planning for housing within the permitted limits.[31] But the Planning Division was more concerned with righting the difficulties created by the unco-ordinated sprawl of the nineteenth-century city. The Housing Division, with nominal responsibility for housing, took no interest in the plans which could make new housing possible. Any policy which seemed likely to permit more construction within the limits of plans was likely to find favour. For reasons which are developed in the next chapter, rent control was seized upon. The failure to seek a more comprehensive solution was partially a lack of will. But it was also a matter of inability. The reasons for this incapacity emerge in the discussion of the research apparatus.

## Research Organisation

Research was not a popular concern of the government or civil service in the 1950s. Nor has it become much more so in more recent times. The civil service of the twentieth century created 'a tradition of government which led to a distrust of scientific method and statistical analysis and which in the past permitted decisions to be reached on data the inadequacy of which would have appalled a schoolboy scientist'.[32] The best that can be said of many departments is that they were so busy as to be unable to do more than collect facts of immediate relevance.[33] Few had the advantage of the Department of Education and Science, which possesses its own Inspectorate and collects masses of data through them.[34] Inclination and capacity combined to establish ignorance and amateurishness as proper procedure.

Recently, departments such as Housing and Local Government have become aware of their own deficiencies in the collection and use of data. A 1963 White Paper asserted:

Information about housing conditions is not as complete as it now needs to be, and the government intends to improve it. It has always been regarded as the responsibility of local authorities to keep themselves informed about local housing conditions, the government relying on the ten-yearly census for the national picture. Since the war the need for additional houses has been so universal that there has not been cause to analyse the make-up of demand or the quality of housing, apart from the slum surveys. Local authorities keep housing lists but these are based on widely differing criteria. The government now intend to collect more comprehensive information by regular and systematic sample surveys, and the necessary arrangements are being made.[35]

But such was not the case in 1955-6 when information was being gathered for the drafting of the new Rent Bill.

The research organisation of the Ministry, as it pertained to rent control, was divided into two parts. The most important, so far as the Ministry was concerned, was the statistical section of the Housing Division, under a chief research officer. The other unit interested in rent control was the housing section of the Social Survey, a division of the Central Office of Information. The Central Office was the chief information collecting agency of the government. The Social Survey did research under contract to various other agencies.

But the Ministry of Housing apparently preferred to reach decisions unencumbered by too much information. One former civil servant directly concerned with rent control has alleged that statistics inevitably embarrassed the Ministry. In any case a policy of disengagement did not seem to require extensive information to assist in the selection of the most appropriate methods of decontrol. Precedent alone seemed to be sufficient.

There were, indeed, evident difficulties in the use of research. A principal obstacle was the transitory nature of demand for accommodation. Consumers customarily listed what they most missed in their present accommodation. Once satisfied, a new series of requirements emerged. At the same time, the householder determined his standards by those prevailing in the community as a whole. What was economically acceptable at one period, need not, with changed conditions both of income and consumption opportunity, remain so. Nor was it easy to determine the 'market'. According to Mr Needleman:

The pattern of a consumer's preferences will depend partly on his taste and partly on what he believes the structure of prices to be. He may

miscalculate the cost of satisfying his wants . . . and where such miscalcula-
tions occur he may not carry out his previously stated intentions. . . .
The activities of the house-movers themselves may alter the structure of
prices.[36]

Thus, it was difficult to foresee how useful research might be.

Moreover, research could not be devoid of political consequences,
and it might prove politically inexpedient. Sometimes research
exposed unsatisfied needs and aroused hitherto dormant expectations,
or raised problems with which the government preferred not to cope
either on pragmatic or ideological grounds. Mass survey research, or
simply the publication of research, stirred expectations of reform
which might be neither feasible nor clearly remediable for the situation at hand. Plans for legislation must not be revealed by preparatory
research. Research and information might somehow force the scope
and direction of political decisions. Research was therefore to be
distrusted and eschewed.[37]

In the case of research on housing, the problem was particularly
sensitive. Economists and social scientists differed fundamentally.
Research from one vantage point raised new questions to be explored.
In the delicate political situation emphasis by research on the
individual served the Labour Party. In part, then, the antipathy of
the Ministry to 'information' was a desire to shield itself from
criticism.

Research required a research unit. As an administrative entity it
would develop a distinct cohesiveness with a prepared position that
asked to be heard. Statisticians usually in the executive or technical
grades, might become a ginger group within the department, presenting views at variance with 'departmental philosophy'.[38] No
Ministry could accept too much of this – witness the difficulties
Brittan describes in the Treasury.[39] But this was especially difficult in
a Ministry as tied to its hierarchy as the Ministry of Housing and
Local Government. The dominance of the Administrative Class and
the character of Dame Evelyn made a parallel source of policy unacceptable.

The embryonic research unit that was operating before 1951 was
largely disbanded in the reorganisation of the Ministry during 1955.
The change of name merely reinforced the disinterest in research.[40]
The technicians who might have acted as a unit in a research group
were distributed in ones and twos to the various Divisions. Their
influence was now limited to their individual capacity through their

Division, through their assistant and under-secretaries. Not only were their contacts to the permanent secretary and the ministers thus limited, but their duties were circumscribed by the definition of the 'terms of reference' within which research would be done. If the Ministry as a unit did not discourage individual research, it certainly discouraged researchers by giving them a relatively low place in the hierarchy.[41] The consequence was that key administrative grade personnel were intellectually superior to their technical counterparts. Since the academics at the time engaged in housing research (the best entered only later) were not as knowledgeable as the civil servants there was no point in consulting them.[42]

The new role assigned to the researcher, after reorganisation, became particularly evident in the treatment of data arising from he 1951 Housing Census, especially the data on the number of new independent households being formed. Dame Evelyn was perfectly aware that the figures indicated that a new view of the housing supply/demand structure was implicit in the research being done on headship.* She pointed out many of the implications in public.[43] Yet she gave no indication that serious policy implications ought to be drawn from the new figures. She certainly never presented either figures or implications to the ministers for their consideration. Nor did she see reason to pursue this research. Nor did she ensure that those Divisions whose policies would have been affected became aware of the available new statistical methods.

The non-Ministry source of information on housing was the Social Survey. Though emasculated during this period it still managed to retain its integrity as an independent research unit. There was a general decline in activity between 1952–8. Only the Ministry of Agriculture used it consistently. Others – Labour, Health, Treasury, Common Service Organisation, Board of Trade, G P O, Transport, and the Department of Scientific and Industrial Research – all used it more often than the Ministry of Housing. The Ministry used the Survey on a small scale in 1946, 1947, 1949, 1950, 1958 and 1959 but quite extensively in 1960 and thereafter. But during the entire period 1951–7 the Survey was not used at all by Housing and Local Government. The only Ministries which used the Survey less were those with

---

* Headship rate shows the proportion of any particular group in the population who are heads of households. This is useful as it enables prediction as to the rate of household formation and the likely future requirements of households based upon estimates of their size related to the age of the head of household.

no great contact with public services or those with substantial independent research organisations.[44]

The Social Survey was not likely to be consulted. The personnel of the Survey and of the Ministry did not get on well together. Perhaps the most important reason was that Social Survey did represent a group with expertise on housing, not committed either to the administrative hierarchy, and thus not subject to direct pressure or to the Ministry philosophy. As such, it constituted a potential political threat. Never was this more evident than in the controversy over the Survey's Report on the 1957 Act (Cmnd 1246). The existence and contents of this document were leaked to the Opposition. One of the figures connected with this leak (though by no means the only possible source) was the head of Social Survey. A parliamentary attack forced the minister to publish this potentially highly damaging piece of research. In fact, no damage was done because no one could understand the Report outside of the small group already reasonably well informed.[45] And indeed, the Survey was not consulted about the 1957 Rent Act.

Both Social Survey and the Statistical Section of the Ministry were engaged in what might be termed applied research. That is, they developed particular policy formulations and analysed the consequences either retrospectively and prospectively.[46] But many other research functions were relevant to the decision-making process. The library of the Ministry maintained an adequate collection of the 'basic books'. Its principal function was as repository of the departmental Papers. Whatever the disadvantages, there were few departments which could so readily consult the thoughts of their predecessors on a given topic. The material was bound and readily available.* The library performed the 'intelligence function' of monitoring the various periodicals for information of interest to the Ministry. A quite respectable card file was kept. But as the staff was small the file was inevitably incomplete. Nor were the categories chosen necessarily those which the harassed civil servant might easily consult.

The research function of most importance, the 'information function', was least well performed. A reasonably systematic collection,

* Save to the scholar! These papers, however, are far less valuable than the outsider might imagine. Those dating from 1933 and 1938 rent restriction legislation contain nothing that would have been of real value in 1956. After all, what good civil servant would allow anything truly controversial into the files, and how much of the significant decision-making is taken without formal memoranda?

analysis and publication of data on current activities was not undertaken until 1966. That the Ministry was forced to turn to the Inland Revenue for the raw data on which it prepared estimates of the consequences of the proposed Rent Act was symbolic of the problem. Virtually the only data published came not from the Housing Division but from the Planning or Local Government Divisions. Partly, this was a reaction to the pre-1951 situation in which data on any problem was readily available on account of the various controls.[47]

The academic community might have filled some of the gaps in research endeavours. But the Ministry of Housing was a notoriously difficult Ministry with which to deal. Few Ministries excelled its capacity to discourage research which might have political repercussions on the Ministry or its policy. Not surprisingly, then, through the middle 1950s only Dr Cullingworth was systematically concerned with housing and rents policy. Even he worked almost completely without Ministry assistance. A factor in this scarcity of concern was the general disinterest in housing problems. Neither the B B C nor the serious Sunday press were interested. Only as an aftermath of the Rent Act was the Rowntree Group brought together to do research on housing and housing policy.[48] The role of other major sources of information, pressure groups and professional associations will be discussed elsewhere.

The possibilities for research prior to the introduction of the Bill were thus quite limited. There was a bias against research and research organisations. No outside help would be accepted and the Ministry would not make provision to do the work internally. The disastrous consequences can be seen by a study of the data available to draftsmen of the Bill.

## Available Data

The defects in the research organisation only partly explained the faulty data upon which decision-making was based. As the collection of data must be an important part of the legislative process, it is important to see how and why these faults arose. Not only does the study of the data help to explain defects in the process *per se*, but it also helps to explain decisions which the participants, with hindsight, recognise to have been mistaken. To survey the government's data alone would not suffice. First, non-governmental data has been surveyed and then the various government sources and procedures.

The principal non-governmental data open to the Ministry was that provided by PEP in its 1949 and 1955 studies. The first concentrated on the problems of the landlord. This report, like that of the Girdwood Commission,[49] pointed to the impossible financial situation in which landlords were placed.[50] The policy conclusions, inevitably, were that rents would have to be raised quite substantially.[51] The second study, done in 1955, concluded that the supply and demand for housing were coming into balance. Only three-quarters of a million more houses were needed to bring the total supply to balance.[52] This was based on the assumption that the birth rate was falling. That this figure did not allow for overcrowding and for the capacity of the population to form more households was ignored in both the policy conclusions of the article and the implications drawn from the article by the Ministry.[53]

Only one substantial piece of government-sponsored research had been undertaken well in advance of the drafting. This was the Report '1953–4 Household Expenditure, Report of an Enquiry into Household Expenditure', done not in quest of housing data but as a general Paper for the Ministry of Labour and National Service, published in 1957. This provided a wealth of data on the rents actually being paid, both regionally and by income group. The following figures (table 6) on Rents, Drink, and Tobacco were used to demonstrate that the average family spent more on luxuries than housing. It was not used by the Ministry of Housing as a fair sample of prevailing rents. The Ministry claimed that the Social Survey sample of 12,911 units (comprising 22,673 persons, compared to 1,000 persons in the average Gallup Poll of the period) was too small to be reliable. Of particular interest are the relatively high figures in the second part of the table at the lower end of the income scale, and the low percentage of 'luxuries' to 'housing'.

Not merely the quality and quantity of the data assembled by the Ministry for the preparation of the Rent Bill should be called into question. Officials and ministers, as well as subsequent commentators, have all pointed to the failure to assemble headship rate data as a major omission. The first opportunity to use this data came in 1952 when the 1 per cent sample of the 1951 census became available, and revealed for the first time the number of concealed households.* In 1952 a departmental Paper was circulated which revealed that head-

* Households which would have liked to occupy separate accommodation but did not.

TABLE 6

*Social Survey's Expenditure Survey,\* 1953–4, for the United Kingdom*

(Average household expenditure – rounded to nearest penny)

| region | rent unfurnished (including rates) | | drink | | tobacco | |
|---|---|---|---|---|---|---|
| | s | d | s | d | s | d |
| Northern | 14 | 5 | 8 | 8 | 17 | 10 |
| East and West Ridings | 13 | 4 | 9 | 0 | 15 | 4 |
| North-West | 15 | 2 | 8 | 7 | 16 | 5 |
| N. Midlands | 14 | 7 | 10 | 3 | 15 | 6 |
| Midlands | 14 | 5 | 10 | 11 | 15 | 7 |
| Eastern | 16 | 3 | 7 | 4 | 13 | 10 |
| C. of London | 21 | 11 | 8 | 10 | 17 | 5 |
| G. London | 22 | 5 | 7 | 10 | 16 | 7 |
| Southern | 19 | 3 | 7 | 8 | 14 | 2 |
| S.-Western | 17 | 3 | 6 | 3 | 13 | 11 |
| Wales | 14 | 1 | 7 | 10 | 16 | 5 |
| Scotland | 12 | 3 | 6 | 11 | 18 | 4 |

| weekly income of household | rent, rates, water | | average payment for | | | | | |
|---|---|---|---|---|---|---|---|---|
| | | | food | | alcoholic drink | | tobacco | |
| | s | d | s | d | s | d | s | d |
| £50+ | 30 | 5 | 162 | 10 | 37 | 8 | 27 | 5 |
| £30–£50 | 29 | 0 | 137 | 0 | 26 | 8 | 33 | 4 |
| £20–£30 | 20 | 8 | 122 | 8 | 18 | 1 | 28 | 3 |
| £14–£20 | 18 | 6 | 99 | 11 | 11 | 6 | 21 | 6 |
| £10–£14 | 17 | 0 | 83 | 0 | 7 | 3 | 16 | 7 |
| £8–£10 | 15 | 6 | 72 | 5 | 6 | 1 | 13 | 6 |
| £6–£8 | 13 | 7 | 60 | 11 | 4 | 1 | 11 | 1 |
| £3–£6 | 12 | 3 | 43 | 5 | 2 | 5 | 5 | 10 |
| under £3 | 10 | 1 | 25 | 6 | 1 | 1 | 2 | 1 |

Source: Ministry of Labour (by Social Survey).

ship data could be of value and had several potentials as a predictive tool.[54] In 1954 the headship rates were used to project local authority requirements. But only in late 1957 did headship come into use for national planning. It was not proposed as a working tool in planning housing until late 1959.[55] But even without this data, that assembled was grossly inadequate.

One of the main charges against the data assembled, by both Social Survey and the Ministry, was inaccuracy. Part of this was

\* Adapted from Ministry of Labour, *1953–54 Household Expenditure. Report of an Enquiry into Household Expenditure, Non-Parliamentary Papers*, 1957.

subsequently seen to be the inadequacy of Inland Revenue's valuation list of property.* Inland Revenue is reputed to contend that the Valuation Office were not in any way concerned with the statistical merit of the exercises which were devised by the Ministry. The data which Inland Revenue drew up ought to have indicated: 1. Address; 2. Description; 3. Rateable value; 4. Gross value; 5. Whether the premise is a dwelling; 6. Whether owned by local authority or owner-occupied.[56] In fact, the Ministry is reported to have asked only for 1939 rent per annum and 1956 gross value, the date of sale, construction, estimated rent of a smaller unit, and subsequently a small random sample of estimated rents. Several criteria made this sample, *prima facie*, unreliable. The Ministry excluded flats or maisonettes. This would seriously distort the view of the housing situation in major cities.

The first request came during early 1956. About three months later the Ministry asked for information on properties about which definite data could easily be obtained due to their sale. Two months later a revision was asked for to take account of the possibility that the Rent Restriction Acts might be repealed and the landlord bear the cost of repairs, insurance and maintenance. At the same time, valuers were asked to provide a larger sample of estimated rentals. But they were specifically enjoined from making any on-site estimates and restrained from too meticulous examination of their own records. In a later circular valuers were asked to estimate rents outside the controlled sector, by way of contrast with those in control. No one allowed at the time for the potential difficulty and inaccuracies. It was impossible for Inland Revenue to know precisely whether the property in question was actually for rent or owner-occupied. Thus both types of housing were included in the sample supplied. Often property on the hereditaments lists had been demolished. The consequence was that the figures presented by the Ministry to the public were almost 100 per cent overestimates of consequences to be expected by enactment of the Rent Bill.[57]

Another source of confusion was the nature of the sample units as against those specified in the proposed Bill. The Bill referred to dwelling units. But these were the units actually being lived in as separate accommodation. Often the hereditaments lists would show several such units which filled a single building as a single dwelling

* The list of rateable values of property upon which rates could be collected by local authorities.

unit. This was especially likely since prior to 1957 there was no reason for landlord or tenant to obtain an apportionment[58] of annual value.

Yet another difficulty was the inability of the government to estimate correctly the proportion of dwellings with rateable values above the proposed control limits which were 'let unfurnished at controlled rents'. It has been suggested that the presentation requirements led to omission of cautions attached during internal circulation. In addition, a certain amount of rounding off beyond the usual took place. From the vantage point of many, the selection of the figure 750,000 for use in the White Paper as the number of houses to be decontrolled represented the whim of the moment; it bore very little relation to the realities of the situation.[59]

As can be seen, estimates of current or future rents such as those presented in tables 3 and 4 of Cmnd 17, the government's explanatory White Paper on the Bill, could have little sound basis. Neither the Ministry which pretended confidence in its figures nor the Social Survey which pointedly remained sceptical could be very definite. The Social Survey was plagued by the failure of tenants to be able to produce a rent book and their complete inability to distinguish rents from rates. Thus the following, substantially different, figures were produced in the Ministry's and Social Survey's calculations (table 7). It seems likely that the Ministry seriously overestimated the number of tenants who, in 1956, were paying low rents and seriously underestimated the number whose rent was already quite close to the proposed limits for increased controlled rent.

TABLE 7
*Householders Paying Rent, by Amount of Rent*[60] (per cent)

|  | social survey % | ministry % | Gallup % |
|---|---|---|---|
| Rent of less than 5s per week | 11 | 23 ⎫ | |
| 5s–10s | 49 | 41 ⎭ | 10 |
| 10s–15s | | 13 ⎫ | |
| 15s–20s | 23 | 8 ⎭ | 32 |
| £1+ | 12 | 1 | 51 |

(Note: Errors due to transposition or categories not shown yield totals less than 100%)

Unpublished, but mentioned in debate and of great importance in the decision-making process, was the estimate of turnover. No very accurate estimate was obtainable. In the end some rough calculation and still rougher generalisation produced a turnover rate of 5 per cent believed at the time to be liberal. In fact, the rate proved conservative.[61]

The government's data was inadequate both because it was poorly collected and because it was poorly evaluated. The difficulties of the Inland Revenue and of Ministry personnel in collecting and evaluating the data requested have remained a source of discussion even today. But even more important was the fact that some data which academics at the time might have thought essential was never collected. The date on density of occupation was barely adequate. None was collected on preference patterns or tenants' priorities in consumer expenditure decisions.[62] Thus basic data was lacking.

What was also lacking was an examination of alternative systems of rent control. No re-evaluation of the controls based on rateable value and gross value, adopted at the instance of the professional associations by Mr Macmillan in 1953, took place. Even without access to Ministry Papers this is still demonstrable. Throughout their statistical inquiries the Ministry never asked for calculations on any basis other than those laid out in the Rating and Valuation Act (1935) in which the distinctions between rateable and gross value were first made.[63] Thus, no new thinking had been done since *Housing: The Next Step.*[64] Indeed, not even the experience of other countries' systems of rent control was examined.

Objections to the disinterest, both as to data and new policy, of the Ministry were not merely academic in origin. *The Times* in a leader of 8 November 1956 complained that statistics were sorely lacking in the Ministry's case.[65] Professor Donnison pointed out that the proposal to amend the Rent Restriction Acts was not sudden. Under the circumstances, he argued, it was a responsibility of the Ministry to do as much research as necessary to assure full and accurate information.[66] Some of the reasons why this was not done will become evident when the relations between civil servants and ministers is examined.

## Relations between Ministers and Civil Servants

Data is collected to enable particular types of decisions to be made. But it is also collected for the particular people who must make the decisions. In 1956 it was the minister and a small group of civil servants who required data to map a new Rent Bill. The character of each member of the decision-making group, as well as their inter-relationships, helped to determine the information collected and the uses to which data was put. Whether to start such an analysis by defining the political role of civil servants or the policy role of ministers is now debatable. To begin by asserting the politics of the civil service should not be construed as necessarily adopting the Tory view of the administrative process.

C. H. Sisson's *The Spirit of British Administration* was merely the most pungent attempt to explain what Tory philosophers see as the role of the civil servant – the wielders of power without any responsibility save a vague 'national interest'. 'They [civil servants' opinions] are a mediocrity arrived at not because they are likely to be true, though sometimes they may even be that, but because in a system of protests and objections a man may hold them and escape without too many rotten eggs plastering his head'.[67] Thus, Sisson contends,

> The practical man . . . cannot afford to be sincere. He must, not only on all questions of value but even on matters of fact, share the provisional delusions of his fellows. It is a discipline, but it is not a discipline of the truth. It requires the muscles and obedience of an acrobat rather than the patience of a philosopher.[68]

This is quite a different conception from the Liberal and published civil service view. For the traditionalists the principal question has been how efficient, how loyal – in the broadest sense of the word – and how good was the advice of the civil servants.[69] It is these parallel visions of the same set of circumstances which must be pursued jointly.

The efficiency of the Ministry's organisation to deal with the Rent Bill depended upon two main characters: the permanent secretary and the most knowledgeable member of the drafting team of civil servants – in this instance the principal.* The character of Dame Evelyn has been frequently reported; her overall dominance of the Ministry, the extent to which it partook of her character, reduced her need for day to day contact with any issue. Though it has been reported that she proposed one of the major additions made to the original drafts, there was no indication that she took more than a general interest in the Bill. In any case, primary responsibility lay with Mr S. W. C. Phillipps, the under-secretary. Though one civil

* Confirmed in interviews with the people involved.

servant was brought in specifically to provide the group with some-
one familiar with past rent-control legislation, none had any recent
experience in dealing with the problems. It was only natural, therefore, that added weight was given to the memoranda of Mr H. Symon
(who had retired from the Ministry to the directorship of a landlord's
pressure group) and to Papers on past bills: for the tendency in times
of transition was to accept what had found favour in the past,
especially when it seemed so suitable to the current situation.[70] Thus,
the authority of the civil servants was somewhat reduced.

The role of the civil servants as decision-makers was made more
complex by the character of the minister. Mr Sandys was well known
for his methods in dealing with Ministry business in general and
legislation in particular. Bevins and Sampson both comment upon
the particular difficulties civil servants encountered in the preparation
of the Rent Bill.[71] Mr Sandys was extremely cautious. He took action
only after listening to many opinions, and often not then. He was
rather slow to accept anything new. Mr Sandys, partly from necessity,
partly from habit, preferred late working hours – and long sessions –
uncongenial to the civil servants. Until February 1956 Mr William
Deedes, the parliamentary secretary, served to protect Mr Sandys
from himself. By modulating the force of Mr Sandys' demands and
by coaxing him to accept at least some of the civil service ways, Mr
Deedes probably made the early part of Mr Sandys administration
more pleasant for the staff than the later. Without himself having any
academic pretensions Mr Deedes was said to have got on far better
with the civil servants than did Mr Powell (who succeeded Mr
Deedes as parliamentary secretary). Mr Powell was an academic
politician. The master of anything he touched, Mr Powell knew what
he wanted to such an extent that advice became almost irrelevant.
Moreover, he was unable to exercise a moderating influence on Mr
Sandys. Indeed, it was said that Mr Sandys had to exercise a
moderating influence on the schemes of Mr Powell. Three such
similar, tough-minded politicians as Mr Sandys, Mr Powell and
Dame Evelyn – all sure of what they wanted – inevitably clashed
often. There is no evidence, however, that this prevented effective (as
distinct from efficient) cooperation on the drafting of the Rent
Bill.[72]

But the consequence of this personal disharmony was stories of
administrative inefficiency that not even the most loyal civil servants
could conceal.[73] Mr Sandys insisted that drafting be conducted in his

presence and with his active participation. He refused to allow the technicians – legal and draftsmen – to carry on without hindrance. Thus the civil service was unable to relieve the Minister of many decisions which they would normally take without consultation.[74] On the other hand, considerable delegation of responsibility remained in matters of policy. It is in this relationship that the misuse of information became evident.

The civil servant ought to present facts, 'however unpalatable'.[75] But the selection of those facts, as to quality and quantity, always depended on the capacity and requirements fixed by the minister. Apparently Mr Sandys either did not require all the data available or, as some insist, could not absorb all that was presented. In any case the amount omitted or ignored seemed considerable. Certainly Mr Sandys and Mr Powell used little if any of the qualifications with which the statements of the statisticians were hedged. Nor did these qualifications appear in the White Paper accompanying the Bill.[76] Moreover, however limited his information, Mr Sandys seemed to consider that he had more than a sufficient base (of information) for the taking of policy decisions.

Perhaps the requirement that a minister be fully informed was less relevant in this case than in others. Mr Sandys readily accepted the views of the Ministry on general direction of policy. Preparation for legislation was carried out with goodwill often lacking.[77] Whether the civil servants were generally pro-Conservative or not, they were certainly all in favour of fundamental changes in the position on rent control, in this sense more 'Tory' than even Mr Sandys found acceptable. In any case, immediate tasks fell upon one of those, whom Professor Neustadt has described as possessing 'the frame of reference which befits a man whose career ladder rises up the central pillar of the Whitehall machine . . . where dwell the seniors of all seniors, moulders of ministers . . . knights in office, lords thereafter. . . .'[78] Such men naturally lead the minister down the 'proper' road.

Thus, data had remarkably little relevance to the decision-making group of its communal efforts. This happened in part because each member of the group was arguing a policy, not presenting information for consideration. In part, this was due to the general agreement on direction that preceded the drafting efforts. In part this reflected the character of the Ministry, of the ministers, and their personal relationships. The consequence of all this for the draft Bill was to be profound.

## Summary

The above setting, administrative and intellectual, determined the climate in which decisions on the Rent Act were taken. The 1954 Act provided both the intellectual base and the legislative reason for a new parliamentary effort. With the change in the rating system and the emergence of parliamentary time the Bill became a possibility. But was the government equipped to take the necessary decisions? Though difficulties in the 1954 Act's administration had emerged, there was no indication that the government was equipped to evaluate these. The discontinuity both of personnel and of divisional responsibility for rent control, not to mention the lack of central control over housing policy in general, made the administration and appraisal of policy difficult. The art of judgment was certainly made more impressionistic by the temporary strangulation of the research organisation and the consequent shortage of adequate data. But the difficulties were increased by problems which had nothing to do with the use and misuse of data. Such little information as was collected passed through the civil service sieve on the way up to senior civil service and political decision-makers. Often the decision-makers did not have even the whole of the inadequate stock of ministry information available to assist in decision-making. But it was in this setting that decisions had to be taken.

NOTES

1 Royal Institution of Chartered Surveyors, *A Memorandum on Rent Restrictions and the Repair Problem*, R I C S, London, 1951, para. 19.
2 *Ibid.*, para. 20.
3 *Ibid.*, para. 21.
4 *Ibid.*, paras 14–17.
5 *Ibid.*, para. 12.
6 Chartered Auctioneers' and Estate Agents' Institute, *Memorandum on the Amendment of the Rent Restriction Acts*, C A E A I, London, April 1952, para. 21.
7 *Ibid.*, para. 24.
8 *Ibid.*, para. 13.
9 *Ibid.*, para. 23.
10 *Houses: The Next Step*, 1953–4, Cmd 8996, *Parliamentary Papers*, xxvi, 1.
11 *Ibid.*, paras 47, 63 and p. 6.
12 *Ibid.*
13 *Ibid.*, para. 91.

14 *Ibid.*, paras 25, 27.
15 *Ibid.*, para. 31.
16 *Ibid.*, para. 1, and p. 6.
17 *Ibid.*, para. 29.
18 *Ibid.*, para. 30.
19 *Ibid.*, paras 32, 34, 35.
20 *Ibid.*, paras 38, 39.
21 *The Economist*, vol. 173, pp. 18–19.
22 *The Real Estate Journal*, vol. 5, no. 1, p. 8.
23 F. Smallwood, *Greater London* . . ., Indianapolis, 1965, pp. 10 ff.
24 J. A. G. Griffith, *Central Departments and Local Authorities*, Allen and Unwin, London, 1966, p. 288.
25 *Imperial Calendar*, 1956.
26 Griffith, *Central Departments and Local Authorities*, p. 288.
27 *Ibid.*, conclusions and p. 289.
28 *Houses: The Next Step.*
29 Ministry of Housing and Local Government Circular 32/56 (1956), Ministry of Housing and Local Government, *Report of the Ministry of Housing and Local Government for the Year 1956*, Cmnd 193, June 1957.
30 *Imperial Calendar*, 1955.
31 M H L G, *Report of the Ministry of Housing and Local Government for the Year 1955*, Cmd 9876, October 1956.
32 Griffith, *Central Departments and Local Authorities*, p. 559.
33 *Ibid.*
34 *Ibid.*, p. 557.
35 *Ibid.*, p. 292; Cmnd 2050, paras 7 and 8.
36 Lionel Needleman, *The Economics of Housing*, Staples Press, London, 1965, p. 50.
37 Louis Moss, 'The Social Survey in the Government Process' (unpublished evidence submitted by the Social Survey to the Heyworth Committee), part III, p. 2.
38 Bevins, *The Greasy Pole*, Hodder and Stoughton, London, 1965, pp. 54–69.
39 S. Brittan, *The Treasury Under the Tories, 1951–1964*, Penguin, London, 1964.
40 Donnison, *The Government of Housing*, Penguin, 1967, p. 353.
41 *Ibid.*
42 *Ibid.*
43 Dame Evelyn Sharp, 'Housing: The Past Ten Years', *Chartered Surveyor*, December 1956, pp. 291 ff.
44 Moss, part II, chart 1.
45 Comment by Professor Donnison to the author.
46 Donnison, *The Government of Housing*, pp. 353 ff.
47 Cmnd 17 (1956) and the appendices to the M H L G Annual Reports for 1956, 1957, Cmnd 193 (1957) and Cmnd 419 (1958).
48 Joseph Rowntree Voluntary Trust, 'Memorandum on the "Housing and Rents Study" ' (dated 10 March 1958, mimeographed).
49 (1953), *Non-Parliamentary Papers.*
50 'Rent Control Policy', *Planning*, XVI, no. 305, no. 7, pp. 131–4.
51 *Ibid.*, pp. 125 ff.

52 'How many houses', *Planning*, XXI, no. 386, p. 188.
53 *Ibid.*, pp. 187 ff.
54 S R 52/15.
55 S R 59/35.
56 P. C. Gray and E. Parr, *The Rent Act, 1957. Report of Inquiry*, Cmnd 1246, 1960.
57 Gray and Parr, *The Rent Act, 1957*, p. 21.
58 D. V. Donnison, *Housing Since the Rent Act*, 'Occasional Papers in Social Administration', no. 3, Condicote Press, Welwyn, 1961.
59 Cmnd 1246, table 6; Cmnd 17 (1957), tables 1 and 2, where these figures were presented to the public.
60 Cmnd 1246, table 6, p. 21; Cmnd 17, table 3; British Institute of Public Opinion, survey 1643, November 1956.
61 Cmnd 1246, pp. 17, 19; Donnison, *Housing Since the Rent Act*, p. 31. Though some surveys had been done, these were not used. In any case, as they excluded movements within Local Authority boundaries they were bound to be inaccurate. Donnison, *Housing Since the Rent Act*, pp. 97 ff.
62 Lionel Needleman, *The Economics of Housing*, Staples Press, London, 1965, p. 49.
63 See above, p. 58.
64 *Housing: The Next Step*, Cmnd. 8996, 1953.
65 *The Times*, 8 November 1956, p. 11.
66 Donnison, *Housing Since the Rent Act*, p. 31.
67 C. H. Sisson, *The Spirit of British Public Administration*, Faber, London, 1959, p. 18.
68 *Ibid.*, p. 21.
69 Sir W. Ivor Jennings, *Cabinet Government*, Cambridge University Press, Cambridge, pp. 120 ff. D. W. G. Wass, 'Ministers and the Civil Service' (reproduced in mimeograph by H.M. Treasury, *c.* 1965, from a Lecture given at the Society of Civil Servants National Summer School, 1964).
70 Sisson, *The Spirit of British Public Administration*, p. 20.
71 See Bevins, *The Greasy Pole*, p. 51; Sampson, *Anatomy of Britain*, Hodder and Stoughton, London, 1962, p. 235.
72 Bevins, *The Greasy Pole*, p. 51.
73 *Ibid.*; Sampson, *Anatomy of Britain*, p. 235.
74 Wass, *Op. Cit.*, p. 8.
75 *Ibid.*, p. 10.
76 See above and Cmnd. 17 (1956).
77 See, for example, the view of H. R. G. Greaves.
78 R. Neustadt, *White House and Whitehall* (Paper for the 1965 Conference of the American Political Science Association), pp. 3-4.

# 5

# In the Administration

The actual drafting of the 1957 Rent Act was shrouded in the security of ministerial discretion and the Official Secrets Act. It was impossible to determine precisely the extent to which those responsible were aware of the problems with which they had to deal. Certain ideas and policy objectives seemed to have dominated decision-making. These were the general priorities within the Ministry, the free market formulations then fashionable within the Conservative Party, the role of the landlord in society and the provision of accommodation, and the overwhelming need to increase the stock of accommodation. I have seen no papers, nor have I been told of any discussions, that indicate that explicit attention was given in advance of drafting to such questions as how many houses to decontrol, how to select them, when to decontrol, whether to permit increases in controlled rent and of what size, how to deal with security of tenure, etc. It would appear that once the decisions in favour of a rise in controlled rent, a step towards total decontrol, and a revision in the disrepair procedure were taken, the clauses were formulated by reference mainly to techniques which had worked in the past and limited by knowledge of the politically possible, both of contemporary and previous ministers. Any evidence on drafting problems of the sort suggested must await the opening of the relevant Ministry papers. But some attempt could be made to evaluate the three major provisions of the act by reference to policy preferences.

Equally hidden from public, not to say academic, view was the cabinet decision-making process. As this must be central to Ministry activity on rent control, this chapter commences with a survey of the cabinet decision-making process as it was seen to have operated in the middle 1950s by several participants and observers. At the conclusion of the chapter, having outlined the basic policy questions and their application to the three principal clauses, something must be said about the role of the Treasury in the legislative process.

This study at the margins was the closest possible to analysis of the executive's decision-making.

## The Decision To Go

The decision-making process must of necessity be largely shrouded. While the civil service façade will occasionally be pierced, the political clues have tended to remain largely inscrutable.

Under normal circumstances the decision to introduce a piece of legislation would be taken after full cabinet consideration of a White Paper. This was the procedure followed in 1954. There was no policy White Paper prior to the 1957 Rent Act. It is impossible to know whether this meant that the policy questions were thereby slighted when a decision was taken. Some time in October 1955 the cabinet did, evidently, conclude that a Rent Bill should be introduced.[1]

By October 1955 dissatisfaction with the Macmillan Act within the Ministry at both the civil service and political levels was acute. No bill was actually under consideration. After clearing away the backlog of bills which died with the 1955 general election, the Ministry evidently put in for time to do 'something' about the rent restriction acts.

The cabinet decision remains obscure. There is no doubt that the cabinet did agree to bring in a rent bill. This is indicated by Mr Sandys' announcement, in December 1955, that the government had determined to bring in a bill. But so general was the understanding that at least one person close to the decision within the Ministry was unaware that any commitment had been made. Indeed, only in late 1955 was a principal reassigned to take primary charge of the Bill within the Ministry.

Government decision-making machinery under the Conservatives became fairly standardised in the middle 1950s. The next stage in a Bill's career, having received cabinet assent, was to go for consideration to the Cabinet Committee on Future Legislation. This committee had two functions. It assigned priority to bills and determined which were to be given over to parliamentary draftsmen. The system of categories devised for priority was fourfold. In category 'A' were those bills guaranteed a place. These included the mandatory measures such as Finance and Estimates as well as bills which had been publicly promised. The Rent Bill may well have fallen into this category, given the statement by Mr Sandys. Category 'B' bills were essential parts of the programme for which time ought to be found. Category 'C' was bills that would be desirable if time allowed but would probably not get parliamentary consideration. Therefore, initially, counsel would not be assigned. Category 'D' bills were bills which might be given time. In effect, these were surely not going to receive time. Evidently in the case of the Rent Bill parliamentary counsel were assigned and the Bill ordered to be made ready.

The next stage in the consideration by a Conservative government was in the Cabinet Legislation Committee. This committee was concerned primarily with the legal validity of bills. But there was likely to be an inevitable overlap with policy consideration.

A committee whose name implies an interest, but which in fact would normally take none, was the Home Affairs Committee. This was concerned with day to day policy issues and was below cabinet level. It normally did not consider legislation.*

Only Sir Anthony Eden, the prime minister, could have blocked approval of the proposal to introduce a rent bill when it was discussed in cabinet at this moment. He did not. There were several possible explanations. A prime minister's presidential capacity depends in part on the general opinion that he is likely to remain in office. Whether for reasons of health or politics, Sir Anthony never gave that impression. There was, therefore, strong reason to believe he could not always be sure of carrying his own cabinet. Solid reason would have suggested avoiding unnecessary dispute with a contentious cabinet member. Prime ministers, furthermore, seldom have had time for home affairs. Even Mr Macmillan, who was notoriously good about keeping an interest in home affairs and had had far wider experience with them than Sir Anthony, failed to take much interest in home affairs after 1959.† The problems of foreign affairs and general administration have really been about as much as a prime minister could hope to handle successfully. For the rest, he was dependent upon the good judgment of the ministers he appointed, safe in the assurance that they, not he, would be blamed if things went seriously wrong. Mr Powell has argued that it was an act of political courage for Sir Anthony to allow the Rent Bill to proceed, even in the negative fashion of not opposing. Certainly housing was controversial. But the knowledge that both Mr Sandys and Mr Powell might resign made capitulation the better part of valour. Indeed, there was no indication that he took the decision very

---

* In this period. But it had done so in the 1930s on both the 1933 and 1938 Rent Restriction Acts.

† This was particularly true of Sir Anthony Eden and Mr Macmillan, though as a generalisation it is not always equally true. Certainly it is not an accurate description of Mr Wilson's concerns.

seriously. He passed over the Bill in his *Memoirs*. Neither he nor his assistants recalled any discussion or papers which bore upon any controversy. This added weight to the general impression at the time that the Bill was not likely to be a major issue.

When revision in what might be construed as an essential principle became necessary it would be reasonable to suppose that cabinet approval was sought. It is unlikely that this would be a matter of debate. It has been said that such approval might be granted in the mass of swift decisions taken at the end of a session devoted to other affairs.

Whatever the details of the decision-making process, one fact remains undisputed. The government became committed to a Rent Bill. They allowed it parliamentary time and started it on its way through the paths of public and parliamentary consideration.

## Policy Priorities

The 1957 Rent Act was concerned with three aspects of the housing problem, so far as it affected privately rented housing; rent increases, repairs, and decontrol. It failed to deal with a fourth, security of tenure; thereby it guaranteed eventual failure. The policies devised to deal with these problems had a common objective, the provision of a larger income to the landlord. Though legislation on the individual problems was not new, the obvious failure of the 1954 Housing Repairs and Rents Act made a new departure in policy desirable.

The three threads were the usual concerns. The new unifying bond was the unique feature. Both Mr Sandys and Mr Powell seemed to agree that the primary intention of the Bill was the provision of additional doses of capital. Most of the arrangements made for each of the three factors – increases, decontrol, repairs – were intended to encourage investment in rented accommodation.*

This politicians' view of policy was not completely shared by civil servants. They suggested that the clauses were drafted not in the light of some new policy but as a result of past experience. The key clauses, it was contended, had substantial precedents in previous Rent Acts. While it would be wrong to minimise this evolutionary view and its significance, it is the politicians' picture of the drafting process that warrants attention.

* Albeit the increase on account of repairs was chancy and long term. Interviews with Mr Powell seem to confirm this, as do Mr Sandys' speeches on the Bill.

Civil service and politician were never in open conflict. Differences in outlook were not even vague recollections (though this could be an error in research). In part this may be because such conflict was not normally discussed and therefore effectively forgotten. Probably the conflict was academic. Each side drafted with a particular set of intellectual requirements. Resolution took place not at the intellectual but at the practical level. The conflict between the requirements of novel policy proposals and conceptions which constituted mere amendment of existing legislation proved insignificant.

## The Free Market

The free market idea was the paper tiger of the 1957 Rent Act debates, before, during and after. It was not, in retrospect, of any relevance in the decision-making process which resulted in the Rent Bill. But so many points were raised in debate by government, Opposition and press, based on free market arguments, that the application of the doctrine in the Bill should not be dismissed casually.

The idea of the free market had considerable indirect influence on the form of legislation. It validated the considerations that were given considerable weight in the determination of policy. The free market had become the utopia for which the Conservative government strove.[2] The assumptions presented by free market ideas led to the conclusion that the landlord got a raw deal in the landlord-tenant relationship because he lacked freedom of action. In a free market, the price of accommodation was the 'market price' – where supply and demand were left to strike an equilibrium. The achievement of the free market, it was thought, would lead to specific consequences for supply and demand, in response to changes in price.

Not everyone accepted the free market formulations. Mr Bevins dissented in the strongest possible terms.[3] What was found lacking in the debates was the solid intellectual base that Mr Powell was afterwards to formulate.[4] In the absence of a coherent theory the debate moved from an abstract discussion of the merits of the free market to a discussion of the specific consequences of the free market. The theory itself was almost irrelevant. It was the government's faith in the landlord's role as the principal supplier of accommodation to let that became the controlling element in policy formulation. The missing link between the debates which took place and those which might have been held was the failure of the government to face the realities of the housing problem as distinct from their reliance on free market theories. It was perfectly evident that the government neither created a sufficiently solid theoretical foundation, even for internal use, nor a firm grasp of housing facts.

Indeed, the government revealed no clear conception of the free market, other than as a tag for its assortment of policy intentions. A principal association was established between the free market and decontrol. The two terms were often used interchangeably. There was some indication that this was intentional.[5] On the other hand, informed backbenchers nonetheless equated the free market not merely with general decontrol but with a specific re-allocation of demand[6] (i.e. to make old Victorian dwellings too expensive for old married couples). The government more loosely associated a free market in housing with a general freeing of conditions. This was one part of the conception for the general reformation of the economy that seemed implicit in government and party statements.

The supply consequences were given almost classical virtues. There might be hardship to individuals in the short run, but in the end each individual was presumed to benefit from the increased availability and flexibility of accommodation. But there was no effort at all, as even Mr Powell was afterwards to require, to formulate semi-practical conclusions on demand: the optimum size and base model under which the free market would operate in the housing field. Nor, despite pretensions, was there any study of the extent to which a free market in housing would, in practice, aid or discourage the general free market goal.

The free market became so intertwined, as it remains with Powellites even to this day, in the meshes of Tory *noblesse oblige* that for every implicit rule or model there were infinite specified exemptions or modifications. The market had to be large, but not too large. It had to be free, but humanity required some regulation. The considerations which led to modification of the theory had no bearing on those which led to the establishment of the market. The ideas never crystallised to dogma, much less to ideology.

The connection of the free market with the Bill was probably largely a consequence of Mr Powell's association. Any case he argued inevitably had free market assumptions relatively more explicit than those presented by any other politician. It was not only that he stressed the free market, publicly or privately, to any unusual extent, but also that the idea was so relevant to the various political quarrels of the period. The tendency of observers and participants was to think in free market parameters. In the housing problem the emphasis was not justified and may have been misleading. For, there were different types of free market arguments intertwined. There was the fairly rigid Powellite model. This was not yet as coherent as it was afterwards to become, but it already contained a set of inter-related assumptions. Particularly lacking was a detailed knowledge of housing facts. Finally, there were many vague assumptions about housing and rent control. In the Rent Act debate the model was inadequate and unconnected to the more generally accepted assumptions. Neither was related to any detailed knowledge. The consequence was intellectual confusion. It was easy to talk about different problems under the same misunderstood title.

## The Landlord

Whatever legislation a Conservative government proposed, favouritism for the landlord for party political reasons would be the charge levelled by the Opposition. The *prima facie* case against the government was clear. The 'property owning classes' had been claimed by the Conservatives, and believed by Labour, to be Tory in their political sentiments as well as in their voting. Despite the polemicists on both sides, a government that invariably favoured the landlords for this reason alone would be unthinkable. But it was certainly true that the government chose measures which did favour the landlords in drafting the Rent Act. They wished to eliminate inequity as between landlords and between landlords and tenant. They wished to encourage repairs. They wished to eliminate the vagaries of control. Most of all they wished to encourage landlords as to the future of privately rented housing. All this necessitated favouritism.

The general increase in rents had an element of social justice. The landlord, Conservatives argued, should be given something like a 'fair rent'. For too long the landlord had provided, in effect, a subsidy to his tenant. Control had kept the price of private rented accommodation well below the market price, or perhaps merely the cost price, indicated by council house rents. But more important, the Tories felt that the landlord had suffered in the past fifty years. Sir Henry D'Avigdor-Goldsmid, Mr Sandys' parliamentary private secretary from 1955–7, argued that 'now we have the privileged tenant class' instead of the wicked landlord against whose depredations

Rent Acts had been required.[7] This viewpoint was not universal. Mr Brooke, for one, attacked landlords at least as much as he attacked tenants.[8] But the landlord could not be slighted.

Whereas the tenant had been the central concern of prewar and Labour rents legislation, the Conservatives were determined that their policy should be properly focused upon the landlord. The landlord was, after all, another kingpin in the free, private enterprise system. He represented an alternative to local authority housing. Having underestimated the importance of local authority and private-owner-occupied housing as a percentage of total supply, the government became convinced that the private landlord, like the small shop keeper, was an essential supplier who had to be encouraged to increase supply at almost any cost.[9]

The general policy at the time was that, non-market alternatives having failed, controls ought generally to be lifted. Although the Conservative government on gaining power in 1951 removed controls on building, landlords could not or would not, under the combined restraint of a difficult market and insecurity of rent control, provide substantial quantities of additional houses to let. To remove controls on rent was, to one way of thinking, to give the landlords what had already been given to their counterparts, the shopkeepers – the ending of rationing and price controls.[10] But it was further intended to encourage landlords to believe that the government was on their side and would remain so. This was not merely the view or hope of the politicians; it was quite widely held within the Ministry.[11] One might call the policy the denationalisation of housing. Mr Sandys came from the Ministry of Supply as a specialist in this activity.[12] He reduced the role of local authorities in the construction of houses to let by altering the system of subsidies. He further limited their activity by encouraging the sale of council houses to sitting tenants and the imposition of differential rents. To this extent, the free market notions had significance in the policy decisions.

But there were other reasons for lifting control. The vagaries of the system were a source of constant complaint. By historical accidents, similar houses next door to one another might have widely different rents. The new Act would level out this discrimination as between landlords, with the tendency to bring all rents up to a higher level. The Minister of State for Scotland pointed out that Scots landlords had not got 'a fair break – or even break as compared to English. . . .'[13]

Not only had landlords to be encouraged to do more, they had to be encouraged to do enough to keep up the existing stock. The cost of repairs, Dame Evelyn noted, had risen three and one-half times the pre-second world war level. But rents remained fixed, and very often at the 1915 level plus the 40 per cent inter-war increase. The innovation of the 1954 Macmillan Act was the recognition that landlords must have sufficient capital to enable them to make repairs. When landlords, assured a fair return by law, failed to make the necessary repairs, this basic assumption was proved false. Subsequently, it was hoped that if more capital were available, some part of it would be ploughed back in the form of repairs. Applied to their favourite type of landlord, the widow or retired person who owned three to five houses or less, the Conservative government made a strong case. The large landlord would also benefit, though not substantially.

Rent increases, for whatever purpose, were not expected to have a great impact on the large landlord. His situation was already an economically profitable one.[14] But obtaining vacant possession, especially by the dispossession of bad tenants or the redevelopment of largish Victorian houses into small service apartments, had been next to impossible under the old rules. After all, the whole purpose of control had been to prevent landlords from exploiting a scarcity situation in time of crisis. This, in the government's view, had been overextended. It was argued that the landlord would not abuse trust in a free market situation, even if it were possible.

The government was in most respects as far removed from an understanding of the landlord's difficulties as the tenant's. This was true even of the broadly composed Central Housing Advisory Committee which contained no landlord or tenant representatives. Few of those concerned with drafting had experienced the petty problems of the landlord-tenant relationship such as the provision of rent books and the collection of rents and rates. They had no conception of the role that rent control had played in the customs relating to houses' repair, maintenance and tenure. Further, the government was unaware of the extent to which housing in large cities, especially London, had fallen into the hands of the property companies.[15] It had no more real awareness of the administrative problems faced by the large landlord than it had of the problems facing the council estate administrators.[16] Whereas the habit of concern for the 'middle classes' might develop some sympathy for the plight of the small landlord, the large landlord had no hope of internal representation. To this extent the large landlord was certainly not intentionally benefited.

But the government certainly exceeded all the recommendations by landlord and professional groups in drafting the Bill. By so far exceeding the landlords' expectations they made possible the charge of 'give away'. With the exception of the Scots, who still felt cheated, landlords were encouraged not to make comments on aspects of the Bill of which they might otherwise have been critical.[17] Why rock so satisfactory a boat?

## Accommodation

If the free market provided a theoretical justification for the 1957 Act, the practical basis for revision lay in the Ministry's conception of the supply and demand for housing. They believed that sufficient accommodation was available, on a statistical basis. Although the stock of accommodation was badly used, it would suffice if redistributed. Much accommodation, nominally ancient, was still usable. The supply-demand equilibrium provided an opportunity to take decisive action on rent control.

All statistics confirmed the Ministry's impression: that there was, overall, enough accommodation for every head. This was made clear in the 1951 Housing Census.[18] Not even regional tables showed important deviations from the conclusion. Trusting the 1954 PEP study which combined census and housing statistics, the Ministry declared that shortly the overall demand for housing would be met. Though the Ministry was undoubtedly aware that other research was leading to divergent conclusions, the senior civil servants chose to ignore their own data in preference to PEP'.[19] The Ministry believed that more housing could be brought into the market if landlords were encouraged to rent rather than sell upon obtaining vacant possession.[20] The system of control discouraged sub-letting.[21] Tenants occupied dwellings larger than their requirements because they could not obtain smaller and cheaper premises.[22] This last argument was not without its significance. The problem of 'doubling up' by two generations was a real one during the postwar era.* As Sir Keith Joseph said:

Hon. members on both sides of the house have told us harrowing tales of what will happen to present tenants of accommodation, but there are no statistics of the unhappiness, misery and frustration existing in the enormous waiting lists of people who cannot move—and cannot even get married – for lack of housing.[23]

The consequences of reshuffling was to be a 'levelling out' of occupancy rates towards the statistically possible mean. Tied into 'decanting' – the movement of population into rationally sized accommodation – was the whole question of mobility. The Ministry's interest in mobility was pronounced. Planning authorities urged the local authorities to make development and redeployment a primary concern. The minister's personal interest in mobility problems was evident. The inhibiting factor was the unwillingness of labour to move from one area to another. The normal British prejudices for locality must be counted a factor but housing was a positive obstacle.[24] A council tenancy could be had only after years of waiting on a council list. To move out of the council area was to forfeit what might be the only chance of comfortable and reasonably priced housing. At the same time one lost all rights if one gave up a controlled tenancy. People therefore tended to stay in one place most of their lives. Workers could not move from areas where industries were declining to new ones. The drift towards already overcrowded areas that mobility might produce was not considered a policy problem. Only in the new towns programmes was any effort made to cater for mobility problems.

Part of the reason for the Ministry's confidence that a substantial rate of mobility could be tolerated was its impression that, given rent restriction reform, considerable quantities of accommodation could be made tenantable. This was first broached in the 1953 White Paper. A great deal of older accommodation, such as the Scottish multistorey tenement, was considered 'basically' habitable. All that was required, in many cases, were some basic structural repairs followed by continual maintenance. As slum clearance could not be universal in any case, this resolved a policy difficulty.[25] But whether the accommodation was itself acceptable, as the White Paper assumed, remained moot. Mr Powell pointed to this assumption at the second reading.[26] Sir Keith Joseph questioned the assumption when he recognised that some of the accommodation 'will not be in such good condition'.[27]

The Ministry held to its conclusion in the belief that only rent restrictions had discouraged repairs;[28] a view shared even by outside experts.[29] It was Ministry doctrine well before the 1953 White

D

Paper. The operation of the 1954 Act only gave added verification. Carefully hedged provisions in the 1954 Act had made repairs increases, and hence repairs, impossible. Given sufficient incentive, the landlord could be trusted to restore his capital asset. In so doing, supplies of poor accommodation would be made habitable and desirable.

The Ministry saw the shortage of accommodation as due to deficits in return and the need for surpluses for repair. They were convinced that housing was underpriced when they compared the low percentage of income taken up by rent by comparison with the large percentage taken up by the various 'immoral' expenditures such as drink and tobacco. Furthermore, the Ministry pointed out that not only had the Rent Restriction Acts produced anomalies, but they had kept rents at a low level as compared with the rest of the economy.[30] Rent increases, the economists concluded, would be good things in themselves: they had deflationary characteristics in that they gave to those who would invest, took from those who would spend. These assumptions were never empirically tested. Such questions as who were the landlords, what were their incomes, what would be done with the increased incomes proposed, were never asked. But these general economic considerations were not dermining factors. The increases were needed to provide accommodation. Policy demanded action.

## Major Sections of the Bill
### Clause One

*Revision of Rent Limits of Controlled Houses in England and Wales*

1. (1) Subject to the following provisions of this Act the rent recoverable for any rental period from the tenant under a controlled tenancy shall not exceed the following limit, that is to say a rent of which the annual rate is equal to the 1956 gross value of the dwelling multiplied by two (or, if the responsibility for repairs is such as is specified in Part I of the First Schedule to this Act, by the appropriate factor specified in the said Part I) together with:

a. the annual amount, ascertained in accordance with the Second Schedule to this Act, of any rates for the basic rental period, being rates borne by the landlord or a superior landlord; and

b. such annual amount as may be agreed in writing between the landlord and tenant or determined by the county court to be a reasonable charge for any services for the tenant provided by the landlord or a superior landlord during the basic rental period or any furniture or shared accommodation which under the terms of the tenancy the tenant is entitled to use during that period.*

The essential question, as put by Mr Powell at committee stage, was 'what coefficient and what multiplier is to be used' in determining the amount of the rent increases to be granted to landlords whose property remained in control. That rents must rise was as much an article of faith with Labour as with Tories.[32]

The reasons offered at various times for increases in rent were not, even by virtue of their number, necessarily contradictory. What was interesting was that different groups who had a voice came to the same conclusions often for far different reasons. The Ministry, i.e. the civil servants, was concerned with two problems: the provision of funds to make repairs possible and the rationalisation of rents to end the anomalies which control and decontrol legislation of the past forty years had produced. Ministers had something more in mind. To them the strengthening of the landlord's position was an objective. The relatively small part of earnings devoted to rent by the tenant was of political significance.[33] It seemed to prove that the tenant received a subsidy from the landlord.

The search for a formula on which to base rents could not have been a very extensive one. Gross rateable value as a base had many advantages. Its use was sanctified by the Inland Revenue, which claimed that the valuations of 1956 represented market rents. Since 1954, G R V had been used to determine what repairs ought to cost. It thus had the added weight of precedent, always dear to the heart of the civil servant. One very senior civil servant remarked that there simply wasn't any alternative at the time. The Ministry, it was suggested, might well have preferred the formula suggested by Mr C. D. Pilcher (a senior member of R I C S, afterwards member of the Milner Holland Committee) to adjust rents not only for market value but also to allow for and discount inflation in the market due to scarcity. But the formula was not suggested until eight years later.[34]

The use of the accepted base would not yield what was thought to be the necessary rent. The Ministry found itself juggling the base, set at 1939 market value, to obtain a current market price. Here the 1954 Act provided a precedent. The 1954 Act based its formula on the increased cost of repairs. The total rent could be fixed by reference to the increased cost of living. This was the basic formula used.

* This text and those in the succeeding sections are taken from the Bill as presented for first reading.

But Schedule One could not be explained so simply. This provided a variety of formulae to encourage the landlord to assume responsibility for repairs. Was this to create an incentive for the landlord to do repairs? Should the incentive take the form of pre-payment, as was chosen in 1956, rather than compensation, as had been chosen in 1953. These questions seemed irrelevant to the decision-making. The primary concern of the Ministry was evidently to finish the work begun by the Macmillan Act – to get repairs done. Thus, no connection was ever drawn between twice G R V and 'fair rent'.[35]

The particular Scottish problems were never separated from the others. The style of construction in Scotland – rows of tenements – permitted only the barest maintenance repairs. Landlords found it virtually impossible to make major improvements individually. In the drafting of this clause, the Scots problem was overlooked.[36]

Though the primary concern of the civil servants was the repairs problem, politicians had other cares. Repairs were long overdue, they agreed. But each individual problem of rent control was viewed in the context of the panacea which they had in mind. Individual steps taken must not jeopardise the government's political future, and hence the chances of encouraging the free market. Under what circumstances was twice G RV chosen? Was it sufficient? There could be no definite answer. But the politicians were at pains to assure that the impact would not be excessive. Mr Sandys pointed out that the cost of living would rise only 2 per cent as a consequence of the increases, and that despite the numbers quoted in the press, only four and three-quarter million houses would be affected. A whole table in the White Paper which accompanied the Bill was devoted to the amounts by which rents of controlled tenancies would rise. This table indicated that the vast majority of increases would be under ten shillings per week.[37] What was the relevance of this table, as against one which would show the new rents, if it was not primarily to allay fears rather than offer promise?

Of equal interest to the government was the relatively small percentage of expenditure which rents represented. The 1953–4 and the soon to be published 1957 figures both showed that the country spent more on alcohol and tobacco than on rent and almost as much on motoring, entertainment and recreation as it did for rent. But this was probably not true of the typical tenant of private accommodation.[38] Salaries had risen by 271 per cent, personal incomes by 211 per cent, rent by only 58 per cent since 1938–9.[39] To a government faced with the need to deflate following an unsuccessful Butler pre-election budget this must have been a decidedly attractive, though perhaps not compelling, argument for rent increases.

Of even greater interest to Conservatives was to ensure that the private, controlled landlord had a return equivalent to that received by the local authority. As the local authorities, who provided regular and adequate statistics, rented their houses at sums not far off from those proposed in Schedule One, the bases were confirmed.[40]

The rationale of the government was that landlords were entitled to some return on their investment, even if houses were in very bad repair. This represented a general shift from Labour policy and the Macmillan Act. Never again ought landlords to lose money due to the operation of rent restriction.[41]

To overemphasise the importance of this clause, or the disputes about it, would be misleading. Ministers and civil servants were probably not overly concerned about political and economic consequences. Precedents, and experience of this type of legislation were quite sufficient. And there was a general consensus among decision-makers at all levels that it was hardly possible for the government to give landlords excessive increases.

## First Schedule: Part II: Abatement for disrepair

*First Schedule: Part II: Abatement for disrepair. Notification of disrepair to landlord*

3 The provisions of this Part of this Schedule shall have effect where the tenant under a controlled tenancy serves on the landlord a notice in the prescribed form stating that the dwelling or any part thereof is in disrepair by reason of defects specified in the notice, and that those defects ought reasonably to be remedied, having due regard to the age, character and locality of the dwelling, and requesting the landlord to remedy them.

*Landlord's undertaking to repair; and certificates of disrepair*

4 (1) If, on the expiration of six weeks from the service of a notice under the last foregoing paragraph, any of the defects specified in the notice remain unremedied, then unless the landlord has given an undertaking in the prescribed form to remedy those defects or such of them as the tenant may agree in writing to accept as sufficient, the tenant may in the prescribed form apply to the local authority for a certificate of disrepair.

(2) Where an application under this paragraph is made to a local authority and the local authority are satisfied that the dwelling or any part thereof is in disrepair by reason of defects specified in the said notice and that all or any of those defects ought reasonably to be remedied, having

due regard to the age, character and locality of the dwelling, they shall issue to the tenant a certificate of disrepair accordingly and any such certificate shall be in the prescribed form and shall specify the defects as to which the local authority are satisfied as aforesaid, stating that the local authority are so satisfied.

(3) The local authority shall not be concerned to inquire into any obligation as between a landlord and tenant or into the origin of any defect; but if on an application by the landlord the county court is satisfied, as respects any defect specified in a certificate of disrepair, that it is one for which the tenant is responsible, the court shall cancel the certificate as respects that defect.

(4) If on an application by the landlord the county court is satisfied as respects any defect specified in a certificate of disrepair that it ought not to have been specified, the court shall cancel the certificate as respects that defect.

(5) Where a certificate of disrepair is cancelled as respects all the defects specified therein it shall be deemed never to have had effect, and where it is cancelled as respects some only of the defects specified therein it shall be deemed never to have had those defects specified therein.

5 Notwithstanding anything in the last foregoing paragraph, a local authority shall not issue a certificate of disrepair until the expiration of three weeks from the service by them on the landlord of a notice in the prescribed form stating that the authority propose to issue the certificate of disrepair and specifying the defects to which it is to relate; and if within the said three weeks the landlord gives an undertaking in the prescribed form to remedy those defects and serves a copy of the undertaking on the local authority, the authority shall not issue the certificate.

6 (1) Where, after the issue of a certificate of disrepair, the landlord applies to the local authority for the cancellation of the certificate on the ground that the defects specified in the certificate have been remedied, the local authority shall serve on the tenant a notice to the effect that unless an objection from the tenant is received by them within three weeks from the service of the notice on the ground that the said defects or any of them have not been remedied, they propose to cancel the certificate.

(2) If no objection is received as aforesaid, or if in the opinion of the local authority the objection is not justified, they shall cancel the certificate as from the date of the application or such later date as appears to them to be the date on which the said defects were remedied.

(3) Where the landlord has applied to the local authority for the cancellation of a certificate of disrepair, and the authority have not cancelled the certificate, the landlord may apply to the county court, and if on the application the court is satisfied that the certificate ought to have been cancelled by the local authority the court shall order that the certificate

shall cease to have effect as from the date of the order or such earlier date as may be specified in the order.

The 1954 Act had failed because the disrepair procedure proved unworkable. Many landlords did not apply for the rent increases to which they were entitled. Penalties could be imposed by the tenant's ability to obtain a certificate of disrepair. Thus, when the landlord applied for the increases, the tenant applied for a certificate. Lest they suffered the automatic loss of the inter-war 40 per cent increase, landlords whose properties had severe structural defects not easily remedied (precisely those who most needed the extra capital the increases would provide) hesitated to apply for the increases. The resultant stalemate affected all.

Part II of the First Schedule was not in preliminary drafts essentially different from the 1954 Act, except that it placed the burden on the tenant. As the Bill moved along in drafting, complications were introduced. The reasons were largely parliamentary. Mr Sandys considered it important to assure members that the procedures would be equally fair to all sides. Consequently, additions were made to eliminate any possibility of partiality, especially by the local authority in the tenant's favour. The new procedure would discourage certificates of repair, a reversal of past policy.[42]

An alternative motivation has been suggested. Some believed that the complications were introduced in order to discourage the use, by the landlord or tenant, of formal legal procedure. It has been suggested that the difficulties placed in the paths of both landlord and tenant were to encourage informal settlements.

There was no doubt, however, that to create a stalemate in disrepair procedures was the intention, and was carried into legislation.

## Clause Nine

*Release from Rent Acts and Furnished Houses Rent Control*

9 (1) The Rent Acts shall not apply to any dwelling-house the rateable value of which on the seventh day of November, nineteen hundred and fifty-six, exceeded, in the Metropolitan Police District or the City of London forty pounds, elsewhere in England and Wales thirty pounds, and in Scotland forty pounds.

(2) The Rent Acts shall not apply to a tenancy beginning at or after the commencement of this Act, and the tenant shall not by virtue of those Acts be entitled to retain possession as a statutory tenant on the coming to an end of such a tenancy: Provided that this sub-section shall not apply

where the person to whom the tenancy is granted was immediately before the granting tenant of the same dwelling under a controlled tenancy.

(3) The minister may by order provide that the Rent Acts shall not apply, as from such date as may be specified in the order, to dwelling-houses the rateable value of which . . . exceeds such amount as may be so specified . . . and an order under this sub-section may be made so as to relate to the whole of England and Wales, to the whole of Scotland, or to such area or areas . . . as may be specified in the order . . .

(7) The transitional provisions contained in the Fourth Schedule to this Act shall have effect in relation to dwelling-houses which cease to be subject to control by virtue of sub-sections (1) or (3) of this section.[43]

The most controversial provision of the 1957 Rent Act was the decontrol of accommodation, embodied in clause 9, which became clause 11 in the final version and its accompanying fourth schedule. The two types of decontrol embodied in the Bill developed from substantially different backgrounds. But they shared some origins. The general desire for 'decontrol' (not merely in housing and rents) permeated all sections of society. This pledge and its fulfilment had helped the Conservatives in the elections of 1951 and 1955. Mr Sandys had earned his right to a place in the cabinet by his success in denationalising steel. Mr Powell, then, was not the only person who believed in decontrol.

The relevance of the doctrine of the free market has been considered. But certainly tables I and II of the White Paper[44] were at least as much to reassure the Commons about the restrictions on decontrol as to point to its extent: reflecting Mr Sandys' political instinct to disappoint no one.

Decontrol by vacant possession appeared in early drafts of the Bill. Although the last departmental committee report on control had attacked this device,[45] it had two supposed advantages: as a logical second step to the decontrol of all new dwellings accomplished in 1954 and as least painful – since it did not, or so it was thought, lead to evictions. There was one major miscalculation. The Ministry was unable to obtain any really accurate estimate of the turnover rate. Although the highest estimate the Ministry obtained was of the order of 4 per cent per annum, it was publicised as 5 per cent. In fact, the figures turn out to be rather higher. At no time was a single figure found reliable. During the second reading Mr Powell used the equally haphazard 125,000 per annum.[46] In retrospect, decontrol by vacant possession was of primary importance. At the time the casual determination of the consequences indicated its relative i͟ significance in the framework of the Bill. The second means, 'slice decontrol' – the decontrol of a bloc of property on some predetermined criteria – was not new. From 1933 to 1939 it had been successful. Mr Symon had argued against it while he was in the Ministry, claiming that conditions would not again be favourable. Once Mr Symon and Mr Wilkinson retired, no one in the department had any reason to recall the special circumstances which made slice decontrol effective. Its advantages seemed beyond question.

But slice decontrol was not included in the original draft. Nor was it a strictly political addition. Mr Powell's idea was to create a free market in one step. His suggestion did not even require parliamentary action, merely an Order-in-Council declaring the state of emergency ended. This would automatically eliminate rent control under the 1939 and subsequent statutes, leaving only those few 'old control' houses which remained in control after 1938.[47] Dame Evelyn's initial attitude to decontrol is reported to have been rather uncertain. But the suggestion to include slice decontrol probably came from her. She argued that if one were using vacant possession to establish a free market, it was necessary to have some sort of free market already in operation to form a standard on which rational economic decisions might be taken. This represented a reasonable compromise with Mr Powell's position.

The 'debate' centred around the limits of 'slice' decontrol. These, theoretically, were needed for two reasons: the requirements of a sample market and the minimising of hardship to participants, as the true free market would not be achieved for several years. The limits were chosen by the ministers for only one reason. Placing the limits only a few shillings lower would bring a considerable fraction of the total accommodation into the free market. Restraint was necessary.[48] The ministers may have so decided under the influence of civil servants who had chosen the limits for other reasons. The figures were suspiciously coincidental with those proposed by Mr Symon. Did Mr Symon lobby for slice decontrol in the department, knowing this to be generally acceptable?[49]

The limits were set, so far as can be determined from the evidence, without any exact estimate of the optimum size of the slice market to be created. Nor was a market of any particular size mooted. The limitation of extent was considered relevant. After all, table II of the White Paper made clear that only something under one-third of all

D*

privately rented accommodation was to be decontrolled immediately. The normal schemes for decontrol were not possible in Scotland. The valuation of property there had not been revised. The base was, therefore, not available. More important, the housing pattern was considerably different from England and Wales. The proportion of rented houses owned by local authorities was considerably larger than in England and Wales. The supply of accommodation was, taken as a whole, shorter than in non-metropolitan England. The Scottish Office had urged a higher limit to be set. That the policy was applied to Scotland at all reflects the generally disorganised state of Scottish housing policy, itself a reflection of the unavailability of statistical information.[50]

The failure to use the decontrol procedures adopted in the 1954 Landlord and Tenant Act was remarkable.* The politicians contended that this form of decontrol would not create a free market. More important, the courts would be required to determine what the free market price should be without any reasonable guideline. Further, while the courts could make determination for the few cases that would arise under the 1954 Act, it would be asking considerably more if this provision had been used in the 1957 Act.

Six months was chosen as the transition period to ensure the Act well under way before the 1959 general election. To make the transition last a year would mean that the Act would come into force too close to the event.

The provision for statutory instrument in sub-section (2) of this clause was never used. Though it was hotly debated at the time, it now has only historical interest. Moreover, there is no data available on the reasons for the inclusion of such a clause. It was obviously desirable to make clear that total decontrol was intended and that the delay inherent in subsequent legislation would not be necessary.

## Interdepartmental Negotiations

In the drafting of the key provisions of the Bill, no mention has been made of interdepartmental negotiations. The reason for this is that senior officials of the Ministry denied that any took place, even with the Treasury. During Mr Macmillan's tenure at Housing and Local Government, the Treasury apparently agreed not to interfere on an

* Under these, the first lease on end of control was fixed, in the event that the landlord and tenant could not agree, by the county court.

item by item basis in housing policy. But most scholars of the period have insisted, nonetheless, that the Treasury continued to play an intimate role because of the Treasury's influence in the shaping of general governmental policy, and hence general Ministry policy.[51] Whenever policy was shaped by 'considerations of national investment', determination would obviously rest with the Treasury. In this instance, the Treasury's explicit interest was in the 'load on the building industry' and the proper distribution of building resources to the various parts of the public sector.[52]

Treasury controls of Ministry policy were made explicit in some respects. *The Annual Report* for 1956[53] fixed as one of the guiding principles under which the Ministry operated the need to minimise public expenditure. This was by direction of the Treasury. The Treasury must have instituted at least minimal checks to ensure compliance.

Circulars 10 and 11/56 of the Ministry of Housing and Local Government[54] instructed local authorities to limit their capital expenditure. This policy, carried over from 1955, virtually necessitated some effort to revive construction in the private sector if the necessary number of houses to let were to be provided. The natural step to increase private enterprise activity was, of course, to remove the principal deterrent – controls. Of course decontrol would at the same time stimulate private construction for owner-occupation, though this was not *per se* controlled. It was against this set of assumptions that Mr Symon argued in the *Real Estate Journal* (see chapter 8, on A L P O).

In addition to the general controls, there is some evidence of specific Treasury interest in the Rent Act. It is said that the Economic Section of the Treasury prepared an exercise on the economic consequences of decontrol. It is further suggested that some of the people who participated in the exercise either werè members of, or had access to members of, the Ministry of Housing's drafting committee. But this is of far less significance to the direction of the Bill than the general controls.

## Summary

The intellectual decisions on policy, the role of the free market, the significance and attitude the government ought to attach to private landlords, and the state of the housing and rental market, were necessary preliminaries to drafting. These determined the form and direction the new Rent Act would take. But when decisions had to be made on particular clauses other problems intervened. Of many decisions about decontrol how much, how, with what safeguards, there is no evidence. There is some doubt that such questions were ever regarded as significant. The guidelines for decisions seemed to have been a combination of the superstitions and prejudices that characterised the Conservative and civil service views of rent restriction at the time the Bill was prepared. Key clauses were as much a reaction to the past as enactments of government policy for the future. There was remarkably little interference, either by other Ministries or by the cabinet, in the preparation of the new Act. The Bill was very much the product of compromise between the different, though not divergent, requirements of civil servants and politicians within the Ministry of Housing and Local Government.

NOTES

1 This process is described, though for a later period, by Ronald Butt in *Power of Parliament*, Constable, London, 1967, pp. 252 ff.
2 J. Wood, *A Nation Not Afraid, The Thinking of Enoch Powell*, Batsford, London, 1965, p. 32.
3 Bevins, *The Greasy Pole*, Hodder and Stoughton, London, 1965, p. 51.
4 See Wood, *A Nation Not Afraid*.
5 G. D. M. Block, *Rents in Perspective*, Conservative Political Centre, London, 1961.
6 Sir K. Joseph, 560 H C Deb.5s., col. 1820; Mr Ramsden, 560 H C Deb.5s., cols. 1809–10.
7 560 H C Deb.5s., col. 1841.
8 567 H C Deb.5s., col. 980.
9 Wood, *A Nation Not Afraid*, pp. 60–1, 63.
10 Sir E. Errington, 560 H C Deb.5s., col. 1803.
11 Dame Evelyn Sharp, 'Housing: The Past Ten Years', *Chartered Surveyor*, December 1956, p. 295.
12 I am indebted for this notion to Professor F. Lafitte, Professor of Social Administration at the University of Birmingham, and formerly *The Times'* social services correspondent.
13 1956–7, H C S C Deb.1. col. 584.
14 See the endless figures cited by Labour of property companies returns ranging from 4–12 per cent p.a. If this had not been so, companies' money would have gone elsewhere.
15 See Milner Holland Committee Report, *Report of the Committee on Housing in Greater London*, Cmd. 2605, 1965.
16 See above, and J. A. G. Griffith, *Central Departments and Local Authorities*, Allen and Unwin, London, 1966, pp. 287 ff.

17 See Discussions of A L P O and N F P O in chapter 8, below.
18 Though not published until 1957, the government certainly had access to its details.
19 Sharp, 'Housing: The Past Ten Years'.
20 Powell, 560 H C Deb.5s., col 1762.
21 *Ibid.*, col 1761; Sir K. Joseph, 560 H C Deb.5s., col 1818.
22 Sir E. Errington, 560 H C Deb.5s., col 1797.
23 560 H C Deb.5s., col 1818.
24 560 H C Deb.5s., col. 1762. (Mr Powell.)
25 *Ibid.*, col 1763.
26 *Ibid.*
27 *Ibid.*, col 1820.
28 *Ibid.*, col 1763.
29 Professor F. W. Paish, 'The Economics of Rent Restriction', in *Lloyds Bank Review*, April 1950.
30 Sharp, 'Housing: The Past Ten Years', p. 296; 560 H C Deb.5s., col. 1775. (Mr Powell.)
31 5 Eliz. 2, clause 1 (1).
32 A view taken even by Bevan. See Conservative Research Department, *General Election, 1955, Daily Notes*, no. 7, p. 9.
33 See speeches of Messrs Hay, Errington, Powell and especially D'Avigdor-Goldsmid.
34 It was embodied in the 1965 Rent Act.
35 *The Economist*, vol. 170, p. 793
36 See explanation of the Scots under-secretary, 1956–7, H C S C I, cols 542 ff.
37 Cmnd 17, 1956, table 4.
38 See The Social Survey Expenditure Study reproduced in chapter 4 (p. 57).
39 1956–7, H C S C, I, c. 175.
40 See the quarterly tables of the L C C and the Ministry of Housing's quarterly returns.
41 1956–7, H C S C I., cols 59 ff.
42 560 H C Deb.5s., cols 2058–9.
43 5 Eliz. 2, clause 9.
44 Cmnd 17, 1956.
45 Inter-departmental Committee Report. *Rent Control*, 1944–5, Cmd 6621, *Parliamentary Papers*, v, 499. (Lord Ridley, ch.)
46 560 H C Deb.5s., col 1766.
47 *Ibid.*, col 1761.
48 Wood, *A Nation Not Afraid*, p. 61.
49 After the fashion of *The Times* under G. Dawson?
50 Indeed, no research on headship was done, and very little work was done by Social Survey for the Scottish office. Letter from the Scottish Office to the author 25 July 1966.
51 S. H. Beer, 'Treasury Control: The Coordination of Financial Policy in Great Britain', *American Political Science Review*, vol. 49, pp. 144–60.
52 Griffith, *Central Departments and Local Authorities*, p. 227.
53 M H L G, *Annual Report for the Year 1956*, Cmnd 193, 1957, p. 1.
54 *Ibid.*

# 6
# Modification

No legislation can emerge from the legislative process without modification, so long as human error and changing requirements persist. The changes made in the Rent Bill were no exception. An understanding of these modifications exposes the pressures that were exerted and with what effect. Exploration will reveal not merely the external pressures of interest groups and parliamentary forces, but those internal to the government and the governing party as well. Some indication is given of the government's standing committee and report stage strategy.

The parliamentary amending process reflected the limitations of delegated and/or prerogative authority. How much was more than symbolic of detailed parliamentary control over the government? Very few Opposition, or even friendly amendments were allowed. The nineteenth-century tradition of compromise to meet the demands of party faction proved unnecessary in the contemporary situation.*

Sir Ivor Jennings has pointed to the variety of pressures that can be brought against a Bill once it has begun its parliamentary journey. Many of these pressures did not affect the 1957 Rent Act. For one thing, this Bill concerned solely the Ministry of Housing and Local Government. Within this department were both the policy makers and the representatives of all who would be asked to administer the Bill, to the extent that these were public servants.† But those who would be most affected were tenants and landlords. Of these the Ministry knew remarkably little. It had not, despite responsibility for local government, any real knowledge of the problems the local authorities had as housing administrators of estates and of rent

---

* Sir W. Ivor Jennings, *Parliament*, Cambridge University Press, 1961, pp. 504 ff. Though Mr Butt argues, in *Power of Parliament*, that backbenchers did obtain concessions and that initial Government strategy had been designed to minimise opposition, I do not think that this leads to the conclusion he suggests: namely that the backbenchers had impact on the legislation. For other factors were at work at the same time.

† Of course, landlords, tenants, etc. operated outside the executive despite notional representation within the Ministry.

restriction legislation. There was thus no internal voice of experience to point to the purely mechanical difficulties which might need to be dealt with. This remained true even after publication of the Bill.

Whereas in 1965 the Ministry consulted extensively with pressure groups, both professional and interested, who could provide some information on the problems the private landlord might encounter,* in 1956 this was considered impossible. With the exception of ALPO,[1] there was no pressure group which was able to exert a significant private influence to alter the course of legislation. Only after publication were the professional and landlord groups able to submit memoranda proposing changes.

In Standing Committee and on Report stage amendments came from backbench government MPs as well as the Opposition. Some took the form suggested by Jennings, i.e. amendments tabled and pushed in an effort to persuade, remind, coerce, the government to accept modification.[2] This was ineffective.† There were also obstructive resolutions, moved with reason but so fundamentally at odds with the policy suppositions of the Bill as to be *a priori* unacceptable. The place of these will be discussed elsewhere. Such a possibility is not recognised in the constitutional literature (other than that on parliamentary rules of order). Indeed, despite many books on 'Parliament at Work' there is remarkably little formal-legal information on the amending process in general.

The amending process in committee was as arduous for the government as for the member moving an amendment. The minister was only rarely informed in advance of the amendments which would be pushed to a division by the Opposition. He could not even be sure which would be debated until the early hours of the morning on the day upon which the committee sat, when the Order Papers were printed. Early in the morning, the principal in charge of the Bill had to reach his desk and consider the amendments tabled for the day. Draft amendments or technical issues had to be considered by the departmental solicitor and parliamentary counsel if legal problems arose. By 9.15 the principal must have briefed his seniors who would

---

* It is reported that consultation with the landlords' groups began even before the planning stages of the 1965 Act, much to the pleasant surprise of at least one leader (Mr H. Symon of A L P O).
† Though some 'demands' by backbench London Conservatives on postponing decontrol were accepted, I doubt that this pressure was a strong factor.

make proposals to the minister. The minister had, therefore, approximately an hour to consider which, if any, of the amendments in the Order Paper should be taken seriously. He had to decide at the same time whether he could accept any amendment in whole or part. Normally the Ministry urged, at the least, that an amendment be re-drafted internally. But there was a natural tendency to reject all Opposition proposals because what could not be fully considered was most probably full of hidden dangers. That any amendments were accepted was a tribute to the flexibility and the readiness of the minister, and perhaps his civil servants, to accept advice, even from the Opposition. Most government-party suggestions worked their way privately. They saw the light of day only when the intent was to bring pressure to bear.[3] Government backbench amendments were not intended for serious parliamentary consideration; in any case the arguments would have been put privately in a variety of ways. Despite all of this, amendments were made.

The most important of the amendments made by the government was to extend the transition period for decontrol from six to fifteen months. This was achieved by a change in schedule IV. Twelve different proposals were tabled, proposing extensions from eighteen months to five years. The government backbench motions were withdrawn when the government tabled its own amendment to provide for a fifteen-month transition. What was the government's logic? The proposal seemed to be at variance with every other suggestion. The Ministry might have been primarily influenced by the RICS proposal for an eighteen-month transition period. In counting the transition period the government, unlike other bodies, counted the time from the publication of the Bill. From that moment both landlord and tenant would have a reasonable idea of what they might expect in the future.[4] Thus while the Bill read fifteen months, this meant more like twenty months from the time the government assumed everyone was aware of the Bill.

One senior politician offered a simpler explanation. The general solution of the government was a two-year transition. If precisely two years were used, decontrol would have taken place at Christmas time. To delay beyond the Christmas holiday meant postponement until March or April, an unacceptable delay. Fifteen months meant that the Bill would begin operation in October, well before Christmas. Dislocations or possible hardships should not strike at an ostensibly joyous season. As this decision required cabinet approval, being a major change in the Bill, sentiment was probably well mixed practical politics.[5]

The length of the transition period could determine the extent of the personal hardships which would arise from dislocations. The Opposition was most comfortable in putting the case of those affected, both as reason for modification and to frighten the ordinary backbencher, who cared at least as much for his constituency's opinion as the government's. Backbench pressure for change was thus substantial.

But the case against change was strong. The longer the transition, the longer the benefits of the free market were delayed and the longer before equilibrium in housing supply and demand could be restored. This delay would strike primarily at the large landlords. Some contended that the large landlords would benefit, not from increased rents, but from opportunities to rid themselves of undesirable tenants and the chance to redevelop.[6] The small landlords benefited primarily from the rent increase. But it was the large landlord who might be able to provide additional houses to let. The delay and the three-year lease option, which provided for early decontrol if a lease were arranged, were disadvantageous to 'economic men'. They knew that they could not obtain the full market rent at first. But the three-year lease deterred many of the large landlords who might have preferred phased increases over a reasonable period. The consequence was to encourage full application of the Act at the end of the transition period. None the less, the amendment on transition was made.

Connected to decontrol were two amendments which prohibited premiums (key money for the grant of occupancy) and extended the minimum notice to quit. Their immediate connection to the original Bill was nebulous. But this Bill was not an original piece of legislation. It sought merely to amend a series of previous Acts, all of which dealt with the problem of landlord and tenant. The addition of new principles could not destroy a conceptual framework where none existed.

The prohibition on premiums reflected the decision of the Ministry to deal at once with what was recognised to be a long standing problem.[7] The decision was a sudden one. Not merely was an amendment introduced in committee, but a further amendment became necessary on Report. The praise received from the pro-tenant rebels was counterbalanced by the criticism of the pro-landlord M Ps.[8] This was to be the sweetener for decontrol.

According to rumour, Mr Quintin Hogg was responsible in the first instance for the proposal to extend the minimum notice to quit to four weeks. Conservative backbenchers of both factions tabled amendments to this effect, which were accepted.[9] A debate on whether this should also apply to council houses was resolved, despite Labour objections, that it should.[10]

These two points plus the transition changes were the major modifications made in the Bill after introduction. Though the remaining amendments were of far lesser importance, they indicate the kinds of concessions a minister felt able to make in the face of not inconsiderable pressure on all sides.

The government made one concession to the Opposition on a significant matter. Mr MacColl, a leading Labour backbencher, argued that the rateable value of a dwelling might be pushed over the limits of control by additions to the rateable value as a result of improvements made by the tenant. In this case, he contended, some arrangement should be made to prevent the landlord from decontrolling because of tenants' expenditures. Mr Sandys accepted this proposal in committee, though the Ministry insisted on drafting the actual amendment itself.[11] A similar concession was made to Mr Graham Page, a government backbencher. The minister agreed in committee, and amended on Report, to provide for compensation to the tenant for major improvements if the tenant left the premises on decontrol.[12] This was the last concession to the Opposition.

Sir Ian Horobin (Conservative member for Oldham) achieved the rare distinction of forcing an amendment over the government's objection. In committee he succeeded in obtaining an amendment which prohibited speculators from benefiting from retrospective aspects of the Bill.[13] This was reversed on Report. The minister argued that the proposal would do more harm than good. In any case, the amendment would have to be removed if only to discourage other attempts in this or any other Bill, at government backbencher initiatives as a dangerous precedent.[14]

In addition to Sir Ian's amendment, one other major backbench proposal was rejected. This was a proposal to limit the rents charged in decontrolled houses, at least initially, to two and one-half times the gross rateable value. Mr Brooke refused to accept this on the ground that it would set a 'fair value' market price outside of London and thus destroy the free market which he was trying to establish as the sole standard.[15]

A great many trivial amendments were proposed, in Committee or on Report, by the government and Opposition and government backbenchers. While these were pertinent to rent restriction, they were not all relevant to the Bill's intentions. Such a change was the proposal to amend clause 10 (2) to prevent decontrol by deception. The landlord should not be able to decontrol unless a substantial rather than purely technical revision was made in the tenant's lease.[16] Similarly, the government agreed not to amend contractual tenancies. The Opposition contended that contracts should not be breached to allow the landlord to raise rent, since they were not to be breached to allow tenants to lower them.[17] This concession was no doubt easier because of government and landlord concern about the principle of breach of contract.[18] The government was further persuaded to introduce a new clause to prohibit an apportionment of rateable value by sub-tenants without the consent of the primary landlord.[19] This was to prevent sub-tenants conspiring to keep all the rateable values within control.

Amendments involving questions of interpretation or general drafting were also offered. These were moved from all sides, and mostly accepted if the intent of the proposal remained in harmony with the Bill. This sort of amendment reflected the Ministry's role in the legislative process. In many cases, the initial drafting proved quite shoddy. It must be a mark against the Ministry when the minister, in moving a drafting amendment says:

> I want to start by apologising to hon. members on both sides of the committee for the extreme obscurity of the words in sub-paragraph (4) of the Bill, but it is not only because they are obscure that I am seeking leave to revise them. Some legal language is, so I understand, necessarily obscure but in fact on further examination it became clear that sub-paragraph (4) as it stands does not provide for every conceivable case and we want to get the wording of the Bill as perfect as possible.
>
> In the course of this further examination I hope it will be agreed that those who are expert in these things have enabled me to arrive at a form of words which, though not crystal clear, at any rate gets many more marks for lucidity than the original words.[20]

In such bills legitimate disagreements could develop among lawyers. The minister had to decide which interpretation to accept. These were not easy decisions to make. On rent control, where the law was so vague, some M Ps, with considerable rent control practice, were as expert if not more so than the Ministry's legal advisors. Second-guessing the courts was a privilege not limited to parliamentary counsel. Nonetheless, the rejections of parliamentary for Ministry advice persisted, in the main, even where government could fall back on nothing more than precedent.[21] However often the rights of the private member might be acknowledged, they remained unrecognised in fact.

It is evident that very few changes were made in the Rent Bill. The reasons mitigating against extensive changes, as has been shown, were partly of substance. But part of the explanation lies in the decision-making process itself. It is this, and the setting in which it functioned, that must be re-examined.

An incoming government or a new minister must often assume responsibility for a particular line of policy with which they do not agree in many essentials. Such a transition can be acutely embarrassing. For, often, there simply has not been time either to understand or reject policy decisions. This was particularly obvious in wartime. One need only recall the relative slow pace of change when Lloyd George and Churchill took power with mandates for rapid change. In peacetime, without the crisis element, the pace of policy transformation is yet slower.

Mr Henry Brooke took office as Minister of Housing and Local Government on 13 January 1957. He inherited a Bill which had not merely been published, but had been given a second reading and was in the midst of consideration by Standing Committee. Within a week of taking office he had to face that committee. He was spared for an extra day by constitutional difficulty.* There was not much time.

Most amendments on the Order Paper were placed by the Opposition with the intention of making party-political points. Civil servants could not judge these, however. The minister, with the advice of his civil servants, had to consider each and every one of the amendments and decide what to do. Especially in the early days, civil servants had also to be trained to the minister's particular style and work habits. He must spend much more time in the early days re-drafting proposed briefs than he did later. The task of the civil service was to develop the knack of giving the minister precisely what he wanted. It was not easy to have to take major decisions at the same time. If only for the reason that the minister did not have time to review all

* He could not be seated on the committee until the Selection Committee met. This was not to be until the afternoon of the day on which the committee resumed work.

the reasoning and papers which led to the original Bill, reconsideration was impossible. In fact, Mr Brooke did not go through the papers. This made reconsideration in detail all the more difficult. But it is quite possible that reconsideration would have made no difference.

The Bill was government policy. In accepting office Mr Brooke accepted the Ministry and policy as left to him by his predecessor. He certainly did not discuss with the prime minister in the few moments allotted to him when the cabinet was being selected his concern about aspects of Ministry policy. He was committed to pilot the Bill through.

Nor could the policy have been revised even if Mr Brooke thought it imperative. The prime minister and cabinet could not take the time to consider the possibility of total revision. Further, at a moment of crisis, both domestic and foreign, when the Conservative Party's political judgment was in serious question, it would hardly be desirable to call a major Tory measure into question. In any case, it was not thought imperative.

For, as has been pointed out, Mr Brooke had no more time for reconsideration than the rest of the government. He was responsible not merely for the Rent Bill but for a variety of other matters from housing construction and local government to water purity and minerals development. There was little time to rethink.

The parliamentary schedule was a further bar. The only reconsideration possible was for change which could be embodied in amendments to be drafted and included as the Bill progressed.

Mr Brooke was hampered in the amending process by lack of intimate connection with the Bill. He came from the Treasury where he had been in charge of taxation and finance problems. While he had experience on the LCC and was hence better acquainted with housing problems than most of his colleagues, he was nonetheless a long way removed. Except in general, he had not given the Bill any serious consideration prior to taking the Ministry. By the same token, he had no time to read the papers critically, to absorb many of the details of the Ministry's intentions. Finally, he had only five weeks to make a major decision on clause 9, relating to decontrol, and to obtain cabinet consent. Changes would have to be cautious.

Mr Brooke's position was not made easier by the particular characteristics of the Ministry.[22] Dame Evelyn and the civil servants were convinced that something had to be done. While other civil servants, even permanent secretaries, might be ignored with impunity, both Mr Brooke and Mr Bevins, like others before and since, were not inclined to challenge Dame Evelyn.[23] Mr Bevins had the impression that 'the Ministry policy' would have been surrendered only with the greatest reluctance.[24] In any case, the ministers could see no alternate plans. At this stage new operative policy could not be developed. To win the civil servants and to examine alternatives required time which was clearly in short supply.

A further deterrent to change was the considerable pressure from the Conservative Party to hold firm. Mr Brooke was far more aware of the difficulties than most of the party, even most of the relevant decision-makers. He was one of the few Tories who was not only a London MP but who also had had some experience with the problems faced by the LCC as a housing owner and as a welfare agency.* The difficulties, as the Allen Committee publications now make clear, were substantially in London, though other areas would be marginally affected.[25] At a time when there was considerable public pressure to hold firm on the Bill, and only limited opposition from London Tories, it required not a little political courage to recognise that there was any need for concessions to eliminate inequities of any sort.

The minister might have been helped by the strength of the Opposition case. But Labour was in a particularly bad position to make a good case in 1956. They had done well prior to 1955 when ministers, fresh from office, could challenge their recently appointed successor with some recent expert information.[26] But after the 1955 general election the ties between ex-ministers and departments dwindled. Opposition 'real information' became less and less relevant. The departmental figures dropped from the scene to be replaced by those without direct experience. Neither Dalton nor Bevan took an active part. Mr Mitchison, who had no direct ministerial experience, and Mr Lindgren, who had been parliamentary secretary, were no real substitutes. The credibility of the attack became moot.[27]

Moreover, the ministers seriously questioned the good will of the Opposition. They believed that though the attack was sincere, it was conducted for party political advantage rather than in a legislative spirit. The Opposition's attack on all points with equal fervour reduced the credibility of their legitimate criticism.[28]

Another dynamic pressure for change ought to have come from

* He was a member of the L C C from 1945–55, for a time leader of the Opposition. He was a member of the Hampstead Borough Council until 1957.

the pressure groups: both professional and landlord-tenant. So far as Mr Brooke was concerned these offered their advice too little and too late. They made almost no comment on the really significant principles of the Bill except for the transition period. Many impartial groups such as the CAB which might have taken an interest were otherwise occupied because of the contemporary social and economic strains produced by the international tensions.[29] The role of such groups is considered elsewhere.

More is said elsewhere about the role of the various Conservative parliamentary pressures. From the Ministry point of view the significant forces ought to have been the pro-tenant London Tories. In fact, they were seen as insufficient in number and quality. They had no real political impact.[30]

Primary responsibility, as civil servants and politicians never tire of saying, rests with the minister. But the parliamentary secretary is not without influence when he chooses to use it. Mr Bevins did not attempt to do so. Civil servants, he has admitted, were frequently able to persuade him. He was impressed by Mr Brooke. Not wholly confident of his own intellectual powers, he was amazed, but accepted the justification for Mr Brooke's self-confidence.[31] Mr Brooke was the only politician of whom he spoke with any degree of affection and sincere praise in *The Greasy Pole*. In any case, Mr Bevins' views on the Bill did not differ substantially from Mr Brooke's. Mr Bevins argued that the housing problem could not be solved by ending rent control. He was suspicious of any intellectual argument, particularly so fluent a case as Mr Powell's free market theme.[32] In consequence, Mr Bevins had no recognisable distinct impact on Rent Bill policies.

In the absence of sufficient pressure to force action, Mr Brooke found himself in a dilemma. He believed that something ought to be done about rent control. But he shared Mr Bevins' doubts as to the means by which this should be done. He did not believe slice decontrol was useful. He would have preferred repair to accommodation as the principal policy goal. Mr Brooke's answer would have been to give the landlord a sufficient return to make repairs. He would have liked to increase rents in stages, perhaps under delegated powers. At the same time, he wished to keep the rent increases under firm political control. Initially, he did not accept rent increases in the decontrolled sector above three times gross rateable value. His reasons for not enshrining this in legislation were explained in his statement on the Rees-Davis amendment.[33]

No one at the time knew very much about the rising number of households in the face of a relatively static population. None foresaw the problems immigration both from the north and overseas would raise. But Mr Brooke might have been more prone to amend had he been aware in advance of all the suppositions on which the legislation was based. As one with some expertise, he might have asked some difficult questions had time permitted. In the absence of good reason to make changes, little assistance from outside, and considerable pressure to maintain the *status quo*, he did not question.

Another explanation put forward for Mr Brooke's failure to make substantial changes has been his 'priggishness'. Both colleagues and opponents use this adjective because Mr Brooke sounds self-righteous when challenged. Mr Bevins praised him for his capacity to take decisions on merit, without reference to their political content.[34] Only his most violent critics and most radical colleagues have questioned this. But 'priggishness', for whatever reason, may help explain Mr Brooke's resistance to change.

In point of fact, only Mr Sandys ever adopted a significant suggestion for change, that of Mr MacColl. He later concurred in all those changes that Mr Brooke made, even if he had not indeed intended them himself. Might he, with his more detailed knowledge of the Bill, and his basic commitment to it, have been better placed to make further concessions? Certainly Mr Brooke was inhibited by the need to make perfectly plain that his concessions were not on points of principle. The conservative influence of the civil service was undoubtedly brought to bear more easily against Mr Brooke than was possible with Mr Sandys. But this is only the ministerial part of the problem of change.

Part of the opposition to change was constitutional. The cabinet had to be, and was, consulted on all major modifications in the Bill. Other ministers' pressures for modification might have encouraged a thorough review. The failure of the cabinet at that time to raise questions was a real barrier to major change. The prime minister may well have been sympathetic to the problems. But he could not take much time, any more than had his predecessors or successors, for domestic reasons. Since prime ministers usually have had time only for foreign affairs and party political decisions, they trusted ministers with the rest. Some have suggested that it was Mr Macmillan, with his memories of Stockton, not Mr Brooke who urged modification of the Bill. No evidence has borne this out.

The principal alterations to the Rent Bill were the extension of the period for transition in clause 9 from six to eighteen months, the prohibition of premiums, and the extension of minimum notice to quit to four weeks. Other amendments for compensation, both to landlord and tenant, for various forms of improvements were accepted. But these, like the more major amendments, in no way altered the principles of the Bill.

Considerable modifications were made. But with the exception of the transition provisions, all were additions rather than changes. Principles remained fixed. Individually, the drafting amendments were significant. Collectively, they were trivial. The textual integrity of the Bill was preserved by the inability of the political masters to decide what was principal and what was detail. Partly, the conservative treatment of the Bill reflected genuine assurance that the proposed course was the right one. Partly, the Bill was guarded by a Ministry with strong commitment and/or ability to impose its will upon politicians. The minister was all the more subject to these pressures because he arrived on the scene too late to make major alterations in policy, both for political and intellectual reasons. He could neither exert pressure at the appropriate moments, nor could he master the details already known by others. The moment for compromises had passed. Moreover, he was subject to strong pressures against change: the party and public commitment, the contemporary political situation, the lack of strong outside sources of information and pressure for change. In the conclusions the implications of these dilemmas for the legislative process are drawn out.

NOTES

1 See below, chapter 8.
2 Jennings, *Parliament*, Cambridge University Press, Cambridge, 1961, pp. 280 ff.
3 Jennings, *Parliament*, pp. 228 ff.
4 567 H C Deb.5s., col 1038; 1956–7, H C S C,I, col 989.
5 Confirmed in an interview with the Rt. Hon. H. Brooke.
6 *The Economist*, vol. 182, p. 366. This view was also held by many of the property companies. The Milner Holland Report suggests that redevelopment was most difficult for these because their property was mostly purpose-built.
7 1956–7, H C S C,I, col 1065.
8 567 H C Deb.5s., cols 973–82.
9 1956–7, H C S C,I, col 1065; 567 H C Deb.5s., cols 982 ff. Order Paper amendment of 25 February 1957 in the name of Mr Monslow and others.

10 1956–7, HCSC,I, col 1149.
11 *Ibid.*, cols 103, 106.
12 *Ibid.*, cols 1137 ff.; 567 HCDeb.5s., cols 1289 ff.
13 1956–7, HCSC,I, cols 872 ff.
14 567 HCDeb.5s., cols 1069 ff.
15 *Ibid.*, cols 990 ff.
16 1956–7, HCSCDeb.,I, cols 955 ff.
17 *Ibid.*, cols 1081 ff.
18 *Ibid.*, cols 109, 339.
19 567 HCDeb.5s., cols 988 ff.
20 1956–7, HCSCDeb.,1, cols 1301–2.
21 The attempt to include Hornchurch in London was rejected on reference to the 1915 Act, to name but one example, 567 HCDeb.5s., col 1102.
22 Bevins, *The Greasy Pole*, Hodder and Stoughton, London, 1965, pp. 54–69.
23 *Ibid.*, p. 51.
24 *Ibid.*
25 *The Impact of Rates on Households*, Cmd 2582, 1965.
26 D. E. Butler, *The British General Election of 1955*, Macmillan, London, 1956.
27 See below, chapters 9 and 11.
28 709 HCDeb.5s., col 96.
29 But see statement on Report, 567 HCDeb.5s., col 991.
30 See below, chapters 9 and 10.
31 Bevins, *The Greasy Pole*, p. 51.
32 *Ibid.*, pp. 51–2.
33 See below, and 709 HCDeb.5s., cols 95–6
34 Bevins, *The Greasy Pole*, p. 51.

# 7
# The People and the Press

Although the Rent Bill would affect great masses of people, this inchoate voice remained unheard in the legislative process. Politically apathetic, most people were never even aware that the Rent Bill was going through Parliament, and the quantity and quality of the information provided either by the government or at the initiative of the mass media virtually ensured disinterest. So insignificant was the role of the mass media that the public, although greatly concerned about housing in general, were not similarly concerned with rent control.

No more public announcement could have been given of the government's intentions on rent control than Mr Duncan Sandys' speech to the Conservative Party Conference in October 1956. Nor was the significance of that pronouncement lost upon the mass media. Yet in this they were given remarkably little direction by party or government. The Ministry's press office evidently did plan to circulate excerpts from Mr Sandys' speech. A circular without other comment was duplicated but, at the last moment not distributed.[1] The official explanation was that the responsibility for circularising such a statement lay with the party. Yet succeeding paragraphs will indicate the extent to which this restraint was to become the key to government and Conservative strategy so far as the general public were concerned.

When the Bill and its accompanying White Paper were published the government issued a mimeographed circular to the press, with a covering letter dated 7 November 1956. This formed the basis of most of the press reports on the Bill. The press statement contained nothing more than the restatement of some of the principal reasons for the Bill, an outline of the salient figures in the White Paper, and a very cursory outline of the principal clauses of the Bill. Of special interest was the statement of objectives:

   a. to provide means for the progressive abolition of rent control;
   b. to establish for houses which remain in control in England and Wales,

revised rent limits, more in keeping with the present-day value of money
and the cost of maintenance; and

   c. to permit, in Scotland, an increase in controlled rents subject to
certain conditions.[2]

Small wonder that these, and not repairs, became the chief concerns
of the newspapers who were dependent upon the government for
their information at this stage. The remaining activities of the
Ministry of Housing press division can be quickly recounted. Two
subsequent releases, one explaining the extension of the transition
period for decontrol and the other on Sir Ian Horobin's amendment,
were issued. Both of them merely stated government intentions.
Thus the Ministry abdicated to the correspondents themselves responsibility for deciding what information the public ought to have
about the pending legislation. Of this *The Times* commented:

> Much of the confused hostility it has aroused might have been dis-
> sipated had the need for reform been the subject of a prolonged campaign
> of explanation. Yet the statistics about the effect of the Bill which Mr
> Brooke's predecessor eventually issued had to be extracted by a clamour
> from the Press for information. Even today government supporters are
> making no sustained effort to justify the reform outside their speeches in
> Parliament.[3]

*The Times* and *The Manchester Guardian* (as it then was) had a
special place as purveyors of information. It was therefore important
to understand the setting within which their lead articles and reports
were prepared. In each case primary responsibility lay with a social
science correspondent. In 1956–7 *The Times*' man was Mr Francois
Lafitte, now Professor of Social Administration at Birmingham
University. At that time the *Guardian*'s correspondent was Mr Derek
Senior, now a freelance writer and consultant and a member of the
Royal Commission on Local Government. Both of these had to cover
a wide range, neither was particularly expert in Rents and Housing.
Mr Senior was mainly interested in local government and planning.
Mr Lafitte was much better equipped on health and social services
and had to cover so wide a field that he could spare little time for
housing.[4] Nonetheless, both could claim, like the principal professional groups, an *a priori* right to be consulted or at least advised
about the progress of legislation in their field. That neither was, in
fact, consulted in advance may reflect on the Ministry's diligence or
deliberate negligence. But it may also reflect an awareness that both
correspondents had come to the minister's conclusions independently.

Both were firmly convinced that the system of rent control was making the housing to let situation more serious than it needed to be. Both were convinced of the need for reform in the law to make it more workable and more equitable. Both had a certain faith in the desirability of decontrol as a means of stimulating not only redeployment of stock but also increase in the privately let stock. It was within the context of sympathy but non-commitment that these two principal papers' policies developed.

Almost as soon as the 1954 Housing Repairs and Rents Act was law *The Times* showed signs of discontent. In January 1955 and February 1956 *The Times* ran articles which indicated the 'Woes of a Landlord' and complained about the failure of the new Act.[5] In July 1956 *The Times* called for prompt and large-scale decontrol, though it also urged an expanded role for local authorities.[6] If the *Guardian* was less sure as to the solutions, it was equally sure as to the need for them. In a series of leaders during the early summer of 1956 the paper advocated that something drastic be done about rent control and praised the approach offered by the Bow Group. But it pointed out, by way of caution, that the free market would not encourage repairs.[7] Though both papers had defined their positions, neither one really prepared their readers for the debate to come.

The first of the press comments on the proposed Bill came on 11 and 12 October, in connection with Mr Sandys' conference statement. Mr Ian Trethowan in *The News Chronicle* and Mr Hunter in *The Daily Herald* both reported that at long last a cabinet decision had been taken and action on rent control was to be expected. The next day came the reports of the conference. *The Daily Mail* and *The Daily Sketch* both reported the speech and commented favourably upon it. *The Daily Mirror* commented that it expected the gross rateable value limits to be £75 and £50 (they were, in fact, much lower). *The Daily Worker* called for 'action'. *The Daily Telegraph* commented favourably on the proposal. These comments betray the haste with which they had to be prepared.

*The Times* and *The Manchester Guardian* took a more considered view of the matter. *The Times* argued that decontrol was needed to secure proper care and more advantageous use of dwellings. But it cautioned that decontrol on vacant possession ought to be limited.[8] The *Guardian* also commented editorially, remarking that it was necessary to restore some measure of reality to housing finance. Rent control, once a defence for the private tenant, had become a hindrance.[9] Thus the stage was set for the favourable reception of the proposed Bill.

When the Bill was published most of the press contented itself with impartial summaries, drawn from the Ministry's own statement.[10] Most intentionally waited until the debate on second reading before delivering judgment. But both *The Times* and the *Guardian* had some reservations. *The Times* pointed out that though the Bill was 'An Urgent Reform' it wanted more information about the consequences. The *Guardian* contended that the system of slice decontrol would prevent 'artificial inflation of free rents: indeed, they may well settle down to something less than is now demanded . . .'.[21] The *Guardian*, however, was concerned that there was no 'safeguard against the hardship of a too abrupt rent increase . . .'.[12] These cautions were to re-emerge only very much later in the debate.

The major reports of the Rent Act debate were those on second reading. *The Times* and the *Guardian* ran leaders on the first day of debate,[13] in which they emphasised the advantages of the Bill and the wrongs it would right. *The Scotsman*, however, ran an editorial in opposition to the Bill because it failed to make allowances for the peculiarities of the Scottish position. But most of the editorial comment came on the second day. The *Telegraph* argued that rents needed to be raised and considered that the dispute was primarily about who should own houses to let. *The News Chronicle*'s position was not very much different, except to urge caution. Not until 24 November did *The Financial Times* remark that the new Rent Bill was 'bold and imaginative'. In short, press comment was generally favourable.

But almost immediately thereafter, the principal papers at least started to express their renewed doubts. *The Times* mentioned the possible dislocations in large urban areas,[14] and the *Guardian* pointed to the possible abuses that landlords might use to get vacant possession.[15] It warned that:

> It is incumbent on the Minister of Housing, having chosen to rely on economic forces to restore some measure of reality to housing finance, to use all the means of publicity at his disposal to ensure that the realities are understood by the potential victims of sharp practices.[16]

Both papers reported the initial amendments on delaying transition and compensation to tenants when Standing Committee A began to sit.[17] And doubts became greater as the committee stage progressed.

By January 1957 *The Times* started to have fairly serious reservations. It said that:

The aims of the Rent Bill are right, but some of its methods are plainly too crude . . . Decontrol comes best when money is cheap and there is ample scope for expanding private house building. This year's prospects are rather different. Those about to be decontrolled need more time for readjustment. The fairest way is surely to keep them within rent control, subject to the same regulated rent increase, for the same nine months as other controlled tenants; and to allow them a further nine months after decontrol, during which, protected against eviction, they can attempt to settle new terms . . .[18]

The *Guardian* was reassured by the comments of Mr A. C. L. Day who remarked in an article on future rents that the rise of decontrolled rents in London was likely to be between two and three times G R V. But, at the same time, previously uncontrolled rents would fall by one-third or even one-half.[19]

After the extension of the transition period complacency became the watchword. The *Express* argued the delay was unnecessary.[20] *The Times* agreed that it was a 'sensible cushion'.[21] Only the *Herald* held that the delay was inadequate.[22] But all agreed that such a move was politically necessary in view of the defeat of the Conservatives in the North Lewisham by-election, supposedly because of public reaction to the Rent Bill.[23] But papers such as *The News Chronicle* still opposed any modification up to that point.[24] All through the committee stage papers like *The Sunday Pictorial*[25] attacked the Bill and even *The Observer* noted the general public concern about decontrol and rent rises.[26] In the end, the serious papers all agreed that no one really knew what would happen, but that whatever happened would not be serious, and the problems caused by rent control really did need solving.[27]

The only major paper to make a serious attack on the Bill was the *Daily Mirror*. With its five million circulation, public concern could well be aroused. When the Bill was published the *Mirror*'s comment read:

Shocks in the Rent Bill. It's pay what we say or get out for 800,000. These are the drastic features of the Bill presented to Parliament. . . . But it will be fought line by line by the Labour Party.[28]

By 17 November the *Mirror* had digested the actual rent increases and contended that there would be no limit to decontrolled rent

TABLE 8
Newspapers Classified by Geographical, Social and Political Community

| Constituency | Social Classification | Political Distribution | Name of Paper |
|---|---|---|---|
| LONDON | | | |
| Dulwich | Urban, light industrial and residential | Mainly Tory | South London Observer |
| Clapham | Urban, light industry and residential | Marginal Labour | Clapham Observer |
| Hackney | Clothing, chemicals | Safe Labour | Hackney Gazette |
| Hampstead | Residential | Safe Tory | Hampstead and Highgate Express |
| Islington | Light industry | Safe Labour | Islington Gazette |
| Streatham | Residential | Safe Tory | *Streatham News |
| | | | |
| London Suburbs | | | |
| Acton | Urban—motors, light industry | Marginal Labour | Acton Gazette and West London Post |
| Crosby | Urban—residential | Safe Tory | Waterloo and Crosby Times |
| Petersfield | Rural, residential, farming | Safe Tory | *Hants. and Sussex News |
| Wood Green | Urban, residential | Labour | Wood Green, Southgate and Palmers Green Weekly Herald |
| | | | |
| Provinces (England and Wales) | | | |
| Aberdare | Urban, mining | Safe Labour | *Aberdare Leader |
| Aldershot | Light industry, residential | Safe Tory | Aldershot News |
| Birmingham | — | — | Mail, Post and Gazette |
| Bradford | Engineering, textiles | Mainly Labour | *Telegraph and Argus |
| Bristol | Light and heavy industry, docks and residential | 4 Labour, 2 Conservative. All safe seats | Bristol Evening Post |
| Cardigan | Farming | Liberal | *Cardigan and Tivyside Advertiser |
| Chesterfield | Mining, steel, engineering | Safe Labour | *Derbyshire Times |

E  TABLE 8—*continued*
*Newspapers Classified by Geographical, Social and Political Community*

| Constituency | Social Classification | Political Distribution | Name of Paper |
|---|---|---|---|
| *Provinces (England and Wales)*—continued | | | |
| Clitheroe | Urban, textiles | Safe Tory | *Clitheroe Advertiser* and *Times* |
| Crewe | Urban, engineering, R.R. works | Safe Labour | *Crewe Chronicle* |
| Guildford | Urban, light industry, residential | Safe Tory | *Surrey Times* |
| Harwich | Urban—farming, tourism, residential | Tory | *Harwich and Dovercourt Standard* |
| Henley | Farming, residential | Safe Tory | *Henley Standard* |
| Kettering | Farming, steel, light industry, urban | Safe Labour | *Northamptonshire Evening Telegraph* |
| Leicester | Urban, hosiery, light industry | Mostly Labour safe seats | *Leicester Evening Mail* |
| Morecambe | Urban, tourism, residential | Safe Tory | *Morecambe and Heysham Times* |
| Manchester | — | — | *Manchester Evening News* |
| Newcastle-on-Tyne | Docks, engineering, shipbuilding | Mostly Labour Tory seats marginal | *Newcastle Journal* |
| Oldham | Engineering, textiles | 1 Labour, 1 Tory | *Oldham Chronicle* |
| Plymouth | Docks, light industry, tourism | Both seats marginal Tory | *Western Evening Herald* |
| Sheffield | Steel, engineering | Mostly Labour, safe seats | *Sheffield Telegraph* |
| Walsall | Urban, steel and engineering | 1 Labour, 1 Tory | *Walsall Observer* |
| Wolverhampton | Steel and engineering | 1 Labour, 1 Tory | *Express and Star* |
| *Scotland* | | | |
| Edinburgh | — | — | *Scotsman* |
| Glasgow | — | — | *Daily Record* |

\* Papers carrying no report of Rent Bill.

(*Note*: Columns 2 and 3 drawn from Mitchell & Boehm)

increases.[29] The paper soon lost interest and the Conservative Bill was left to run its course, unmolested from this source at least.

Though it would be difficult to provide full documentation, it seems evident that the press was poorly informed about housing. The quality and number of journalists capable of writing sense about housing—or understanding a leak when they got one—were nothing like that of the journalists specialising on (say) education, or the motor industry, or the fashion trade.[30]

The reactions of the local press, especially the Greater London newspapers, were not as generally favourable to the Bill as the nationals. Most of the reports in the local papers concerned activities of the area: a council's protest, a local Labour Party function, the meeting of a new tenants' association. And comments were widespread mainly during the end of January and beginning of February. The London newspapers were generally in opposition, especially papers for the middle-class dormitory areas such as Lewisham.[31] But it is difficult to draw a reasonable profile of local reaction to the Bill.

What can be done is to trace the extent to which the Rent Bill was discussed in the local press. To do this a sample was taken containing a local newspaper from the constituencies of the four ministers responsible for the Bill and the various members of the Standing Committee (whose newspapers might find it profitable to report a matter in which the local MP had a particular hand). In addition selected areas were added to give the sample an additional middle-class dormitory bias. Thanks to the habit of members with constituency interests dominating Standing Committees, the sample included a proportion of every community likely to be affected by the Bill, especially in London. Table 8 gives a profile of the regions selected. To determine the extent of press comment the papers listed in table 9 were checked for the three issues following the debates on second reading, Report, third reading. In the case of the dailies, the newspapers on the days of debate were also considered. Of the thirty-five newspapers so considered, fourteen had no report whatsoever on the Rent Bill during that period. These are indicated in table 8 by an asterisk next to the name of the paper. Nine other newspapers, including all but two of those from London, and all the newspapers from the London suburbs (not previously asterisked) carried no reports on the debates themselves. What they did carry were reports on the various local forces at work against the Bill. These activities were reported in the issues surrounding the Report

TABLE 9
*Papers which Reported the Rent Bill in Parliament*

| Newspaper | Report on Second Reading | Report on Report and Third Reading | Other Reports |
|---|---|---|---|
| Hampstead and Highgate Express (weekly) | None | Reports Third Reading debate | Threats of eviction (30N), fights by tenants, tenants' meetings, letters by many |
| Islington Gazette (weekly) | Own MP's speech | Own MP's Third Reading speech | None |
| Birmingham Post (daily) | Parliamentary Report | Parliamentary Report and front page | Editorial on Second Reading-'Rationalising Rents' |
| Crewe Chronicle (weekly) | Editorial on Second Reading | Brief report on Report Stage | Report of constituency speech |
| Henley Standard (weekly) | None | Report of own MP's speech | None |
| Northamptonshire Evening Telegraph (daily) | Report on Mitchison's and Lindgren's speeches | Parliamentary Report | 'Tory' claims anti-rent Bill campaign will flop in an article |
| Newcastle Journal (daily) | Yes | Comment on Rees-Davies amendment | None |
| Oldham Chronicle (weekly) | Yes | None | Mentioned in connection with party meeting |
| Sheffield Telegraph (daily) | Yes | Yes | None |
| Express and Star (daily, evening) | Report of Powell | None | None |
| Scotsman | Yes | Yes | Editorial on Second Reading |
| Daily Record (evening) | Yes | None | Article attacking Bill by Labour MP |

and third reading. But, of course, some local papers did carry comment on the Bill in Parliament.

The summary of papers carrying reports on the Bill in Parliament is given in table 9. The principal conclusion to be drawn from this table is the surprisingly slight coverage given, even though in every case local MPs were actively involved. Only a partial explanation can be found in the more immediate significance to these papers of the Dr Bodkin Adams trial and the release of Archbishop Makarios from detention. There was no indication here of the clamour which *The Times* claimed was raised by the press.[32] Only the middle-class community was offered anything like adequate debate by its local press. Apparently, few viewed the debate in progress as worthy of local coverage.

What was the role of the sound media during all of this? Here too no conclusion could be drawn with any great precision. *The Listener*, which reproduces the most significant of the BBC sound and television broadcasts, printed only two items on the Rent Bill. One was a radio talk given by Mr Day, the other a party political broadcast given in May 1957 by Mr Brooke, Sir Ian Horobin and Mr Geoffrey Rippon. In this they attempted to refute the principal concerns of the Labour Party and further argued that Labour's scheme of municipalisation was impractical.[33] Another broadcast was given during the debates in which experts from the professional groups appeared. But this was not reported and the only references to it appeared in a professional group's own minutes.[34] From these indications, radio and television had no great impact.

Before trying to measure the impact of radio and press, notice should be taken of the attitude of one major journal, *The Economist*. The roles of *The New Statesman and Nation* and *The Spectator* are considered in the discussion of the political parties to which they have attachments. Though the circulation of *The Economist* was not large, the quality of its audience made it an important source of public pressure. Reaching as it did the decision-makers and others who influenced opinion, it served as a mediator between the public and the government policy-maker.

Throughout the early 1950s *The Economist* had maintained that rent control was a form of subsidy and that in any case it prevented an ultimate solution of the housing problem.[35] *The Economist* applauded the 1954 Housing Repairs and Rents Act as a first, if very inadequate first step.[36] When the Rent Bill (to become the 1957 Act) came out *The Economist* was on the whole satisfied. It pointed out that working-class families, despite the new increases, would still be housed quite cheaply.[37] It approved of the gross rateable value formula,[38] though it thought the limits of decontrol should be much lower.[39] But it did have reservations about the vacant possession principle:

> The expedient of releasing dwellings as they fall vacant was tried before the war, when it did not work well. Experience then suggested that the arrangement tends to embitter relations between landlords and tenants, and that its effects are very slow.[40]

But *The Economist* concluded that general reform was in order:

> The system of rent control is a wholesale subsidy against the generation which wants to get married and build up a family, and against people who have to move in an automotive age—in favour of a selected class of (largely middle-aged) people who are holding on to far more accommodation than they need in enjoyment of squatters' rights.[41]

This referred to the families which had continued to live in rented accommodation after recontrol in 1939, with the security and low rent provided for under the Rent Restriction Acts. These people, *The Economist* was contending, would have moved to smaller accommodation as their children grew up were not their oversized dwellings so cheap and secure. Though it accepted the need for amendment on transition as a political necessity, it argued that the hardship postponed was the very thing to be desired.[42] That many of *The Economist*'s arguments, such as those cited above about the 'decanting' process, were based on false premises, and/or information even more inadequate than the government's, should be noted. Certainly the line taken by this journal helped popularise a respected point of view which was shared by the government.

All the foregoing merely set the scene as the various media portrayed it. To what extent was this view held or adopted by the public? We must rely almost entirely on the work of Gallup Polls for the answer. The other principal polling body, Research Services Limited (Mark Abrams) had no special information on rent control. N O P had not yet been organised. To make this analysis it would be well first to look at the state of public opinion at the time when the Bill was being drafted and debated and then at public reaction to relevant questions.

Even in 1957 the state of the parties, as measured by the opinion polls, must have been of interest to politicians.[43] Table 10 indicates the relative position in public favour of the political parties during the crucial months when the Bill was being drafted and debated:

TABLE 10

*Voting Intentions (in Percentages of Total Sample)*

|  | January 1956 | February 1956 | March 1956 | April 1956 | May 1956 | July 1956 | August 1956 |
|---|---|---|---|---|---|---|---|
| Poll No. | 455 | 458 | 460 | 462 | 464 | 467 | 470 |
| Conservative | 40 | 38·5 | 36 | 35·5 | 36·5 | 36·5 | 36·5 |
| Labour | 41 | 40 | 38·5 | 39·5 | 40 | 41·5 | 42 |
| Liberal | 6·5 | 8 | 6 | 6·5 | 7·5 | 7 | 5 |
| Other | 0·5 | 1 | 0·5 | 1 | 1 | 1 | 0·5? |
| Don't Know | 12 | 12·5 | 19 | 17·5 | 15 | 14·5 | 16 |

|  | September 1956 | October 1956 | November 1956 | January 1957 | March 1957 | April 1957 |
|---|---|---|---|---|---|---|
| Poll No. | 471 | 473A | 1643 | CS1705 | No no. | CQ17 |
| Conservative | 36·5 | 36 | 37·5 | 39 | 31 | 35·5 |
| Labour | 39·5 | 40 | 38·5 | 43·5 | 40·5 | 43·5 |
| Liberal | 8·5 | 8 | 7 | 6 | 6 | 5·5 |
| Other | 0·5 | 1 | — | 1 | 1 | 1 |
| Don't Know | 15·5 | 15 | 17 | 10·5 | 21·5 | 14·5 |

Source: British Institute of Public Opinion

During the crucial period of drafting, and indeed until some time after January 1957, the Conservative position was never particularly disadvantageous. True, the polls showed a gap of 1–4 per cent. But an election was not due for a considerable time, and the number of 'don't knows' was still rather high. The worst months for the government were July-August during the Suez crisis and the months immediately following the resignation of Sir Anthony Eden. Reasonable politicians would accept these declines in popularity as inevitable, and not necessarily as irreversible trends. But any politician must view a minority position with concern, and there was plenty of evidence that Conservatives did so. Similarly, Labour were aware of their potential strength. But while this might affect party policy, party preference was not necessarily reflected on selected issues.

The public seldom considered housing to be an important responsibility of government. This could be seen from a list of problems
facing the government offered to the sample in January and November 1956 and January 1957 (table 11).

TABLE 11
*Priorities for the Government*

|  | January 1956 | November 1956 | January 1957 |
|---|---|---|---|
| Poll No. | 455 | 1643 | SC1705 |
| *ISSUES* | | | |
| Foreign Affairs: | | | |
| Middle East, Cyprus | 32 | — | — |
| Suez-Hungary, Russia | — | 71 | 38+4 |
| Anglo-American relations | — | — | 9 |
| Oil, Fuel, Petrol | — | 7 | 11 |
| Balance of Payments | 8 | 1 | — |
| Housing | 5 | 3 | 5 |
| Social Services | 3 | — | — |
| Others | 11 | 8 | 1 |
| Don't Know | 15 | 7 | 4 |

Source: British Institute of Public Opinion

This was not unusual. In 1959 Gallup reported similar priorities.[44]
Even as a factor affecting individual families, the public rated housing
slightly. In two surveys conducted in February and November 1956
housing, though in second place, was mentioned by only 9 and 7 per
cent respectively of those questioned as a family problem which was
most urgent. Cost of living was always first and health/education a
close third or equal.* Under the circumstances, the Conservatives can
hardly be accused of having courted political disaster by an attack on
rent control. For, if they bothered to inquire, they would be aware
that they were not judged on domestic policy to any great extent. Of
course, being politicians, they may have preferred adherence to the
superstition that such issues did matter.

Data on public reaction to rent control prior to the introduction of
the Rent Bill was limited and disjointed. When asked about the total
abolition of rent control in August 1956 a clear majority opposed it.

* British Institute of Public Opinion (Gallup Poll), poll numbers 458,1643. In
July 1966 those concerned about housing amounted to 5 per cent; immediately
after the Second Reading of the Rent Bill those concerned rose from the 5 per
cent recorded on 10–11 November to 7 per cent recorded on 22–5 November.

And there was only a slight majority of Tory voters in favour.[45] But when queried about Labour policy, only 6 per cent were aware of 'Homes of the Future'.

In their survey conducted between 22–3 November 1956 Gallup Poll asked a series of questions about rent control.[46] This was done as a matter of information. There was no sponsorship. As the only profile in existence from that period about the view and information possessed by tenants, the summary should be studied with care. 19 per cent of those questioned expressed a desire to move immediately; a further 13 per cent found their present accommodation unsatisfactory but adequate; 20 per cent thought their landlord very good and 30 per cent thought him good (this included all types of landlord). But 52 per cent preferred councils as landlords, 21 per cent private owners and only 5 per cent companies. Many did not even know whether their houses were controlled or not (44 per cent). When asked what the consequences would be if rents were raised, 19 per cent said they would work overtime, 17 per cent cut down on smoking, 14 per cent on food and housekeeping, 9 per cent on clothing and 28 per cent on other things (other alternatives were also possible). When asked to choose between Labour and Conservatives 40 per cent chose Labour, 39 per cent Tory, 21 per cent didn't know. When asked about the Rent Bill itself 33 per cent approved, 35 per cent disapproved, 7 per cent hadn't heard of the Bill and 25 per cent did not know. But when asked which party dealt best with housing problems 37 per cent said Tories, 34 per cent Labour, 24 per cent did not know. Perhaps the most important discovery was that 38 per cent believed themselves unaffected by the Rent Bill, only 18 per cent thought they would have to pay more rent (though 39 per cent knew they were controlled). Only 4 per cent believed that as a consequence of the Bill they would get repairs done, only 1 per cent contemplated moving in consequence. 37 per cent didn't know what would happen. The public was clearly confused.

In January 1957 Gallup asked 'Should the government continue with its new Rent Bill which will permit most controlled rents to rise or wait until conditions are more settled or abandon the Bill altogether?' The results, tabularised opposite (table 12) indicate that once the transition concession had been made, there would be a general predisposition to accept the Bill. Even Labour supporters seemed to have been not unalterably opposed to the measure. But a substantial number did not know and did not care.

TABLE 12
*Poll on the Rent Bill (January)* [47]

|  | Total | Conservative | Labour | Liberal | Don't Know |
|---|---|---|---|---|---|
| Continue | 24 | 41 | 7 | 41 | 19 |
| Wait | 34 | 37 | 30 | 33 | 32 |
| Abandon | 29 | 12 | 47 | 18 | 26 |
| Don't Know | 13 | 10 | 16 | 8 | 24 |

Source: British Institute of Puplic Opinion.

Indeed, there was every indication that the public remained totally confused to the end. In August–September 1957, when nothing had in fact occurred (only notices had been issued), the survey asked people whether they had been affected by the Rent Act. Their replies are given in table 13.

TABLE 13
*Poll on the Rent Act* [48]

|  | Total | Conservative | Labour | Liberal | Don't Know |
|---|---|---|---|---|---|
| Yes | 25 | 18 | 29 | 21 | 26 |
| No | 63 | 77 | 58 | 68 | 55 |
| Don't Know Yet | 12 | 5 | 13 | 11 | 19 |

Source: British Institute of Public Opinion.

In April 1958, despite the implementation of controlled increases, figures were similar. In a series of questions on rent control policy the public expressed their general preference for municipalisation and general opposition to the decontrol of houses and the Rent Act itself. Indeed, 47 per cent of those questioned (including 27 per cent of Conservatives) favoured repeal of the Act. But even so, the general support for Tories as the party best able to deal with housing persisted. [49] As a commentary on the state of public information, it should be noted that never less than 25 per cent confessed ignorance.

The failure of the government to provide adequate information may have added to the state of public ignorance. The press, though generally favourable to the Bill, did not seem to have delineated the issues for most people. The quality press and magazines, by not debating among themselves, aroused no great debate among their readership (no flood of letters to the editor, etc.). Radio and television seem to have been uninterested. The consequence of this

E*

general malaise seemed to be that the public were ill-informed, misinformed, and unaware of a 'great debate' which might affect the lives of many.

## NOTES

1 Ministry of Housing and Local Government, W.6.15/56/120.
2 Press Release, paragraph 5, 7 November 1956, MHLG.
3 *The Times*, 20 February 1957.
4 Comment to the author by Professor D. V. Donnison.
5 *The Times*, 17 and 18 January 1955, 7 February 1956.
6 *The Times*, 13 July 1956, 'Freeing Rents' (leader).
7 *The Manchester Guardian*, 30 July 1956, p. 6; 25 June 1956, p. 6.
8 *The Times*, 12 October 1956, p. 11.
9 *The Manchester Guardian*, 12 October 1956.
10 *The Manchester Guardian*, *The Times*, *The Financial Times*.
11 *The Manchester Guardian*, 8 November 1956, p. 8.
12 *Ibid.*
13 *The Times*, *The Manchester Guardian*, 21 November 1956.
14 *The Times*, 8 December 1956, p. 11.
15 *The Manchester Guardian*, 14 December 1956.
16 *Ibid.*, 14 December 1956, p. 10.
17 *The Times*, 14 December 1956; *The Manchester Guardian*, 21 December 1956.
18 *The Times*, 23 January 1957, p. 9.
19 *The Manchester Guardian*, 6 January 1957, p. 6.
20 *The Daily Express*, 20 February 1957.
21 *The Times*, 20 February 1957, p. 9.
22 *The Daily Herald*, 20 February 1957.
23 *The News Chronicle*, 15 February 1957; *The Times*, 16 February 1957.
24 *The News Chronicle*, 11 February 1957.
25 *The Sunday Pictorial*, 8 January 1957.
26 *The Observer*, 3 February 1957.
27 *The Daily Telegraph*, 29 March 1957.
28 *The Daily Mirror*, 8 November 1956, p. 12.
29 *Ibid.*, 17 November 1956, p. 6.
30 Comment of Professor D. V. Donnison.
31 *The Kentish Mercury*, 9 January 1957; *The East Anglian Daily Times* (Ipswich), 26 January 1957.
32 *The Times*, 20 February 1957.
33 *The Listener*, 9 May 1957, pp. 754–5.
34 RICS. MSS.
35 *The Economist*, vol. 176, pp. 840–1, 1010–11.
36 *Ibid.*, vol. 172, p. 721.
37 *Ibid.*, vol. 181, p. 767.
38 *Ibid.*, vol. 181, p. 117.
39 *Ibid.*, vol. 181, p. 226.

40 *Ibid.*, vol. 181, p. 488.
41 *Ibid.*, vol. 181, p. 117.
42 *Ibid.*, vol. 182, pp. 624–5.
43 R. Rose, *Influencing Voters*, Faber, London, 1967, p. 155.
44 D. E. Butler and R. Rose, *The British General Election of 1959*, Macmillan, London, 1960, p. 71.
45 BIPO, poll number 470.
46 *Ibid.*, poll number 1643, question 10.
47 *Ibid.*, poll number CS 1705.
48 *Ibid.*, poll number CQ 67B.
49 *Ibid.*, poll number CQ 41.

# 8
# Pressure Groups

## Legitimate Pressures

One of the democratic assumptions has been that citizens influence government to act in their interest. The problem in the modern complex state was how the government, however democratic its form, could best be made to serve the people. Who were the people? They were divided into a variety of groups – economic, social, political – with varied capacities for affecting action in their own interests. Within each there were stratifications both as to needs and power potential. The individual with the greatest need of assistance might be least effective in making his wishes or needs known or understood. He knew so little of power strategy that he often continued as a member of the party in power even though his needs were ignored. Since most recipients cannot identify or define what they want of the government, the responsibility for policy formulation must rest elsewhere.

The dilemma for modern government was how to determine what needs to be done for individuals in the public interest with or without pressure from citizen groups. The competition among the groups for government action evoked what we have come to call 'pressures', a pejorative word. Members of interest groups changed as the issue changed. The effectiveness of groups in making their point and winning acceptance for it (these are not necessarily the same) might vary even though the members remained the same and the issue unchanged.

In this chapter the activities of the interested pressure groups in connection with the 1957 Rent Act are outlined. Pressure group literature has provided convenient categories with which to view the various groups in perspective. In addition, the activities of the various groups are delineated.

Pressure groups obtained 'authority' from any of three principal sources: material – total or partial control of the resources to be regulated; informational – a supply of information or propaganda; and public support. Certain of the pressure groups involved with the

Rent Act possessed elements of both material and informational support. The two landlords' pressure groups, the Association of Land and Property Owners, and the National Federation of Property Owners (A L P O and N F P O), had considerable if not total support from landlords who controlled the materials about which legislation was being undertaken.

They had in addition, along with the two principal administrators of land, the Royal Institution of Chartered Surveyors and the Chartered Auctioneers and Estate Agents Institute (R I C S and C A E A I), a virtual monopoly of the supply of information – given the failure of the government to obtain much of its own. Indeed, it was the information they could supply, not their membership (however large the total they represented), that gave the professional associations so potentially influential a place in the legislative process. This was true to a lesser extent of the Association of Municipal Corporations. The tenants' associations and trade unions were dependent for their authority upon public support. On the one hand the tenants' bodies could never show the membership necessary to acquire authority; on the other, the unions did not choose to expend their stock of authority on this particular issue. All these sources gave the pressure groups some right to speak 'in the public interest' but in reality for the special interest of their respective constituents.

The moral issue as to whether pressure is legitimate or illegitimate was virtually irrelevant. Only the direct payment of money to a member of the government or to a civil servant could constitute an illegitimate pressure, and that was not involved in this instance. But at what point might undue influence, a command of propaganda funds, or intimacy with the power structure, pass the bounds of decency and become undesirable? The extent of influence thus achieved could be ascertained by studying the operation of the pressure organisation itself, the techniques used, and their effectiveness. But the ultimate test was the degree of success. That which is bad always seems less evil if it fails. That which is good, is good at least in part because it helped achieve the ends intended.

None of the organisations concerned with the 1957 Rent Act had had the power to compel negotiation which Eckstein has ascribed to the B M A.[1] But some, the professional associations and Association of Municipal Corporations, did have the capacity to command attention for their views, by the government and parliamentarians. Others, the landlords' pressure groups, had information available which they presented to the government. But for the most part this seems to have been ignored, as was the slighter evidence of the tenants' associations. It was thus mainly those groups who could claim the privilege of consultation that contributed helpful data to the Ministry and the decision-making process.

But more significant, on this occasion, than the right of consultation was the capacity to influence. Again the professional associations had a dominant place. They possessed officials corresponding to those of the Ministry and in day to day relations with the Ministry. This gave them, in some sense, a privileged position. But seemingly the greatest influence on the government could be exerted by a pressure group, the ALPO. Their capacity came from the intimate connection of Mr Harold Symon, formerly a civil servant in charge of rent control matters and latterly secretary of ALPO, to his former colleagues. For it was the capacity to influence decisions before they were taken that in this as in most legislation constituted a significant advantage. Though NFPO could attempt to influence decisions, often through very powerful spokesmen, their influence was exerted after the fact. How significant the influence of any of the groups was will be shown in subsequent discussion.

The main force of the landlord, and the only force of the tenant groups, was their capacity to arouse public support for their cause. In this they were only occasionally successful. The landlord groups may have had some success in the middle 1950s but by 1956–7 their propaganda seemed to have ceased to be effective. Tenants' associations never had the impact which a mass-based organisation required to be successful. The consequence of these failures was to further limit the effectiveness of the organisations as pressure groups.

The various groups operating under a variety of conditions used all the techniques available to them; though of course, given the differing circumstances these techniques were differentially effective. The vast proportion of the data in this chapter deals with written efforts – either informal or formal. The memoranda and letters to the Ministry or to politicians were of the greatest importance. The printed material for distribution to the press was intended to have impact. The care taken in the preparation of these was considerable. Yet this touched only at the tip of the pressures. Far more extensive were the unreported conversations and meetings, both public and private. It would be premature to draw conclusions as to effectiveness – before the evidence has been examined.

The pressure groups and the techniques they used, as presented in this chapter, hardly cover the full range indicated by the literature on pressure groups. Indeed, it will be seen, there are only the gentlest hints of any extreme procedures, such as those denounced by H. H. Wilson.[2] The very 'normal' fashion in which the pressure groups were seen to operate provides the principal surprise.

But the activity, and application of techniques, can be understood only by a survey of the pressure groups and their role in the legislative process. In the following pages the role of the tenants' associations, the trade unions, the professional associations (RICS and CAEAI), and the Association of Municipal Corporations, and the pressure groups with landlords' interests (ALPO and NFPO) are delineated and explained.

## Tenants' Associations

By comparison with the landlords, tenants found it harder to develop effective organisations, a characteristic they shared with other consumer groups. The lessons of Captain Boycott had to be learned anew.

Part of the difficulty in organising the mass public was that tenants were not all affected in the same way by the Rent Bill. The owner-occupier and the council tenant were largely unaffected. This accounted for about 59 per cent of the total. The variety of landlords, both in the nature of their property and their relations to tenants, posed a further obstacle to general tenant organisation. For even where tenants lived in a single row of houses the interests of the inhabitants varied quite widely, depending upon the landlord of the particular dwellings, and outside London landlords might be as numerous as houses. Finally, the significance of the new Act became evident to most tenants only when a notice of eviction or increase in rent was served. It was difficult to explain to tenants what would happen. It was harder for them to see the need for action.

Only one 'national' organisation of tenants existed in 1956–7: the National Association of Tenants and Residents. The secretary at that time was Mr T. W. Vernon. Operating through a variety of local associations, it was difficult to organise effective public demonstrations. A mess petition rally in Trafalgar Square on 17 March failed because only about two thousand turned up. Representation from outside London was very sparse indeed.[3] Because the organisation was connected through some of its members with 'far left', including Communist, causes, the local trade union councils and Labour parties refused the organisation assistance and support. Indeed, they went out of their way to quarantine local tenants' associations to prevent them from becoming fronts for Communist political activities, as in the case of the Holborn and St Pancras Workers and Tenants' Defence Committee.[4] An efficient central organisation was, of itself, insufficient to generate effective pressure.

The Haldane Society played a minor role. A meeting, which included representatives of the Plasterers, Tobacco Workers and Furniture Trade Operatives, thirty Labour Party organisations, seventeen Co-ops, twenty-two trades councils, twelve plant councils, one hundred and eleven individual trade union bodies and nineteen tenants' associations, may have passed a resolution, but it was otherwise ineffectual. *The Daily Worker*'s story indicated that it had Communist backing.[5]

Any distinction between long-standing tenants' associations and *ad hoc* protest groups was largely irrelevant. Quite often groups in either guise formed and dissolved and re-emerged. An examination of the available data fails to reveal meaningful patterns for differentiation. The principal organisation which existed prior to the debate and took an active part in the debate was the Key Flats Association, composed of the tenants of London County Freehold and Leasehold Properties (known as Key Flats). Other large size organisations were the Greater London Tenants' Association, the Hampstead Anti-Rent Bill Association, Battersea and Chelsea Tenants Security Association, Hornsey Tenants Anti-Rent Bill Association, and the North Paddington Security of Tenure Association of Conservatives, all *ad hoc* bodies, some with Communist sponsorship.[6] Of particular interest was the Communist-dominated West London Rent Bill Committee which was violently attacked by the Labour front bench.[7] Many small tenants' associations were meeting during the debate but took no public part in it, like the Clare Court Tenants' Association. They may have found the impact of the Rent Bill unclear or felt inadequate in an essentially 'political' debate.[8] But many did become involved, such as the Gillingham Council Tenants' Association,[9] the West Kensington Tenants' Association,[10] and the Kew Bridge Court Tenants' Association.[11] Generally, though some exceptions have been cited, the protest was distinctly London-and-middle-class oriented. This limited the impact, which 'mass-based' efforts might have had.

Not even the Communists could escape this problem. The special role of the convinced Marxists, including party members, fellow travellers and Trotskyites, in tenant associations organised at local levels explained their failure to exert effective political pressure. Certainly *The Daily Worker* provided one of the largest sources of coverage for tenants' associations, and an excellent clue as to the left wing or Communist sympathies of one or more of the leadership. The West London Rent Bill Committee, the Greater London Tenants Security Association, and NATR attempted to coordinate national or regional activities, but they were doomed to fail in a climate where diverse political opinions were more important than common causes.[12]

But the local associations did their best to arouse the public. Among these were Wandsworth Tenants' Defence League,[13] Croydon Housing Campaign Committee,[14] Battersea Tenants' Association,[15] Birmingham Tenants' Association,[16] Islington Tenants' Defence League.[17]

The principal activity of all tenants' associations, large or small, Communist or otherwise, was making the public aware of and activated with respect to the Rent Bill through meetings, pamphlets, telegrams, canvassing. Parliamentary protests by telegram took a variety of forms. Those of the Hampstead and Hornsey bodies were typical. Hampstead's telegram was short and dogmatic: 'Why not twice gross value as ceiling for three year agreement? Only way to avoid hidden premium. What reasonable landlord could object? You know we speak for thousands.'[18] The Hornsey Tenants Anti-Rent Bill Association was more general. It followed the Labour party line all the way. Recognising the need for action, it asked for security of tenure, limits to increases on decontrol, stricter disrepair procedure and retention of rent tribunals, and was accompanied by a petition of three thousand signatures.[19] Others lobbied directly.[20] All of this received little or no attention in the national press and not much more in the local press. It certainly had no political impact, nor any effect on government decision-making.

The only protest to attract any significant attention was the rally in Trafalgar Square and the delivery of a protest to the prime minister. It evoked some rioting but no change in government policy. Even the Communists could gather only slight support on this occasion. *The Daily Worker* listed only four 'respectable' non-Communist groups which participated: the London District AEU, Deptford TC,

Briggs Bodies, and Holborn and St Pancras South Labour Party.[21]

Smaller meetings might have been equally valuable because they could attract local publicity and spread the gospel. Such meetings were held by West London Rent Bill Committee and St Marylebone Tenants' Association, among others.[22] But there was no indication that very many such meetings were held, nor of any significant local response.

The petitions, protests and lobbies of the tenants' associations all failed to achieve any political impact – on Parliament or the executive. The protests were not sufficiently representative of an affected interest to command attention. That all such protest, with the odd exception, may well be ineffectual is perhaps the best explanation for the failure to obtain recognition. But the principal problem was the large number of tenants, especially outside of London, who remained silent. For visible apathy was the major counter to such protest as occurred. And such apathy was inevitable given that the majority of working-class tenants would not be affected because they were council tenants or had rents close to the new limit. It was, perhaps, Labour Party ignorance of this change in patterns of occupancy that made their Opposition so militant. The working classes were not the private renters they were thought to be.

## Trade Unions

The trade unions were the largest organisations which represented people likely to be tenants affected by the Rent Bill. Yet virtually no protests were heard from the unions during the debate. The reasons for this are to be found in the decisions the unions had already taken about housing, and about their own role in essentially political questions.

Decisions on housing policy were taken, mainly in 1954, in response to two separate pressures: draft resolutions of the International Confederation of Free Trade Unions, and the Housing Repairs and Rents Act. In 1954 the T U C in conjunction with I C F T U, accepted the principle that housing ought to be a social service and that housing subsidies should be provided. But the T U C did not accept total municipalisation of housing. It insisted that any rent increases which repairs mandated be tied to wage increases.[23] The next year the T U C added the proviso that owner-occupation was an integral part of the housing scene, though it should not impinge on provision by the public sector of houses to let.[24] But this policy was adopted only after the Macmillan Act of 1954 had been enacted. The TUC's activities on the Macmillan Act were both precedent for and forerunners to its activities in 1957. In December 1953, the General Council of the TUC objected to the Housing Repairs and Rents Act, because it did not remove the anomalies of control, the repairs increase was insufficient, the machinery for disrepair was already condemned, and the Scots increase unjustified. At the same time, the council urged that the government and the local authorities be encouraged through low interest loans to take steps to promote new construction.[25] The member unions were unimpressed with the General Council's efforts. At conference, by a vote of 4·351 million to 3·269 million (majority 1·082 million) the Congress carried a resolution, against the advice of W. L. Heywood of the General Council, calling for a campaign to repeal the Housing Repairs and Rents Act. This was reiterated in 1955, though on this occasion emphasis moved towards the type of accommodation the Government provided.[26]

The debate in 1954 had focused on two aspects of the housing problem. The Foundry Workers opened the debate by arguing that 'rent is robbery' and that safeguards to tenants were more important than protection of token old ladies. The Tobacco Workers, pursuing the point, contended that the Act was nothing more than a giveaway. Both called for a campaign to *repeal*. To this motion the General Council took exception. The repeal of rent legislation was virtually impossible, though some amendment might be achieved. More important, some rent increases were viewed as necessary to make repairs possible and the present system of rent control was not 'fair'.[27]

By 1956 attention was redirected from the provision of housing to let to the size of houses and their financing through subsidies. The attrition policy in cutting standard size and ending general subsidies of the government led to a TUC protest which received a negative letter from the minister.[28] The motion, carried by voice vote, was a composite of eight motions and an acceptable version of none. The Civil Service Clerical Association concentrated on the availability of adequate houses to further the mobility of labour.[29] The Building Trades Workers charged that the government was ignoring the social service element in housing and, consequently, increasing the hardship of those seeking to form families.[30] The resolutions of the

Woodworkers, Tobacco Workers, and Scottish Painters all complained about the high rate of interest and difficulty of access to the Public Works Loan Board by local authorities. Their concern was with the slowdown of construction and the consequent impact upon their own members, a sentiment echoed by the Post Office Engineering Union for other reasons.[31] The Building Technicians attacked the ending of building controls, the credit squeeze and other disorganising elements in the housing market.[32] And the Post Office Workers again demanded the repeal of rent and housing subsidies legislation.[33] The resolutions showed a strange combination of social concern and self-seeking.

In this setting the TUC General Council faced the publication of the 1957 Rent Act. In a sense the TUC was to see 1954 repeat itself. In a letter dated 12 December 1956 and circularised to the Trades Councils as circular 54, the General Council complained of the hardships and the threat of eviction that faced many tenants, and of the serious shortages of housing in London, Liverpool, Birmingham, Manchester, Sheffield, Leeds and Glasgow, clear evidence that the free market would not work. Mobility would be decreased through fear rather than spurred by the availability of accommodation. Finally, they contended that there was no positive assurance that repairs would be done. They called upon the government 'to suspend parliamentary action' on the Bill.[34] The support of the TUC for the Labour Party line was affirmed at the same time.

In March 1957 the General Council rejected an NUR resolution which proposed a one day work stoppage because they could not 'accept this suggestion to use industrial action to attain a political objective. In informing the union of this decision, the General Council recalled that they had explicitly rejected such a policy, even in connection with the government's military activities in the middle east, and drew attention to the Labour Party's campaign. . . .'[35]

The history of this decision was not without irony. The general secretary of the NUR, Mr J. Campbell, himself opposed the step his executive committee had instructed him to take in presenting the resolution calling for action. He contended that 'however much trade unionists disliked the provisions of the Rent Bill it had to be recognised that the government had an elected majority in Parliament which was prepared to support them'. This was one of those rare cases where a militant segment successfully stampeded the moderates. Many resolutions calling for industrial action were received at Unity

House (Headquarters of the N U R). The general secretary replied with the orthodox views that:

the union's national executive committee had already considered the recent measures taken by the government and had strongly condemned the proposed abolition of the Rent Restriction Acts . . . that the policy of the union was to oppose any amendment or repeal of the Rent Restriction Acts and to give full support to the policy of the Labour Party . . . and that a protest had been made through the Trades Union Congress, the Labour Party and the NUR Parliamentary Group with a view to arousing the electorate in a demand for a general election.

To those branches who called for industrial action the general secretary explained that the trade union movement was opposed to the use of industrial action to achieve a political object.[36] But one branch, Manchester, persisted.[37] Its resolution was placed before the executive committee:

That we call upon our N E C to request the T U C and the Labour Party to request the T U C and the Labour Party to organise the whole of the Labour movement in a stoppage of work for one day as a protest against the introduction of the new Rents Act.

An alternative resolution having been defeated by a vote of eleven to twelve an amendment was carried by vote of twelve to eleven stating:

That having considered the appeal of our branch, and having regard to the fact that the government is determined to rush this Bill through Parliament we endorse the views expressed by the branch and instruct the general secretary accordingly.

The unpleasant effect on public opinion due to the imposition of the parliamentary guillotine weighed heavily in the N E C decision. At conference this resolution was repudiated by a vote of forty-four to thirty-three.

On 4 April 1957 the T U C General Council finally acted. They sent a circular to all branches in which they reported the failure of the letter of protest and the advanced state of consideration by the Lords. They reported that:

The NEC of the Labour Party therefore have initiated a nation-wide campaign through their local and regional organisations to draw attention to the way in which the Bill will affect the local housing and rents position and as a consequence many local Labour parties are organising campaigns which are related to the specific circumstances in their own localities. Some trades councils are already participating in this local activity and the General Council's view is that trades councils can play a useful part in cooperating fully with the local Labour parties on this issue.[39]

But, throughout, the activities of trades councils were negligible. The annual report of the London Trades Council for 1956 noted a resolution 'Condemning the Tory Government for its callous proposals to remove the protection of the Rent Control Acts from millions of tenants'.[40] In 1957 the Council demanding 'that the Minister of Housing . . . drop this iniquitous Bill and declaring our whole-hearted support to the T U C in their protest to the Government',[41] called attention to participation in an October 1957 demonstration but was conspicuously silent on the N A T R demonstration earlier in the year.[42] As an organisation whose members were most widely and most obviously affected the non-action of L T C was particularly notable.

But the activities of most trades councils and union branches were not much more impressive. Possibly, many held unpublicised meetings. Many more did not begin to act until after the Bill was through Parliament. While the Bill was in Parliament little was done. The Electrical Trade Union and London North District of the Amalgamated Engineering Union, and London District of the Associated Society of Locomotive Engineers and Firemen,[43] Bermondsey Trades Council and Labour Party,[44] Gloucester Trades Council,[45] Hove and District Trades Council,[46] Sheffield and District A E U,[47] Aberdare Valley Trades Council, and Mountain Ash Trade and Labour Council.[48] The E T U in Hendon,[49] and the National Union of Agricultural Workers in Dorset,[50] all held meetings at which anti-Rent Bill resolutions were passed. They called for withdrawal or serious amendment to the Bill. Some, such as East Grinstead Trades Council, also sent letters to the government.[51] The only common characteristic among these organisations was their connection to large urban areas and/or their degree of militancy.

The attitudes of the trade unions were not inexplicable. Their members were affected primarily by the rent increases for controlled premises rather than by decontrol. Whatever their complaints, they were no doubt aware that the impact would not be as considerable as the government expected. Further, they did have some doubts about the justice of a non-increase doctrine. The T U C did not issue instructions until too late to have much impact. Many trades councils preferred to leave political activities to the Labour Party, in which they had a considerable voice at the constituency level.

The inactivity of the T U C and its constituent elements was explicable both on grounds of policy and the fear of a revival of 1926. For effective opposition depended, in part, on the presentation of a suitable alternative policy. The unions had become committed, through the Labour Party, to the municipalisation of rented accommodation. But the unions were not particularly satisfied with this possibility. Unable or unwilling to devise an alternate policy to that of the government and the Labour Party, the trade unions remained silent. But whatever the reason, the unions' inactivity prevented the emergence of an effective tenants' lobby.

## The Royal Institution of Chartered Surveyors

As the senior professional body dealing with land, the Royal Institution of Chartered Surveyors' (R I C S) primary function has been to train and examine chartered surveyors. The titles of F R I C S and A R I C S have been highly prized, whose holders, as professionals, have been in constant demand, without the restrictive practices characteristic of the legal profession. Its members have served as managers of property as well as experts on planning, valuation, construction and transfer.

The senior members of the Institution have been regarded as much members of the Establishment as the permanent secretaries of the Ministries, and indeed perhaps more so, as their claim to status has been *ex persona* not *ex officio*. This, and a large establishment which was equipped to staff committees of member-experts, gave the Institution a prime right to be consulted on all legislation relating to rents.

These consultations took several forms. When the Bill was published, the Institution's Parliamentary Committee prepared a report issued in the name of the Institution. This covered a wide variety of matters, both general and specific. In addition, specific proposals were made for changes, and comments were published from time to time. In the normal course of things, the civil service would consult with the assistant secretary of R I C S in charge of rents on technical points. The assistant secretary might or might not ask members of his committees for expert advice. In 1957 the assistant secretary, Mr Robert Steel, was a barrister and himself the author of several books on rent restriction. His participation in 1954 and earlier established a basis of informal contacts between the organisation and the Ministry. In addition there were informal contacts between senior members of the RICS and the minister. While at the time the president, Mr Bull, did not know Mr Sandys personally, others certainly did. Informal exchanges took place both before and after publication of the Bill. These were two-way. Mr Sandys consulted on key provisions. Professional friends called particular problems to his attention. This was all quite proper. Finally, members sent letters to newspapers to pursue their own positions on the Bill quite apart from the activities of the Institution as such. The institutional background to these consultations was of some interest; it helped explain the advice given.

The members of the RICS shared the prevailing sentiment that something had to be done about the anomalies of control. Although it was agreed that the increase in rent proposed in clause 1 was not sufficient to make repairs possible, the increases were accepted as the maximum that would be politically possible, at least so far as the government was concerned. In consequence there seemed no point in attempting to get these limits raised, once the Bill was published. If any individuals were consulted prior to the Bill's publication, it was in a very informal way. At the same time, there seemed to be a general understanding that the increases were merely transitional. The minister indicated that he intended to use his powers of decontrol or action to further increase controlled rents after a reasonable interval.

The emphasis in the RICS proceedings was on form. Though they presumably had foreknowledge, the minutes of the Parliamentary Committee of 6 November 1956 said only:

The assistant secretary reported that the Queen's Speech to Parliament early that day had foreshadowed a Bill to amend the Rent Restriction Acts and other legislation which might prove to be of interest to the profession. On a proposal by the chairman (44), the committee:

(a) agreed that the chairman should appoint a special subcommittee to examine the Bill to amend the Rent Restriction Act; and

(b) requested that every effort be made for the observations prepared by the subcommittee to be submitted through the Parliamentary Committee to the council before they were presented to the minister of Housing and Local Government.

One person appointed to this committee, an LCC official, withdrew, presumably to be disassociated from the committee report. The special concern that both the Parliamentary Committee and Council should have an opportunity to consider the memorandum before publication reflected the traditional concern of the organisation about participating in discussions with political ramifications. These, it was feared, might jeopardise the organisation's position as a source of neutral expertise. Indeed this was all the more necessary given the great interest many members had in the organisation's statements.

Prior to the meeting of the subcommittee a number of its members, and many who were not, submitted memoranda to the assistant secretary on various issues or non-issues which might be discussed. They were helpful in a variety of problems, including the errors in valuation[52] and the need for amendments to any number of clauses, including 5, 9, 16 and the 1st and 5th schedules.[53] When the committee met, it decided to make no observations on the formula for calculating rent limits. The reasons were explained. It asked that landlord's election on repairs be clarified, that local authorities be encouraged to make loans to landlords to do repairs, that clause 1 (7) (4) be clarified. It urged that houses not actually declared unfit, but in a clearance area, be allowed the increase, that clause 2 (2) (c) (i) be clarified, that the landlord should be subject to fines only for wilful mis-statement under clause 2 (3). There was no comment on clauses 3, 4, 5, 2nd schedules.[54] However, the committee concluded that the Scots clauses (6–8) were less satisfactory and accepted a strong statement from the Scots section. It insisted, however, that some parts of the Scots' presentation be modified. Typical of the organisation's concern were the assistant secretary's remarks:

> Whilst the subcommittee agreed that these statistics were valuable, they did not think it would be wise for the Institution to use them, since they originated with the National Federation of Property Owners and Factors of Scotland, or at any rate have been widely circulated by them. It seemed to the subcommittee that it would undermine the value of our comments if they could be linked in any way with the landlords' case.[55]

How did these decisions come to be taken? Without detailed minutes and with memories vague, one could only conjecture. This being the case, any comment now must be mere speculation. Attendance lists were not notably revealing, except that members who might be expected (or were known to be) the more liberal were, quite accidentally, all absent when the crucial discussions on de-control limits occurred. This probably affected the delay before the Institution proposed an extension of the transition period. At least one 'conservative' member suggested in a memo that most of the proposed suggestions were pointless, that drafting errors were largely in the minds of the reader, etc.[56]

The Scots section of RICS was consulted as to the drafting of Scottish clauses. At a special meeting, the Scottish section opined that 'there are some provisions which do not seem to go far enough in helping prevent the deterioration of many dwelling houses. . . .' They insisted that clause 6 (1–2) did not provide enough to make repairs possible. The anomaly in the situation, they complained, was that landlords in England and Wales had been able to get rent increases that were not granted to the Scots.[57] It can be seen that this had strong impact on the relevant sections of the memorandum, as finally published.

The memorandum of the RICS to the minister, which was published and circulated, announced the consensus position of the Institution. It deplored that, 'for too long, rent control in its present form has resulted in disrepair, prevention of necessary improvements and premature obsolescence'.[58] If the necessary repairs were to be made, local authority assistance must provide the necessary capital.[59] Clause 2 (2) (c) (i), which provided for a limit on rent increases for houses in clearance areas, ought to be narrowed to encompass only those houses actually unfit.[60] Provisions for specifying landlord and tenants' division of responsibility should be clarified.[61] In addition to several suggestions on points of detail and drafting, the memorandum urged that:

> Six months is too short a time for this number of tenants to arrange their affairs. In very many of these cases, the tenants will be able to reach agreement for a new lease of the premises; in others they will prefer to seek other accommodation. But in either event, a longer period will be necessary to allow a smooth transition.[62]

The RICS recommended either no increase in rents, or at least no loss of control for eighteen months. Alternatively, incentives ought to be given to those landlords and tenants who agreed on three year leases.[63]

The memorandum was sent to the minister, signed by the secretary, with the expression: 'My council hope that you will be able to accept the proposals which they make'. Copies were also sent to Dame Evelyn and the principal in charge of the Bill, and to the senior parliamentary officials concerned. To Mr John Hay, who asked what comments RICS would make on the Bill before the memo was ready, the assistant secretary indicated that many landlords would need capital to make repairs. The minister should be persuaded to write a loan assistance programme into the Bill.

The only issue raised by the Institution which received widespread public attention was the suggestion for a longer transition period. This proposal was publicised by the president of R I C S, Mr W. P. A. Bull, in a letter to *The Times* in terms similar to those of the memorandum. This proposal was subsequently adopted by the Ministry.[64]

One problem raised during the committee stage gave rise to an additional memorandum. Sir Ian Horobin had proposed to prevent profit taking by landlords who acquired their property after the Bill was published and could then more easily obtain the advantages of vacant possession, R I C S strongly criticised this amendment in a public memorandum on the grounds that it would not have the effect intended. Because there were emotional objections to allowing 'profit making', R I C S proposed, as an alternative to the Horobin amendment but maintaining its spirit, that the government delay the operation of the Act for two years in respect of properties acquired between publication of the Bill and mid-March. This was rejected by the government.[65]

A problem not discussed by the R I C S, security of tenure, was raised by Mr G. R. Judd and Mr C. D. Pilcher, two of R I C S's most senior members, in a letter to *The Manchester Guardian*. Their efforts to focus attention on what proved to be the real difficulty in decontrol were futile. But their ideas were accepted by the Labour government when amending the 1957 Act. How accurately they caught the essence of the problem:

> The Rent Bill contains provisions which are inconsistent with the recent trend of legislation. One of the objects of the Bill is to deprive tenants of dwelling-houses of their *prima facie* right to retain possession, whereas tenants of all kinds of premises within the very wide definition of part II of the Landlord and Tenant Act, 1954, and all agricultural tenants, have such a *prima facie* right. We are not expressing an opinion on the principle of security of tenure, for it is not the point we raise; but we are surprised that the aspect of the present Bill referred to above has received scant, if any, attention. We suggest that it merits serious discussion before the Bill becomes an Act.[66]

A very cautious professional organisation thus confined itself to issuing a series of memoranda which evaded main issues, however vital to the success of the Bill. Though the memoranda made valuable contributions, their political sensitivities prevented comment on key clauses. Of course, they also recognised that any comment on key clauses after publication was futile. But they were, by an excuse, able to avoid consideration of the real problems raised by rent increases, decontrol, repairs. It was their prescient members who were afterwards to be powerful in the Ministry's councils.

## The Chartered Auctioneers' and Estate Agents' Institute

The Chartered Auctioneers' and Estate Agents' Institute (CAEAI) was thought much the junior professional association concerned with land. The prestige of its members, the quantity of staff, the skills which it taught, all were seen to place it below the RICS in stature (though in fact it was often chance whether men joined RICS or CAEAI, and most large firms had partners in both who specialised in 'General Practice'.) Yet its contacts with the Ministry were reasonably intimate. If, unlike the RICS, the CAEAI could not claim the right to be consulted, its advice could hardly be ignored.

The responsibility for parliamentary activity lay with the Parliamentary, Rating and Legal Committee, advised by the deputy secretary, Mr Watt. After publication of the Bill action was taken.

The committee considered what arrangements should be made in due course for a memorandum or an article on the Rent Act:
Resolved to Recommend:
that Mr L. A. Blundell and Mr V. G. Wellings should be invited to write a suitable article for the Journal, to be published as soon as possible after the Act is passed. . . .

And they proposed to make representations about agricultural cottages (clause 1); existing contracts (2–1); clause 2 (2) (c) (i), on landlord's election for repairs; proof of fraud in notices (2–3); landlord's right to make improvements; the transition to decontrol; and an increase in length of notice to quit.[67] It can be seen that these concerns were those of men relatively more involved with landlord's problems than the surveyors, and also in need of more assistance from their professional organisation.

Indeed, the CAEAI had already been consulted by two Conservative politicians. Mr John Hay had written on 13 November 1956 to say:

I am chairman of the Conservative Members' Housing Committee which will be considering the Bill in detail shortly, and I should therefore be glad to know of any views or amendments which you would like to put forward. We would be in a position to discuss these with the minister and if necessary raise them in debate.[68]

Sir Ian Horobin had mentioned to Mr Watt that he was thinking about an amendment to prevent certificates of repair where landlords were actually trying to clear up the repairs. He had evidently asked for an opinion.[69]

By 4 December 1956 the CAEAI was ready to publish its memorandum, though it first circulated the memo to interested figures, including those politicians such as Sir Ian who had requested assistance.[70]

The memorandum was very similar to RICS's, though there had been no consultation. The Institute welcomed the main objectives of the Bill and noted that 'its' suggestion on new valuation techniques (using GRV) had been adopted.[71] This was in line with previous Institute policy stated in a letter by its president, Mr O. D. Blake, to *The Estates Gazette* in July 1956.[72] The Institute pointed out, in the memorandum, that for agricultural cottages with low gross values, the increase would not be sufficient. They proposed that the transition to decontrol should be at least twelve months.[73] The memorandum also dealt with a variety of minor points. On the whole, it was only in details, such as length of transition to decontrol, that the RICS and the CAEAI were in discord.

But the members of the CAEAI were not in complete agreement with Institute policy. The chairman of the Liverpool-North Wales Branch had a wholly different set of proposals.[74] And Mr C. D. Pilcher, who had also played an important part in the RICS negotiations, sent a series of comments in disagreement.[75] Indeed, Mr Pilcher was a member of the Parliamentary and Rating and Legal Committee which had charge of the CAEAI's representations. It should be noted that not until years later were the two bodies, the RICS and the CAEAI to achieve joint policies on common concerns.

Later on the Parliamentary and Rating Committee again dealt with the problems of clause 2 (2) (c) (i) about the payment of rent for houses in a clearance area, but not themselves unfit. The CAEAI issued a further statement on this topic.[76]

During the debate the organisation was consulted by both Ministry and politicians. In January, the Ministry consulted, very informally, about the availability of statistics on new rents after decontrol.

A Mr Hickenbotham of the Ministry of Housing [the assistant secretary on the Bill] spoke to me by telephone this morning to enquire whether the Institute had any information about the sort of figures at which landlords were thinking of fixing the rents of properties decontrolled under the new Bill. I gathered from Mr Hickenbotham that he would have spoken to the secretary had the latter been available. . . .

Mr Hickenbotham wished to make it quite clear that he was not asking the Institute to take any steps in the matter on behalf of his Ministry but that, if information should happen to come our way, it would help him if we could pass it on to him.[77]

Even earlier, the chief officials of the CAEAI had met at Westminster with Sir Eric Errington.[78] The officials were also in contact with the property owners' associations through Sir Ian MacTaggart.[79]

But the main purpose of the CAEAI was to assist its members in coping with the new problems the 1957 Rent Act would pose. To do so it had commissioned a journal article by experts. It had the professional assistance of Mr R. E. Megarry, Q C, the leading authority on rent control. Its president was busy addressing branch meetings. At several of these he urged members to persuade their 'clients to be reasonable in imposing rent increases'. He was considering whether when the Bill has become an Act these remarks should be published in the Journal with the blessing of the council.[80] Mr Megarry, too, had addressed the CAEAI meetings at which he said 'This is indeed a pretty awful Bill, there are no two ways about it'.[81] Thus, meetings were not merely to inform members, but also to encourage activities which, as officials must have known, would make further Ministry action on rent control possible.

The activities of the CAEAI were nothing like as important as those of the RICS. The lesser role reflected suspicion by those concerned of the relatively intimate tie thought to exist between the organisation's members and rental problems, and the organisation's lack of concern about the details of a Bill which was, in principle, satisfactory. Indeed, the most important part of the group's activities were, no doubt, those designed to make landlords more aware of the problem, and make their members better able (by pushing amendments) and better prepared (by publicity) to deal with the new problems that would arise.

## The Association of Municipal Corporations

Local governments by themselves could do little to influence national policy, however intimately they were concerned. Like Members of Parliament, each local authority had only a limited store of credit with the Ministry of Housing and Local Government. Most local authorities prudently refused to waste this on lost causes or causes not of immediate concern.[82]

But the Association of Municipal Corporations was virtually obliged, by its constituency (the various municipal corporations other than London), to take some action. Certainly no other organisation could offer comparable evidence on the administration of housing policy and rents. But even this association entered the fray only with the greatest caution. For, like the other professional associations, circumspection on any matter with 'political' ramifications was the rule. Its membership, both Tory and Labour, made this all the more necessary.[83]

Despite the need for caution, the Housing Committee of the A M C issued a strong Report. They insisted that 'the local authority would be faced with an impossible task if they were called upon to rehouse the evicted tenants. . . .'[84] In their opinion, long waiting lists for local authority housing should give the government pause.[85] The only group to raise the issue of decontrol on vacant possession, they remained sceptical of Ministry assurances that there would be no problem.[86] On the question of the amount of increase that ought to be allowed to landlords who received local authority grants, the Ministry sanguinely argued that these grants were no longer necessary. The committee vowed, apparently unconvinced, to raise the question yet again, should the Ministry be proved wrong.[87] The association objected that local authorities had already paid a 'sweetener' (in the form of a cash subsidy) to continue possession and maintain rent levels in requisitioned houses. The Ministry argued that this merely preserved the right of possession, and that the Ministry could not discriminate against the landlord of requisitioned property.[88]

The most serious complaint of the A M C was the proposed disrepair procedure, which was to be administered by local authorities. Following the advice of a Public Health Inspectors' Report,[89] the Housing Committee concluded that the procedure would not work. The tenant, they contended, 'would have little experience with the types of proceedings required'. The delays provided were pointless.

The 1954 procedure, they claimed, made more sense. If this could not be applied, they urged that the public health inspectors be given the right to amend the tenants' complaints to include whatever additions the PHI might see warranted.[90] The Ministry responded to this question as one of 'details'. At the association's conference with the minister he recommended that it be taken up with the officials of the Ministry.[91]

The final report of the association reflected the consultations that took place on these and other issues. Only on the transition to decontrol did they continue to protest. For the rest, they concluded that they had done the best they could and concentrated on drafting errors.[92]

The membership of the Housing Committee, primarily responsible for A M C memoranda on rent control, was rather large. The political (i.e. councillor) membership came from Birmingham, Deptford, Finchley, Manchester, Plymouth, Gosport, Hornsey, Lincoln and Chesterfield. They were joined by the town clerks of Darlington, Stafford, Manchester, Newcastle-upon-Tyne and Swindon, and the city treasurers of Hull and Peterborough. In this group the pressure to act did emerge. The Metropolitan Boroughs Standing Joint Committee themselves decided to send a delegation to the minister. Shoreditch M B C invited the Housing Committee to send a representation at the same time. Though the Housing Committee disapproved, the council of A M C decided to accept. Only for this reason was a delegation present at the meeting, on 18 February 1957, with Mr Brooke. Not unexpectedly, the dominant voice was not the Housing Committee but the M B C's who, both politically and from self-interest, had more to say and more reason to say it.

Though, unlike the records of any other group, the A M C's showed not merely their own reasoning but also the replies given by the Ministry, there was no indication that the Ministry made concessions to the views of this professional group. Indeed, they seemed to be outside the normal channels of consultation, as the Ministry contented itself merely to answer queries put to it, rather than consult the A M C in advance in areas where A M C members had special competence. This was rather different from the role of the professional groups with acknowledged interests on the one hand, and the landlord groups with vested interests on the other.

# The National Federation of Property Owners

The oldest of the landlord 'pressure groups' was the National Federation of Property Owners (N F P O). From its inception as an organisation in Newcastle in 1888, its focus on problems in the north remained predominant. Only in 1927 did the organisation finally become London based. History had an impact on this organisation. Even in 1956 the bulk of its members (either direct or through one of the regional associations) had been small property owners who were dominant in the north rather than the larger landlords of the south.[93] In recent years the N F P O gained fame through its association with Cmdr Marten of Critchel Down. But most crucial to its history were its secretaries. In 1942 Mr Reginald Sizen left *The Evening News* to take over the job. His experience as a journalist naturally led him to favour those techniques which would 'make news'. Thus in the early 1950s he succeeded in 'placing' a variety of stories which demonstrated the poverty of the landlord and the need for the reform of the Rent Acts. The combination of press releases, fed articles and speeches to be delivered by M Ps was intended for subsequent publication and publicity.[94] These articles did not appear in *The Times* or *The Manchester Guardian*. At the same time, he strengthened the organisation's house journal to provide a vehicle for publishing the activities of the organisation.[95]

As events leading to the Rent Act began to unfold, several coincidences conspired to give the N F P O a particularly strategic position. Its president after January 1956 was Sir Eric Errington, who was, at the same time, president of the Executive Committee of the General Purposes Committee of the National Union of Conservative and Unionist Associations. The N F P O's legal assistant was Mr John Hay, who was at the time chairman of the Conservative backbenchers' Housing Committee and secretary of the London Municipal Society (the central organisation of London Conservatives). This should not be viewed as a conspiracy. Sir Eric's connection to the property world was of long standing. Mr Hay's position was, according to Mr Sizen's recollection, an accident. Indeed, strictly speaking, Mr Hay's firm, not he, were the legal consultants to N F P O. In 1957 few lawyers combined the need to make extra money with the particular expertise which rent restriction work required. Mr Hay was in that position. This was only a part of the N F P O's parliamentary resources.

F

The NFPO's parliamentary representation was considerable. Mr Richard Hornby was MP for Mr Sizen's own constituency. On the whole, Mr Hornby tended to be cooperative in parliamentary affairs. He did not approve of clause 9, decontrol, but Mr Sizen hoped to convert him.

We think that any watering down of clause 9 would be most detrimental to the provision of new homes from existing accommodation. Sir Eric Errington had a letter in *The Times* of 25 January. I wonder whether you would care to follow it up.

It may save you a certain amount of trouble if I enclose a draft of the type of letter I have in mind though no doubt you will wish to write it in your own way if the subject appeals to you.

It is being suggested that I should speak on the Rent Bill to branches of the Tonbridge constituency. If I can spare the time I would be pleased to do so but I should not like to feel that you and I had different views about the Bill in general and clause 9 in particular.[96]

But Mr Hornby was by no means in Mr Sizen's pocket.[97] Among the MPs who were representatives, or potential representatives for NFPO were Mr Biggs-Davison,[98] Sir H. Butcher,[99] Mr R. F. Crouch,[100] Mr Finlay, Sir C. F. Grey,[101] Sir I. Horobin, Sir H. Legge-Bourke, Sir G. Lloyd, Mr G. Page and Sir W. Wakefield.[102] The peers included Lords Meston (chairman of POPO, the London branch of NFPO), Conesford, Broughshane and Ridley (the last three being the so-called independent unionist peers). The forms of contact were varied. To some MPs Mr Sizen wrote reminding them that they had agreed to 'help this federation in its parliamentary troubles on appropriate occasions'.[103] To others he pleaded for support of a more general character.

The position vis-à-vis the Lords was more intimate. There, the pressure group official took responsibility for organising the debate. Once a group of Lords were agreed on a position, the pressure group wrote the amendments and the speeches, and all but arranged the order of amendments.[104]

The first stage in the battle over rent control organised by NFPO was a press campaign in 1951. This was based upon the need for an increase in rents to pay for repairs. Owners could not meet repairs costs at current prices out of prewar rents.[105] In the statement a 25 per cent increase was suggested. There was no indication that NFPO was aware of the significance of the RICS proposals to alter the very bases of control and so obtain extra funds for the landlord.[106]

While the 1954 Housing Repairs and Rents Act was in Parliament the president of NFPO, in a letter to the minister, complained that it would be impossible to do repairs under the 'onerous' conditions established in the Act to qualify for the repairs increase.[107] The proposals of the NFPO proved considerably more moderate in the important respect of security of tenure than those finally adopted by the minister. In 1955 the NFPO proposed to decontrol rents, but not possession. If new negotiation on rents proved futile, either landlord or tenant could appeal to the courts for adjudication. The proposal was signed by the then President and the chairman of the Rents Committee.[108] The 1955 NFPO Conference was equally conservative. Representatives from the north tended to be more conservative than those from the south and west, who favoured rapid decontrol.[109] It was in this setting that policy on the Rent Act was to be shaped.

During the critical summer months of 1956 Sir Eric Errington apparently kept his own counsel. His party position would indicate that he was informed as to the basic contents of the upcoming Bill. But he did not inform Mr Sizen as to its contents, and even after Mr Sandys' Llandudno speech (where the outlines were revealed to party conference) he wrote to an associate saying that 'one does not know how the matter will eventually pan out. . . .' But the details he thought were still very much open.[110] Consequently, the NFPO was caught unprepared. Without the machinery for rapid decision-making, it was unprepared to offer a set of amendments or proposals for change before the opening of the committee stage.

Far more important was the clash within the organisation as to tactics and objectives. The conflict of interest between party and pressure group rose somewhat above the surface. Sir Eric urged the organisation to keep quiet, answer as few challenges from tenants as possible, and await the inevitable Tory largesse.

Basically I feel that the less publicity we have the better. The purpose of publicity is to get what you want: when you have got it then the best thing is to keep quiet. However, various people have written to the newspapers already and made the Bill a matter of public comment and it has consequently been necessary to refute their arguments and to put our own point of view. I am convinced, however, that we should confine our publicity efforts to destroying our opponents' case on such important matters as clause 9.

It follows that, if we distribute leaflets in any quantity, the Labour

Party will circulate counter-leaflets, then we shall have to reply and so on, ad lib. I am sure we should be doing a disservice to ourselves if we helped to fan the Socialist agitation into flames.

... To sum up, I think we have now reached the stage of in-fighting in which we must do our best in both Houses and that to enter into a slanging match with the Socialists would be inadvisable.[111]

Mr Sizen shared this view. He discouraged attempts to follow up scaremonger stories in the popular press on the ground that they often had more the appearance of anti-landlord stories than substance. In at least one case the conclusions of such an article proved quite acceptable. And of course, if the subject of the article were a member of one of the local associations the result could be embarrassing.[112]

In January 1957 disagreement between Sir Eric and Mr Hay on the one hand, and Mr Sizen on the other emerged. Although a memorandum of suggested amendments had been prepared, both Mr Hand, chairman of the Subject Committee of N F P O, and Sir Eric refused to sign it: the latter because of his party position, the former because he was convinced that such suggestions could better be left to Mr Hay.[113]

There was evidence that this dispute did not start in 1957. When the Bill was published, Mr Sizen wrote 'In general we are pretty satisfied with the Rent Bill'.[114] But he preferred not to push the matter of repair grants to enable landlords to make repairs. Mr Sizen did, however, believe in 'red-baiting':

Speaking quite personally, I welcome this sign that auctioneers and estate agents are taking notice of the trend of legislation. I have no doubt that you have pointed out to them that, if the Socialist housing programme ... comes to pass, then there will be no sales, no auction, no valuations, no insurances—in fact, no nothing for professional people.[115]

He persisted with the usual channels of communication, memoranda both public and private, directed both to civil service and to the minister. Privately, he complained of efforts to muzzle him. He remarked: 'Certainly some people do seem afraid of their own shadows and certainly afraid to defend their own interests! However, I will try to find some other line of approach.'[116] Indeed, some of the left wing of his organisation wanted the N F P O to caution landlords on the bad economic consequences of taking advantage of their new position to raise rents exorbitantly.[117] Since this came from one of his senior members, he adopted it with certain reservations.[118] All this made the task of publicity quite difficult.

The process of 'public' pressure took three forms: informal communication to the Ministry, formal communication to the Ministry, and letters to the press. Some of this was pressure undisguised by a surfeit of information. In other instances a considerable body of data was collected *ad hoc*.

Informal communication was of two kinds. A number of comments on particular proposals were directed to Dame Evelyn. Typical was one on clause 9: 'I have had a point in connection with decontrol under clause 9 of the Bill brought to my attention by our affiliated association at Leeds. I enclose a memorandum which has been prepared by the solicitor to the Leeds Association and I should be glad if the point could be investigated.'[119] The principal memorandum submitted to the Ministry was published shortly thereafter in *Property*.[120] Some of the points were purely technical. But some were quite controversial, and a remarkable proportion of them were taken up by MPs or peers. Two amendments of a relatively controversial nature were accepted by the government on Report, and later in Lords,[121] those on premiums and construction. This was quite a reasonable proportion for a single organisation to achieve.[122] Another separate memorandum was sent on the subject of houses with a rateable value under £10. The cover note urged that, since concessions were to be made to the middle-class tenants affected by clause 9, some concessions might also be made to the 'poor' landlords who owned dwellings with value under £10.[123] Attached to this letter was a detailed analysis of the problem, including tables collected from a wide variety of towns. The Report concluded that a considerable number of such houses were part of the nation's stock and that landlords would be unable, even with the proposed increases, to get anything like the funds necessary to put them into tenantable condition. An increase in rent limits, low cost loans from local authorities, and early decontrol were recommended.[124] This recommendation had no impact and it was thought necessary to have Sir Eric Errington follow it with a letter to the minister on 10 March 1957. In the letter he referred to his own second reading speech and asked Mr Brooke to give answers to a variety of problems that affected the small landlord, repeating the proposals made in the memorandum.[125] These official communications did not have much impact. Mr Sizen commented to Mr Thornton-Kemsley, MP

(Conservative, Angus and Mearns) about one Ministry reply: 'It is a typical Ministerial reply, dodging the real issue and basing the reply on assumed and incorrect facts.'[126] But this seemed to be the most that NFPO could obtain.

This was true despite the representations made by both Sir Eric and Mr Hay to the Ministry. Indeed, Mr Hay even used information about the Ministry's own plans to advise the NFPO on its strategy in public presentations.[127] It did not seem to have much effect.

The public debate in *The Times*' letter columns could not be ignored. Only one or two letters sent in Sir Eric's name were accepted for publication. The one which was not accepted concerned the fears of middle-class families in Bebington, which were reported by a special correspondent. In the letter Sir Eric argued that the tenants did not need to fear higher rents because increased accommodation would become available and ultimately prices and rents would fall off. He conceded that those on fixed incomes (e.g. pensioners) would meet hardships but argued that 'intelligent cooperation between owners, the local authority and tenants should prevent or mitigate' this. He concluded that:

Inevitably difficulties will arise. Through its members, the National Federation of Property Owners will do its utmost to ensure that the transition period from tight control to a free market shall be made as smooth as possible in order to restore the happy relationship between owner and tenant which artificial restrictions have so much impaired.[128]

A much stronger letter, attacking the proposals of the RICS for an extension of the transition period was accepted. Dated 22 January 1957, Sir Eric argued that 'In my view . . . [the] pool [of accommodation] is large enough to prevent the transitional confusion which Mr Bull fears, and anything smaller would not produce the desired impact on the housing shortage'. He argued that the sooner the Bill was in operation, the sooner more and more accommodation would be provided to let. He contended that tenants who now occupied premises larger than they required would be glad of the chance to move into smaller, perhaps cheaper accommodation.[129] But this public confidence was not shared in private. In a letter of 25 January 1957, Sir Eric confessed: 'I think it may well be that decontrol down to £40 in London may be a bit precipitate but, generally speaking, I don't think that decontrol down to £30 in most parts of the provinces, and at any rate in Liverpool is too sudden.'[130]

Indeed the NFPO was unhappy at the decisions to modify the Bill taken by the government at the committee stage. A statement, written by Mr Sizen, was published and subsequently appeared in *Property*.[131] In it, the NFPO complained that the revisions made the Bill 'legislation for the sitting tenant, not for the homeless (and certainly not for the landlord)'. They argued that the clause would delay conversions and that the premiums clause would benefit the unscrupulous, since there would be no need for premiums when the free market operated. 'The federation's advice to property owners was not to treat their tenants harshly or unfairly, since the time was not distant when a reputation as a good landlord will be a valuable asset'. They concluded bitterly that 'Mr Brooke has given way, not so much to his political opponents as to the pressure organised by the sitting tenant'.[132] But this was still to be preferred to the Labour alternative of municipalisation.

Very little was said in the NFPO publications about Labour's 'Homes for the Future'. Mr Hay commented that even Labour Party supporters were not happy with a document that was 'both unrealistic and expensive'.[133]

All this campaign was carried out without the cooperation of the other pressure and professional groups of similar view. The professional bodies avoided giving any impression that they might be 'tainted' by their association with pressure groups. Often they pursued this to extremes. Thus, when cooperation was suggested, Sir Eric remarked that

I doubt myself if the estate agents as a body would help us to distribute the leaflets. You will remember what happened in the case of our Rent Petition when the professional bodies sent either instructions or advice to their members to have nothing to do with it.[134]

But during 1956-7 there was little contact even between the NFPO and the ALPO. This was not for lack of possible lines of communication. Mr Sizen and Mr Symon were personally friendly. Sir John MacTaggart, and subsequently, Sir Ian MacTaggart were distinguished landlords and members of both executive committees. Sir Ian certainly interested himself in the affairs of the NFPO and served as chairman of the propaganda committee. He succeeded Sir John as a member of council during 1957. But he made no effort to force the two groups into a single action policy, or to take joint lines on the issues raised by the Rent Act. Nor was there any exchange of information: hence the

NFPO's ignorance of the terms of the Bill prior to its publication. A divergence of interests and personalities between the two organisations seems to have been the central problem in effecting cooperative action. The ALPO was a splinter group of the large landlords principally in London and the south. They had broken away from the NFPO for three reasons. The large council of the NFPO was not conducive to the expeditious conduct of business. And, however dull, when a man came from the north to London he expected to be heard if only because of the trouble he had taken to come. Thus, whereas the ALPO councils did their business in relatively brief time, the NFPO meetings dragged. The division between small and large landlords was significant. For the small landlords, increases in rent and provision of capital funds were more important than tax credits. But, increasingly, following the abolition of Schedule A tax on owner-occupation, the large landlords could do well despite the Rent Restriction Acts. Their property was newer or at least converted. Repairs posed less of a problem. Finally, there was personal animosity between Mr Sizen and some of the ALPO landlords. This need not have had any impact, judging from the success of Sir Ian MacTaggart's efforts to reunite the two during the Rented Homes Campaign, a landlords' anti-rent control effort; but in 1957 he made no such effort and the result was disharmony and a disservice to the landlord interest.

The roles of Sir Eric Errington and Mr John Hay were ambiguous. Where did they stand? Did their role in both the NFPO and in Conservative Party counsels constitute a conflict of interest? A definite answer, in the absence of minutes and impressions by those with whom they associated, must remain in doubt. Political motivation undoubtedly helped support the Bill through. But this was born not of self-interest but of policy:

> There is bound to be upset to some extent whenever an effort is made to restore private enterprise and I think, when we are satisfied that we are doing the reasonable thing, it would be a mistake to postpone it any longer than we must, bearing in mind the next general election. Don't you agree that an awful lot of people shout for freedom and when they get it and it personally doesn't suit them, they are rather apt to turn round and criticise? I have every sympathy with the middle classes but they must take a long view in our present political difficulties.[135]

Though the NFPO concentrated on parliamentary activity and had considerable parliamentary assistance, it proved able to modify only slightly the proposed Rent Act. As a group attempting to exert pressure on the Ministry it was notably less successful than the A L P O, whose activities are considered in the next section.

## The Association of Land and Property Owners

The other big landlord pressure group was the Association of Land and Property Owners, together with the Associated Owners of City Properties, whose separate identity was only nominal.

In 1939 the Association of London Property Owners had separated from the National Federation of Property Owners because, according to their own historian, they found they could represent the interest of the large London landlord better as a separate organisation. The discovery that there was a difference in interests between the small and large property owners was to have a profound impact on the structure and nature of the lobby.[136] The Land League, a gentlemen's organisation composed of landlords all over Britain, merged with the London Property Owners in 1953 to form the A L P O as it then became.

The focus of the association was determined by its officials. Its secretary until 1956 was the former general manager of London County Freehold (Key Flats). Directors on its council were recruited from most of the principal landowning companies in the Greater London area. The companies represented were City Offices Co., Key Flats, Sun Insurance Office and Sun Life Assurance, Wates Ltd, Hillier, Parker, Hay and Rowden, Westminster and Kensington Freehold, Goddard and Smith, Western Heritable, Exchange and General Investments Ltd, London Investment and Mortgage, Town Investments, Bernard Thorpe, Kemp and Hawley and Regional Properties Ltd. Viscount Buckmaster, the president in 1956, was an A L P O man, but most of the 'distinguished element' came from the old Land Union list; Lord Brocket, Major Sir Albert N. Braithwaite, Lord Dynevor.[137]

The organisation divided its functions into three parts: research, public lobbying and private lobbying. The publication of the *Real Estate Journal*, a more focused and less authoritative version of the *Estates Gazette*, represented the research effort. The A L P O also provided an advisory service and held periodic meetings on topics of current interest. As a public lobby it attempted to maintain 'an organised body of opinion recognised as the qualified mouthpiece of

F*

large-scale property owners to which Parliament, press and public can look for enlightenment on all matters appertaining to property ownership. . . .' On the unofficial side it attempted to influence Ministries and local authorities on matters of concern where the 'interest of property owners seem to be adversely affected'.[138] Its role as advisor to private members during the passage of the Town and Country Planning Bill (1947) gave it considerable cause for pride.[139]

But the formal structure and activities of the organisation did not reveal in themselves its true import in the 1957 Rent Act debates. To understand this, it is necessary to see the particular role of the ALPO's director, Mr Harold Symon, CB. He entered the organisation direct from a long term at the Ministry of Housing, which began in 1934, and ended as under-secretary of the Local Government Division where he had been concerned with rent control and rating. As to his commitment to the landowning interest there has been no question. Property, he insisted, was the key interest in society. Since the Reform Bill, he claimed, its power had been whittled away more than was just. His ties to the Ministry remained intimate. Long after his departure from the Ministry and the Rent Act debate in 1958, he became the subject of a parliamentary fracas, the 'sticky labels incident'. At that time he obtained a set of addressograph labels used by the Ministry of Housing which he turned over to a subsidiary organisation with which he was concerned. The information he divulged was trivial, but its reflection of his continued intimacy with the department should be viewed as significant.[140]

The intimacy of the director with the Ministry civil servants had a natural impact on the style with which the group presented its case. Primarily, its contacts were through him, and highly informal.[141] The director made his points, not in formal memoranda but over the luncheon table. The strategy was, in the words of Mr D. Walker-Smith, MP, 'the art of the possible'. Mr Symon felt free to push with his former colleagues as much as he thought they could reasonably be expected to accept. To him, as perhaps not to others, the civil servants were prepared to pay close heed. Undoubtedly this gave him and his organisation a favoured position. The ALPO statements of policy could anticipate Ministry intentions, and hence the ALPO suggestions could be closely in line with policies acceptable to the Ministry. Moreover, the ALPO had advance warning of Ministry activities. This worked to the Ministry's advantage as well. It was of vital importance that civil servants with specialised interests be able to discuss ideas with knowledgeable people. Pressure group officials can be quite useful as sources of advice on the desirability of particular policies.[142] Against the advantages of close contact to the Ministry, the ALPO had to overcome structural difficulties. Unlike the small landowner, who recognised his dependence upon the property associations, the large landowner often felt he could 'go it alone'. The consequence was that dissent and non-cooperation were more common in the ALPO than in the NFPO. Not only did this make data for memoranda harder to come by, but it also meant that attendance at council was poor and agendas of little significance.

The organisation was 'non-political' only in the loosest sense. It did not explicitly support the Tory government, but probably most ALPO members did so. The anti-landlord attitude of the Labour Party ensured an anti-Labour tone to ALPO statements.[143] This was probably an advantage while there was a Tory government. The ALPO's pro-Tory members were quick to criticise the 1954 Macmillan Act and White Paper as incomplete and insufficient to do the job intended. But aside from an editorial, no effort was made to campaign against the Bill.[144]

In 1955 the organisation decided to submit a memorandum on the Rent Restriction Acts to the minister. A subcommittee was established consisting exclusively of large London landlords. It met twice, on 28 September and 20 October 1955. The memorandum submitted on the 30 October was, however, largely the work of Mr Symon. The main concern was not with rent increases but with obtaining possession and increases for fringe activities such as services (this was of particular importance to key flats). Mr Symon outlined the position the organisation should take on the debates then raging within the Ministry on the proposals for a new Rent Act.

Significantly, a considerable proportion of the proposals made by the ALPO subsequently found a place in the Bill in one form or another. This can be seen from an examination of the ALPO's principal proposals. Four categories of houses, the ALPO memorandum suggested, should be decontrolled: 1. Flats let with substantial services; 2. Houses falling vacant; 3. Post 1939 lettings; and 4. Houses with rateable values in excess of £45 in Metropolitan London and £35 elsewhere. The Bill provided for decontrol on vacant possession and a slice decontrol almost identical with that proposed by the ALPO.

The A L P O proposed a one year transition period to decontrol. After this, it suggested, tenants should be able to get a three year lease at terms to be agreed upon voluntarily if possible or determined by the county court as was arranged under the Landlord and Tenant Act (1954). The Ministry adopted a shorter transition period and added the lease principle as an amendment.[145]

On rent increases, the A L P O memorandum suggested that the limit on the amount for which repairs increases could be claimed should be raised to thrice the G R V. This was about the amount actually received when account was taken of the new valuations and general rent increase provisions of the government's Bill.

Another suggestion subsequently adopted in a different form was that future stages of decontrol should be made possible. The A L P O proposed that after two years the limits of control be reduced to £35 and £20 for London and elsewhere respectively. The Ministry in fact exceeded this in providing general authority for change in the limits of decontrol.

These proposals were presented to the Ministry by a formal deputation. Subsequently some 'formal' consultations took place.[146] The *Real Estate Journal* carried an original idea of Mr Symon's which contained elements appealing to those who wished control and housing to be considered in the broader context of social policy. He argued that the situation which had made decontrol possible in 1933 and in which private enterprise could replace public construction of housing to let could not be duplicated in the middle 1950s because economic conditions were unfavourable. Rather than limit decontrol, those hurt by decontrol should be compensated through a system of tax allowances. This could be recovered from the landlords through Schedule A.[147] Although this suggestion was not taken up, it reflected a recognition by both the civil servants and landlords of the role which taxation could and did play in the housing scene. Ten years later, the implications of taxation problems were still being discovered.

With the publication of the Bill, the A L P O council on 12 November appointed a subcommittee to prepare a Report.[148] A total of nine points were raised. These were: 1. The possibility of eliminating all mixed premises from control; 2. The definition of rent recoverable; 3. The possibility that landlords might do repairs without tenants' consent; 4. Obtaining decontrol of sub-tenancies where the principal tenant was decontrolled; 5. Decontrol of houses for demolition to further *bona fide* development; 6. a further definition of maintenance; 7. An increase in compensation given to landlords of requisitioned houses; 8. A request for the definition of law where a lease providing for a rent increase under control affects a premise to be decontrolled; and 9. A request that the time to obtain revaluations for assessment be extended.[149] Mr Symon decided, however, that only two of these, the request regarding requisitioned houses and that regarding possession, should be put in the memorandum.[150] He made a distinction between what could be done privately and what might reasonably be pushed publicly.[151] Only a single public meeting was held on the new Bill, in December 1956. It was well attended, a symbol of landlord interest. This conference forced the inclusion of requisitioned houses in the A L P O memorandum.[152] All these proposals were really in the nature of detailed comment rather than challenges to the principal of the Bill.

Like the N F P O, the A L P O issued a statement in which landlords were discouraged from attempting to make too great a profit from decontrol. An editorial in the *Real Estate Journal*[153] of January restated what the council had already asserted in a press release;[154] that landlords would be foolish to forfeit the goodwill of their tenants and be caught with empty houses. This statement was accepted for publication only by the *Estates Gazette*; *The Times*, *Financial Times* and *Manchester Guardian* accepted letters from Mr Symon on this issue.[155]

Unlike the N F P O, the A L P O could claim that a substantial part of the 1957 Rent Act could be found in the A L P O proposals prior to publication. But after publication, it seems evident that the A L P O's role declined. It has been suggested that this reflected Mr Symon's inexperience with the lobby side of the landlord's case. To what extent did the A L P O's success reflect merely the fact that the A L P O's ideas were designed by Mr Symon to correspond to those he knew to be in favour at the Ministry? Or did the A L P O's success indicate that Mr Symon had chosen the proper timing and proper approach to maximise the influence a pressure group could exert on the Ministry?

## Summary

The dominant conclusion which emerges from the activities of the pressure groups engaged in the 1957 Rent Act debates was the advantage which a known supply of information gave to particular groups. The two groups which were known by the Ministry as reliable sources of advice and information and whose staff were well known in the Ministry, the RICS and the ALPO, had easiest access and seemed to have made the more significant contributions to the Act. The other groups had lesser impact, down to the purely public pressure of the tenants' associations which had none.

The advantage possessed by the RICS and the ALPO lay not merely in the ease of access they possessed, but the time at which they could exert influence. Unlike the other organisations, they were able to influence decisions before the White Paper, or basic policy decisions, let alone a Bill, were prepared. The influence may not have been much in this case, and it is particularly difficult to trace, being essentially informal and private.

There was little mention, by any of the participants, of 'the national interest'. Each pressure group consciously attempted to improve the position of its clients. But there was remarkably little use of border-line tactics to achieve objectives. Indeed, the questionable practices involved matters of ease of access either to the Ministry or to the Conservative Party. Most of these have been discounted as trivial by contemporary observers.

Perhaps the reason for restraint, and the success of information suppliers, lay in the uncertainties that clouded the debate. Neither Ministry nor pressure groups could be sure precisely what arguments were valid and what information most relevant. Indeed, each side had had, during the previous five years, a 'turn' at self-righteousness.

But the most significant conclusion from the point of view of the study of pressure groups is the small role which any and all of the groups played in the legislative process. Their information, their pressure, their publicity, seemed to have little impact on the decision-making process. The pressure groups seemed to be but another influence operating very much at the periphery of the decision-making process. Indeed, a great deal of supposed 'influence' may appear in retrospect to be mere self-touting. In a situation where the special expertise of the pressure groups, the supply of information and favourable public opinion, could have little interest for the decision-maker, the effectiveness of pressure groups as mediators between public and government was considerably reduced from the norms which pressure group theory has led us to expect.

# NOTES

1 H. Eckstein, *Pressure Group Politics: The Case of the British Medical Association*, Allen and Unwin, London, 1960.
2 H. H. Wilson, *Pressure Group: The Campaign for Commercial Television*, Secker and Warburg, London, 1961.
3 *The Times*, 18 March 1957, p. 8.
4 *The Daily Worker*, 30 March 1957.
5 *Ibid.*, 11 March 1957.
6 *The News Chronicle*, 15 March 1957; *The Times*, 29 January 1957, p. 11.
7 *The West London Observer*, 25 January 1957.
8 Interview with Mr R. Rawlings, formerly hon. secretary of the Clare Court Tenants' Association and other London tenants' groups.
9 *The Chatham Observer*, 1 February 1957.
10 *The West London Observer*, 1 February 1957.
11 *Ibid.*, 25 January 1957.
12 *The West London Observer*, 1 February 1957.
13 *The Daily Worker*, 8 February 1957.
14 *Ibid.*, 5 March 1957.
15 *Ibid.*, 30 January 1957.
16 *Ibid.*, 29 January 1957.
17 *Ibid.*, 11 March 1957.
18 567 H C Deb.5s., col 1347.
19 Telegram of Mr H. Sterne, secretary, Hornsey Tenants Anti-Rent Bill Association.
20 West Kensington Tenants' Association, *The West London Observer*, 1 February 1957.
21 *The Times*, 18 March 1957, p. 8; *The Manchester Guardian*, 18 March 1957; *The Daily Worker*, 18 March 1957.
22 *The Daily Worker*, 5 March 1957; *West London Observer*, 1 February 1957.
23 Trade Union Congress: *Report of Proceedings at the 86th Annual Trade Union Congress (1954)*, the T U C, London, 1954.
24 T U C, *Report . . . (1955)*, para. 176.
25 T U C, *Report . . . (1954)*, para. 269.
26 T U C, *Report . . . (1955)*, paras 464–5.
27 *Ibid.*, para. 25.
28 T U C, *Report . . . (1956)*, paras 374–6.
29 *Ibid.*, resolution 50.
30 *Ibid.*, res 72–4.
31 *Ibid.*, res. 75.
32 *Ibid.*, res. 76.
33 *Ibid.*, res. 77.
34 T U C, Circular 54; see T U C, *Report . . . (1957)*, para. 351.
35 T U C, *Report . . . (1957)*, para. 351.
36 Letter of Mr S. Greene, now general secretary of the N U R, to the author. His reference number, GS/455/11.
37 *The Times*, 18 February 1957, p. 5.
38 Letter of S. Greene, GS/455/11.

39 Circular 78; see T U C, *Report* . . . *(1957)*.
40 London Trades Council (1952), *Annual Report* . . ., *1956*, p. 4.
41 London Trades Council (1952), *Annual Report* . . ., *1957*, p. 4.
42 *Ibid.*, p. 12.
43 *The Daily Worker*, 23 February, 12 March and 9 April 1957; *The Times*, 18 February 1957.
44 *The South London Press*, 22 March 1957.
45 *The Citizen*, 23 May 1957.
46 *The Brighton Gazette*, 23 February 1957.
47 *The Sheffield Telegraph*, 25 February 1957.
48 *The South Wales Echo–Evening Express*, 8 March 1957.
49 *The Hendon and Finchley Times*, 1 March 1957.
50 *The Dorset Daily Echo*, 6 May 1957.
51 *The East Grinstead Observer*, 15 February 1957.
52 Royal Institution of Chartered Surveyors M S S: Jennings, 15 November 1956.
53 R I C S MSS, Dowse, 19 November 1956.
54 R I C S MSS, Brief Notes of a Meeting of the Parliamentary (Rent Bill) Subcommittee of Monday, 26 November 1956.
55 R I C S MSS, assistant secretary to Millar, 5 December 1956.
56 R I C S MSS, Doc. 78.
57 R I C S MSS, Notes of a Meeting of the Special (Rent Bill) Subcommittee of the Scottish Branch of R I C S, 21 November 1956.
58 R I C S, *Memorandum to the Minister of Housing and Local Government on the Rent Bill*, R I C S, London (Mimeographed, December 1956).
59 *Ibid.*, para. 4.
60 *Ibid.*, paras 5–6.
61 *Ibid.*, paras 8–9.
62 *Ibid.*, para. 18.
63 *Ibid.*, para. 20.
64 *The Times*, 22 January 1957, p. 9.
65 R I C S MSS, memorandum of 5 March 1957.
66 *The Manchester Guardian*, 18 April 1957.
67 Chartered Auctioneers' and Estate Agents' Institute MSS, Parliamentary and Legal Committee, 27 November 1956, item 3, 408/3038 (their reference).
68 C A E A I MSS, Hay to F. C. Hawkes, 13 November 1956.
69 C A E A I MSS, Watt to Ryan, 3 December 1956, 408/3038.
70 C A E A I MSS, Watt to Horobin, 4 December 1956, 408/3038.
71 C A E A I, 'Memorandum of the Council of the Chartered Auctioneers' and Estate Agents' Institute', *The Estates Gazette*, vol. 169, pp. 6–7.
72 *The Estates Gazette*, 7 July 1956, vol. 168, p. 13.
73 C A E A I, 'Memorandum', *The Estates Gazette*, vol. 169, pp. 6–7.
74 C A E A I MSS, Ryan to Watt, 5 December 1956.
75 C A E A I MSS, Watt to Pilcher, 12 December 1956.
76 C A E A I MSS, Minutes, 24 January 1957, item 8.
77 C A E A I MSS, Watt Memorandum, 4 January 1957.
78 C A E A I MSS, Watt to MacTaggart, 5 December 1957.
79 *Ibid.*

80 C A E A I MSS, Memorandum from Watt, 29 April 1957.
81 *The Journal of the Chartered Auctioneers and Estate Agents Institute*, 1957, pp. 261 ff.
82 1956–7 H C S C Deb.,I. cols 480, 1305.
83 'Rent Bill Report (Housing Committee) Supplement', *The Municipal Review*, August 1957, pp. 148–52. A Report of the Housing Committee of the A M C. Report dated 9 January 1957.
84 *Ibid.*, para. 17.
85 *Ibid.*
86 *Ibid.*, paras 19–20.
87 *Ibid.*, paras 25–8.
88 *Ibid.*, paras 35–8.
89 *The Municipal Journal*, vol. 64, ii, pp. 2019–20.
90 *Ibid.*, paras 42–6.
91 *Ibid.*, paras 7–8.
92 'Housing Committee Report (Final) Supplement', *The Municipal Review*, December 1957, pp. 234–5.
93 Miss B. Taylor, 'The National Federation of Property Owners History' (MS. n.d.).
94 National Federation of Property Owners, *The Voice of the Press Demands Rent Reform*, N F P O, London, 1952.
95 See *Property*.
96 N F P O MSS, Sizen to Hornby, 30 January 1957, 217/712.
97 N F P O MSS, Sizan to Sutton, 30 October 1956, 19/218.
98 *Ibid.*
99 N F P O MSS, 238/328.
100 N F P O MSS, 25 September 1956.
101 N F P O MSS, 804/847.
102 N F P O MSS, 793/860.
103 N F P O MSS, Sizen to Wakefield (no marks).
104 N F P O MSS, Sizen to Hand, 397/448.
105 N F P O MSS, statement of 6 December 1951, p. 2.
106 *Ibid.*, p. 4.
107 N F P O MSS, 19 November 1953.
108 N F P O MSS, Proposals to Amend the Restriction Acts, 24 October 1955.
109 *Property*, June 1956, pp. 6 ff.
110 N F P O MSS, Errington to Sutton, 16 October 1956, 149.
111 N F P O MSS, Errington to Sutton, 5 February 1957, 623/740.
112 N F P O MSS, Sizen to Hand, *Re*: article in *The People*, 7 February 1957, 253.
113 N F P O MSS, Sizen to Ling, 30 January 1957, 455/699.
114 N F P O MSS, Sizen to Ling, 4 December 1956, 257/399.
115 N F P O MSS, Sizen to Aspell of Leicester Auctioneers' and Estate Agents', 21 December 1956, 429/487.
116 N F P O MSS, Sizen to Cmdr Marten, 15 February 1957, 794/843.
117 *Ibid.*
118 N F P O MSS, Doc. 253, and see above.
119 N F P O MSS, Sizen to Dame Evelyn Sharp, 28 December 1956, 450/499.

120 N F P O, *Property*, March 1957.
121 *Ibid.*, parts 4 and 7 of memorandum.
122 *Property*, March 1957, sent as letter on 1 February 1957.
123 N F P O MSS, Sizen to Brooke, signed by Hand, 13 February 1957, 724/814.
124 N F P O MSS, Hand to Brooke, 16 February 1957, 814/848.
125 N F P O MSS, 47/132.
126 N F P O MSS, 23 January 1957, 590/642.
127 N F P O MSS, Hay to Hand, 23 January 1957, 538/641, Sizen to Goldring, 7 December 1956, 226/418.
128 N F P O MSS, 2 January 1957, 42/519.
129 N F P O MSS, 22 January 1957, 519/630.
130 N F P O MSS, Errington to Beavan, 672.
131 *Property*, March 1957, pp. 7 ff.
132 *Ibid.*, p. 5.
133 *Ibid.*, pp. 5, 15.
134 N F P O MSS, Errington to Sutton, 5 February 1957, 623/740.
135 N F P O MSS, Errington to Beavan, 672.
136 *The Real Estate Journal*, vol. 1, no. 2 (April 1951), pp. 298–9.
137 *Ibid.*, vol. 4, no. 1 (June 1953), back page.
138 *Ibid.*, vol. 1, no. 12, p. 325.
139 *Ibid.*, p. 326.
140 594 H C Deb.5s., cols 971 ff., and 595 H C Deb.5s., cols 399–400.
141 Though Mr G. D. M. Block was parliamentary consultant to the A L P O during this period, he did not affect the A L P O's policy or use his influence within the Conservative Party. His responsibility was solely for a column on parliamentary activity entitled 'Whitehall Chimes' in *The Real Estate Journal*.
142 Suggested to the author by Professor D. V. Donnison.
143 *The Real Estate Journal*, vol. 7, no. 5, p. 105.
144 *Ibid.*, vol. 4, no. 7, p. 159.
145 *Ibid.*, vol. 6, no. 6, p. 145.
146 *Ibid.*, vol. 6, no. 7, pp. 176 ff.
147 *Ibid.*, vol. 7, no. 3, pp. 76–7.
148 *Ibid.*, vol. 7, no. 12, p. 160.
149 *Ibid.*, vol. 8, no. 1, pp. 6 ff.
150 *Ibid.*, pp. 6 ff.
151 *Ibid.*, vol. 8, no. 4, p. 105.
152 *Ibid.*, vol. 7, no. 7, p. 161.
153 *Ibid.*, vol. 8, no. 1, p. 1.
154 *Ibid.*, p. 7.
155 See *The Times*, 7 December 1956, p. 11.

# 9
# Combat

Sir W. Ivor Jennings has remarked of Parliament:

> The British governmental machine is, in spite of its many defects, one of the most efficient constitutional structures of the world. It is reasonably efficient because it can be criticised. It is reasonably just because its actions are proclaimed to the people by those who have no cause to praise it. It is, in short, a good system because it rests upon Parliament and, through Parliament, upon the willing consent of those who are governed. The dogs bark in Parliament; if there were no Parliament they might bite.[1]

Whether this is true or not, it is certainly the spirit that lies behind most surveys of Parliament, and even colours the views of MPs and Lords. To evaluate the validity of these views, only Parliament watched in the process of its principal function can provide an answer. Did the Commons come to grips with the issues posed explicitly or implicitly by the Rent Act? What were the arguments in the general debates, in committee, and on Report? What were the devices used to improve parliamentary consideration? In this case, what was the role of the guillotine and the petition? What was the place of the House of Lords in the debate? How concerned was the body by a fairly explicit attempt to usurp functions embodied in delegated legislation? It was these devices and debates that gave colour to the parliamentary aspects of the legislative process. How responsive, responsible and efficient was Parliament in its deliberations upon the 1957 Rent Act? Were the failure to profit from expertise and the general inability of the Opposition to put its case failures of institutions or merely the people who worked within them?

## Contrast

Rhetoric, not analysis, characterised the debates on the Rent Act. There was to be no dialogue between two sides. Arguments presented by one side were incomprehensible to the other. The Labour Opposition never confronted the genuine difficulties of the landlord; the

Conservatives never empathised with the effect of dislocation problems on the working classes.

Class barriers, class misunderstandings, class quarrels (if only latent) provided both explanation and cause for the false dialogue. Of the Conservative view, Mr Lindgren (deputy leader for Labour on the Bill) remarked:

> How can an ordinary person be a Tory MP? A representative of vested interests cannot be an ordinary person. . . . There is talk about making accommodation available. I got married in 1926. I was then a railway man. My money was 57s. a week and I got the house in which I now live at 25s. a week. It is a three-bedroom parlour type house. Have the Hon. Gentlemen opposite ever lived on a wage of 57s. and paid 25s. a week rent?
>
> When I had to do that, I could not pay the rent unless I had a lodger. Of course, if I had been a Tory I would have called him a paying guest, but the real reason we had the lodger was that we could not afford to pay the rent. I had a family, and I am still living in the same house.
>
> *Sir Eric Errington:* The Hon. Gentleman is pretty comfortable then.
>
> *Mr Lindgren:* I am pretty comfortable says the Hon. Gentleman, and that is what worries him. The family is now grown up, married and gone. The lodger has gone too. But it is true that we have a spare bedroom, and the third bedroom I am using as a study. Apparently it is really shocking that I should have a spare bedroom. We are underoccupied. Only my wife and myself occupy this house to which we went when we got married, and we have got a spare bedroom. I can easily invite my daughter or my son to come and spend the weekend with us. This is shocking so far as the Hon. Gentlemen opposite are concerned; they do not like the ordinary working man to have a spare bedroom. . . .
>
> Being a Tory minister, he could have two houses, but so far as we are concerned being representatives of the working class, we cannot have a spare bedroom.[2]

Labour remembered, all too well, not merely the hard times during the interwar period, but also the immediate postwar shortages, the social dislocations as well as the privation.[3] Tories did not recognise the extent to which working-class expenditure varied as between parts of the working class, nor the extent of the sacrifices made to pay additional rents.[4] Several Labour MPs warned that the only consequence would be a round of wage demands to cover the increases.[5]

Coupled with fear was class hostility. In no country is the landlord a figure of merit in the folk culture. One Labour MP demanded:

Are the charges of usury unfounded? Are the charges of lack of social conscience unfounded, and the charges that they have ruined the health of our people? . . .
  If the Bill were being considered against the background of enlightened landlordism, there would be a different reaction, but it is because we know so much about the past activities of these people that we oppose the Bill.[6]

Anything which benefited landlords must, *ipso facto*, be wrong. It was the British version of the Viennese proverb: 'Even landlords die'.

Although Mr Brooke understood and sympathised with this position to a certain extent,[7] the basic attitude of the Tories was sympathy mixed with concern for the landlord. This has been documented in the section on government policy. During the debate, Conservatives gave no indication that they understood the origins of the Labour M Ps' concern. Whether the Bill could be presented as anything other than a 'landlords charter' was moot. The government and its backbenchers failed in debate to eliminate this label; they never tried. Indeed, throughout the debate Tory M Ps were complaining about the sorry plight of the small landlord and how fifty years of rent control had crushed him. Bad landlords some Tories accepted as a possibility, but argued that these were a small minority. The few bad did not justify withholding aid from the many good.
  The Tories, except for the plight of the small landlord, tended to ignore the social case. On purely economic grounds something had to be done about the housing situation; they were offering a rent increase and some form of decontrol. Economic realities had to be faced. Whatever the truth of the Tory case, it was irrelevant in the debate. They succeeded in evading the Opposition's attack. That the public and press accepted the Tory alternative was, nonetheless, evident and to their advantage.[8] The argument was one not of ends but of means. The government and Conservative Party portrayed themselves as providing physical plant, by any means possible. The Opposition insisted that people must be housed as individuals and citizens. To the Opposition it was people, not property that required the government's attention. Property, not people, won this round.

## General Debate

The debate on second reading was the most significant of the debates. The government and Opposition had a chance to express their intentions. The press and the public could understand this non-specialist debate. But in the debate on the Rent Act no effort was made to pin-point the opposition to the Bill through an amendment. Instead, attention was concentrated by some show of debate upon the decision of the government that the committee stage should be taken upstairs rather than on the floor, as precedent seemed to require. This was the subject of a division. The focus emerged by the presentation of the Ministry case and the replies to it by the Opposition.

Mr Powell outlined five reasons for introducing the Rent Bill; underoccupation, mobility, repairs, anomalies and consensus on the need for a general rise in rents.[9] The Labour reply, by Mr Mitchison, concentrated on the giveaway aspects of the Bill. Such passages as 'Do the Hon. Members opposite . . . really wish to be responsible for starving a considerable number of people and increasing the mortality rate among those who occupy these houses . . .?[10] are typical of the Labour appeal. There was considerable Labour and Conservative attention to the size of the rent increases. While Labour backbenchers like Mr C. W. Key attacked the size of the increase,[11] Tories like Sir Eric Errington argued it was too small to achieve the purposes of the Bill.[12] The parties were playing their traditional roles in the debate. Labour complained that the landlord was not to be trusted.[13] Tories complained that controls themselves were dangerous and should be eliminated.[14]

But the Scots proved themselves a nation apart. Even Tory Scots M Ps who favoured the Bill in its application to England and Wales had doubts about its application in Scotland. They pointed to the harm rent control did. But they also recognised that the solution which might serve as an ameliorant in England and Wales could be explosive in Scotland.[15] The Secretary of State for Scotland emphasised, on the other hand, that the provisions for Scotland, though included in an English Bill, were really sufficiently different to take account of Scots interest.[16]

Mr Callaghan's argument, in concluding the debate, was far more moderate than Mr Mitchison's had been in the opening. His primary contention was not that the principles of the Bill were wrong but that the Bill would not achieve the ends desired. He conceded that people would pay more for better housing, that repairs were necessary, that misallocation and anomalies needed to be corrected. But he argued that the greater danger in practice might well be dislocation and consequent hardship.[17] All this, Mr Sandys conceded, was possible. But a first step had to be taken, and he proposed to take it immediately.[18] Of course, genuine hardship must be prevented, but he preferred the use of the welfare (provision for those in need) rather than the social service (provision of housing to all) principle, as the Labour Opposition had suggested.[19] In any case, Mr Sandys' figures did not justify the exaggerated fears of the Opposition as to the extent of the hardship likely to develop. In 1933 the same fears had been expressed, but decontrol had worked smoothly, he reminded Labour.[20] The rise in the cost of living, as a whole, would not exceed 2 per cent, and the vast majority of households would not be affected at all.[21] But these were merely debating points. Conservatives and Labour were really arguing different cases.

Third reading was, necessarily, rather anomalous. There could be no major alterations in policy or detail. It was merely a last chance for government and Opposition to exchange blows, and these were more formal than real. The Conservatives, indeed, were more concerned to close ranks within their own party than with the Opposition. Mr Bevin's accusation revealed this concern most poignantly:

Of course, it is no secret that a few of my Hon. Friends, whose ideological rectitude I should never dream of questioning, have been just a bit restive in recent weeks. Indeed, their untiring support for the principles of the Bill has almost been equalled by their longing to drive a coach and horses through it.[122]

The reservations of the Scots Tories were partly assuaged by the Scottish Office officers. The attitudes of Mr Price, Mr Finlay and Mr Gresham Cooke were generally encouraging to the government but each was restrained on his own particular point of concern – transition, decontrol, the availability of houses, repairs.[23] Mr Hay, cautious in his praise, saw some advantage for the future of private landlords.[24] Mr Brooke, in his summation, reaffirmed the various guarantees as to the consequences of the Bill – that rents would not rise too much, that new accommodation would become available, that disrepair machinery would work impartially.[25]

The Labour attack on the government varied from the fiery speech of Mr Mahon to the mild conclusion of Mr Mitchison. The general emphasis of Labour's attack far exceeded the mild criticism made by Mr Callaghan during second reading. Labour had discovered that if it could not win parliamentary victory it could at least be passionate in the hope of future electoral success. But the subsequent acceptance of the Lords' amendments remained *pro forma*; there was yet another debate but it had no impact on the legislation.

One final gesture remained. When the Commons were summoned to hear the Royal Assent to the Act the Labour Party refused to leave the Commons to attend, as an indication of the party's commitment to repeal the Act at the earliest possible moment. But this was not a revolutionary gesture – merely one of those postures of which M Ps are fond and the public uncomprehending.

## Standing Committee

The commitment of the Bill to the committee stage upstairs, rather than on the floor of the House, was primarily a time-saving device. The six days needed to put through the Rent Bill were grudgingly acquired. But the Standing Committee could be an equivalent hurdle. Without a guillotine and with standing orders that permit endless and repetitious debate, Standing Committee consideration could drag on indefinitely, as Professor Crick has pointed out in his analysis of the difficulties inherent in Standing Committee operations.[26] A substantial proportion of the committee must be within reasonable distance for the period in which the committee is sitting. Committee meeting dates conflicted. The task, on both sides, of preparing the material needed in committee was gargantuan.

The advantages to be gained by either side from Standing Committee did not merit the effort. Since Standing Committees were usually not very well reported in the press, both government and Opposition, but especially the Opposition, got no propaganda advantage from the debate. This reduced the chance of the Opposition to win significant concessions. Concessions on principles have seldom been given. Concessions on lesser points would normally be given on Report after a concession at committee. Since a government amendment irrespective of its source was associated with a successful Opposition appeal, the Opposition won no advantage from its efforts. The Opposition could hope only for the chance to talk the Bill to death. And this, of necessity, at some stage or another, could be prevented. The government's impatience was determined by the parliamentary timetable which settled the dates on which Report and third reading had to occur.

Committee debate could serve the government well. The minister could collect advice on matters of detail, especially in drafting, to supplement the efforts of his own apparat. Pressure groups which did not have, or did not realise the importance of, direct access to the

Ministry could present their case at the committee stage. A wider national consensus in support of a major piece of legislation could serve party as well as national interest. To what extent was the possibility reflected in the activities of government and Opposition? The amendments offered should be measured qualitatively and quantitatively. The quantitative analysis below outlines amendments by subject. Table 14 on page 166 indicates the origin and section of party from which amendments sprang.

Serious amendments were pressed to division or withdrawn. Many were never debated. Those moved by the government were all accepted, though not on all was a division asked. The amendments not pursued failed for two reasons. Some were duplicate amendments which the committee chairman elected not to call. Others the Opposition elected not to pursue to facilitate the operation of the guillotine (once the government decided the maximum time they would allow, the Opposition had a free hand to allot time).

Attention was focused on the most controversial clauses where the maximum amount of political credit could be amassed, even if no concessions were to be expected or obtained. The disproportionate number of amendments for the principal clauses documented this phenomenon. Clauses 1, 2 and 9 and schedules 1 and 4 and clause 6 took the vast proportion of the Opposition attack. More significant was the number of divisions on Opposition amendments (i.e. those which struck at the core of the Bill and were sure of defeat). After clause 2 there were substantially fewer divisions. At this point the guillotine was imposed. On the most important sections dealing with decontrol, clause 9 and schedule 4, there were fewer divisions than on earlier major clauses.

The large number of government amendments differed qualitatively from those offered by the Opposition. Included in the government's amendments were not only the actual changes to be made in the Bill but also amendments to other sections of the Bill consequential upon the fundamental change. Though fifteen changes were made in schedule 4, most of these simply involved changes because of two concessions on clause 9.

The relatively small number of government backbench amendments, except over clause 9, and the failure to press for their adoption, were symbolic of the role the government MPs played during this stage. The significant exception to this was the division over Sir Ian Horobin's amendment to clause 9. Four of the remaining government

# TABLE 14
## Amendments at Standing Committee: Origin, Subject, and Action

| Section | Opposition number | Opposition division | Government Backbench withdrawn | Government Backbench number | Government Backbench division | Government withdrawn | Government number | Government division |
|---|---|---|---|---|---|---|---|---|
| Clause 1 | 25 | 9 | 1 | — | — | — | 2 | — |
| ,, 2 | 27 | 11 | — | — | — | — | 2 | — |
| ,, 3 | 5 | n | — | — | — | — | — | — |
| ,, 4 | 8 | n | 1 | — | — | — | 2 | — |
| ,, 5 | 4 | n | — | — | — | — | — | — |
| ,, 6 | 13 | 5 | — | 7 | — | — | 1 | — |
| ,, 7 | 3 | n | — | — | — | — | — | — |
| Schedule 3 | 6 | n | 1 | — | — | — | — | — |
| Clause 8 | 4 | 2 | — | 1 | — | — | 2 | 1 |
| ,, 9 | 28 | 6 | — | 7 | 1 | — | 2 | 3 |
| Schedule 4 | 11 | 2 | 2 | 1 | — | — | 15 | — |
| Clause 10 | 10 | 1 | — | — | — | — | 4 | — |
| ,, 11 | 1 | — | — | — | — | — | — | — |
| ,, 12* | 4 (1) | (1) | — | 1 | — | — | 1 | — |
| ,, 13 | — | — | — | 2 | — | — | — | — |
| ,, 16 | 6 | — | — | 1 | — | — | 4 | — |
| ,, 17 | 1 | — | — | — | — | — | — | — |
| ,, 18 | 6 | — | — | — | — | — | — | — |
| New clauses | 10 | 3 | 1 | 3 | — | 1 | 2 | — |
| Schedule 1 | 39 | 6 | 5 | 2 | — | 1 | 4 | — |
| ,, 2 | 1 | 1 | — | — | — | — | — | — |
| ,, 5 | — | 1 | — | 1 | — | — | 1 | — |
| ,, 6 | 4 | — | — | — | — | — | 3 | — |
| ,, 8 | — | — | — | — | — | — | 9 | — |
| New schedule | — | — | — | 2 | — | — | — | — |

* An amendment moved initially by government backbench, division forced by Labour.

backbench amendments were discussed, before being withdrawn. The rest were placed to give backbenchers the chance to express their point of view or to allow them to apply very gentle pressure. The Opposition withdrew a relatively large number of amendments which would have yielded limited if any political advantage. Only a few, such as that in clause 1, reflected a genuine withdrawal as a result of a government promise to look into the matter on Report. Table 15 indicates who took responsibility for amendments.

TABLE 15
*Movers of Significant Amendments at Standing Committee*[28]
(These are the persons who spoke first on amendments. Often Government amendments were accepted without debate, other amendments were withdrawn.)

| Government | | Government Backbench | | Opposition Frontbench | | Opposition Backbench | |
|---|---|---|---|---|---|---|---|
| Bevins | 1 | Horobin | 4 | Mitchison | 13 | H. Butler | 2 |
| Brooke | 4 | Page | 1 | Lindgren | 5 | J. Butler | 2 |
| Browne | 4 | | | Fraser | 1 | Blenkinsop | 2 |
| | | | | MacColl | 5 | Evans | 1 |
| | | | | | | Gibson | 1 |
| | | | | | | J. B. Hynd | 7 |
| | | | | | | Jenner | 4 |
| | | | | | | Key | 1 |
| | | | | | | Lawson | 2 |
| | | | | | | McInnes | 4 |
| | | | | | | J. Silverman | 5 |
| | | | | | | Sparks | 5 |
| | | | | | | Willis | 5 |
| Total | 9 | | 5 | | 24 | | 41 |

The relatively small number of significant (i.e. amendments important enough to be considered) government amendments should be noted. Far more fascinating was the complete absence of any pro-landlord amendments. Pro-landlord amendments were tabled in several instances. All were withdrawn. To what extent this would indicate the marginal use made by landlord pressure groups of parliamentary publicity as compared with other occasions is moot. Certainly, as was pointed out in chapter 8, the parliamentary stage, if not the public process, was used.

A total of fifty-four English resolutions, half moved by the Opposition frontbench, were discussed. An average of three amendments was taken up at each sitting, one for every forty-three minutes the committee spent discussing the Bill (three sittings were lost in procedural wrangles; each sitting lasted two and one-half hours). This was not very much time to analyse the major principles raised. Indeed, most points got only cursory attention.

These figures do not present a total picture. To obtain this, stem qualitative questions about the conduct of debate, the nature of the Opposition's attack and the government's response should be answered.

One of the eccentricities of British parliamentary life is the backbencher's obsession with his private rights. Thus, Mr Thornton-Kemsley (Conservative, Angus and Mearns), an otherwise docile backbencher, complained that aside from the discourtesy of not informing his own backbenchers in advance, the government was being unreasonable in demanding time in committee. 'We are not, and should not be, professional politicians.'[29] He insisted that all sittings beyond the customary two per week be held in the afternoon.[30] In this he was supported by other backbenchers. Ultimately an arrangement was reached, but none was ever really satisfied.

Part of the government backbenchers' wrath at extended sittings arose from the knowledge that they could take only a small part. For it was a cardinal rule that government M Ps were to be seen in division but not otherwise heard, however valuable their contribution. Their route of protest was by letter or through the Whips. Sir Ian Horobin (Conservative, Oldham) remarked:

> The most succinct committee points can be made by people who have knowledge, as some of us have . . . and that is why we get ourselves put on these Standing Committees – but we all know that as a matter of practice one is begged and implored by one's minister, however important may be what one has to say, to say it to him privately, but not to say it to him here, because it would hold up the proceedings.[31]

The Opposition had been equally concerned about meeting three days a week. For their senior members, too, had professional engagements in the morning.[32] To this complaint they added the traditional Opposition protest that whereas the government had staff, they have had to do their own research and ought to be given adequate time to do it. The speed required left the Opposition at a disadvantage in 'formulating and discussing' its criticisms properly.[33] The government, were they in Opposition, would protest bitterly at the 'ruthless speed' demanded by the government.[34]

All these protests were ceremonial only. Both backbenchers and Opposition appreciated the limitations of parliamentary time. In fact, none of the considerations discussed had any impact on the pace at which the Bill was considered.

Approximately three hundred columns of Committee Hansard were devoted to clause 1, concerned with increasing rents of properties remaining under control. In retrospect this clause was relatively unimportant. Sir Eric Errington was not far wrong when he accused the Labour Opposition of attacking the clause on the grounds that all tenants were saints, all landlords, devils.[35] Two principal amendments were introduced: the first by Mr Evans (Labour, Islington) attempted to reduce the amount of the rent increase[36] and the second by Mr Mitchison (Labour, Kettering) attempted to establish rent tribunals (rather than the county courts) to settle rents.[37] Both were attacking amendments bound to be rejected.

Various minor amendments ranging from the sublime to the ridiculous were moved on clause 1. Some were concerned to eliminate from the new Act all tenancies paid for by the National Assistance Board.[38] Others tried to persuade the government to uphold contracts which called for lower rents than those permitted by the new control. But Mr Powell wanted to do everything possible to raise rents.[39] This was later reversed by Mr Brooke, in a similar discussion on clause 2.[40] Most amendments were even more detailed, covering fewer tenants.

But relatively little time was devoted to the exact amount of the increase. Mr Powell argued that the government had to determine, perhaps arbitrarily, what constituted 'fair rent'. Even *The Economist* questioned the relevance of the particular levels selected.[41]

Clause 2 was concerned with slums and disrepair procedures. The principal Opposition amendment sought to exempt slum houses from increases in rent, and, indeed, that those scheduled for demolition should be rent free to the tenants. Mr Mitchison's amendment on this point was relatively moderate.[42] Mr Sparks (Labour, Acton) moved an even stronger one to include all unfit houses, not merely those scheduled for demolition. The government took the position that the landlord was not at fault because he happened to hold slum property.[43] They argued that as long as the landlord had responsibility he was entitled to rent.

The Opposition also sought to revise the proposed disrepair procedure to maintain the system used under the 1954 Act. The essence of their position was that the landlords would not do repairs in any case.[44] This was rejected.[45]

A variation on the Opposition's theme was Mr Robert Jenkins' (Conservative, Dulwich) proposal to amend those provisions relating to the lowest category of houses to include not merely houses condemned for demolition under slum clearance but also those condemned under various public health ordinances. The government was able to yield to Mr Jenkins on this point.[46]

Scottish clauses became a case apart. Typical of Scots concern to maintain their own forms was the statement by Mr Willis (Labour, Edinburgh):

> It has been the tradition in dealing with Scottish legislation that we have a discussion on 'shall' and 'may'. No Scottish Bill would be worthy of the name if we did not have that discussion. In spite of the spinelessness of the present Scottish ministers in allowing Scottish legislation to be subject to a guillotine, there is no reason why we should not maintain this cherished tradition. It is true that we shall have to cut the debate, but we should not allow the tradition to fall into abeyance.[47]

The Scots politically, as well as in other respects, lived in a world entirely their own. In theory they dealt only with the Scottish Office, never with English ministers. They expected, and this was true whether from government or Opposition benches, that the Scottish Office would take decisions independently of the English.[48] In rent control this would have been relatively easy, as there was considerable variation between the housing conditions and legislation as they applied in Scotland as against England and Wales.

This differentiation was a source of concern to Tory backbenchers. They argued that the consequence had been that landlords in Scotland were considerably worse off than those elsewhere in the United Kingdom.[49] The Scots Office shared this view.[50] The focus of the debate was on the repairs problem. Labour MPs took special pleasure in attacking Scottish landlords for their failure to make repairs since the 1923 Act increases.[51] Nor did they miss the chance to accuse the Conservatives of pro-landlord, anti-tenant activity. One particularly virulent speech concluded:

> Does not the Hon. Gentleman realise that the landlords of Scotland have regarded their properties—and even their tenants – as a dripping roast, which will go on dripping forever? Does not he realise that he is putting forward a proposal which means that the bones of old age pensioners will be squashed to provide a little more gravy for the landlords?[52]

The extent of the rent rise became only a minor issue in the debate on Scots clauses. The case of the Opposition rested on the premise that slum housing ought to be destroyed, not preserved. Since the property had already yielded a return of two or three hundred per cent, the landlord no longer had a justifiable capital stake in it. Its capital value, they declared, was nil. Amendment after amendment sought to reduce the amount being offered or to modify the procedure by which the landlord could obtain the increase, or by which he might be restrained from obtaining it. The Solicitor-General for Scotland and the Joint Under-Secretary of State both openly acknowledged that the clauses were intended to give an increase to the landlord (unlike the 1954 Repairs increase) regardless of the state of disrepair.[53] (Decontrol applied to Scotland, but affected so few houses as to be trivial.)

The general line the Scottish Office took on technical amendments, including the shall-may debate, was to cite established precedent. Again and again Mr Browne pointed to a particular phrase or to the length of a particular notice as merely a repetition of the form which became precedent as a consequence of this or that preceding Act.[54] Concessions, such as they were, followed the English model. Thus the transition period of rent increases was extended in both its stages, as a concession to the Opposition.[55]

Opposition and government debaters ought to have been embroiled over clause 9. Instead the attack was partially misdirected, partially submerged by the announcement that a concession would be made on transition but made in another section of the Bill.[56] The Opposition was hampered by the dissident Tory MPs who got equal propaganda value from their own radical proposals for delay in decontrol. Thus, Mr Mitchison concentrated considerable fire on the 'Margate mutineers' who tabled many motions attacking transition and then, when Mr Brooke introduced his own more moderate proposals, withdrew their own.

That was, as it were, the hoisting of the pirate flag, the 'Jolly Roger', down on the river outside the Isle of Thanet, and the Margate mutineers duly appeared on the Order Paper carrying cardboard daggers, and with blackened faces, prepared to go on board the ship of state. I never thought they were much of a lot anyhow, but they have proved to be, as indeed I expected, the same . . . minstrels with the old, dirty blues who have appeared on the beach at Margate so often before, and on this occasion had just got themselves up as a pirate band.[57]

The various amendments on the order paper proposed delays in decontrol from twelve months to five years. In addition, the 'Margate mutineers' tabled amendments to provide further security of tenure for the poorer tenants. The panoply of amendments tabled by the Opposition were mostly wrecking amendments, though some had the merit of proposing genuinely useful (though not always unbiased) technical changes.[58] The government backbench points were dealt with by Mr Brooke in a series of amendments.[59]

In the debate on clause 9, the major argument was about the provision of accommodation. The government argued that there was, or would be, sufficient accommodation to make a free market workable. Conservative backbenchers shared this view, even some of those backbenchers who had argued for a delay in transition.[60] The government further contended that the provision of the free market would mean substantial additions to the pool of houses to let.[61] The Opposition cited the length of council house lists, the failure of the government to make a convincing case on under-occupation, the admission by the Scottish Office that there remained an acute shortage of housing in Scotland.[62] Some London Tories joined in this attack. Mr Jenkins produced a case where it was rumoured that tenants would be thrown out to let the property to Americans.[63] The government was unsympathetic and determined.

The Horobin amendment on profiteering from decontrol was a particular effort to deal with the fears of shortages and the profits that might be made out of scarcity. This was carried because the entire Opposition, and Sir I. Horobin, Mr Jenkins, Mr Cooke (Conservative, Twickenham), and Dame Joan Vickers (Conservative, Plymouth), voted in favour, leaving the government four short of its usual majority. This did not occur again in the Bill's progress toward law. Indeed, government backbenchers were very careful that it should be the only occurrence. Sir Ian Horobin, at a later stage in the debate noted that 'we cannot get into the habit of voting against the minister' but hoped that the minister would consider a proposed amendment on Report.[64]

The amendment to the transition period was made in schedule 4. This offered the opportunity for a discussion on the use of county courts rather than tribunals and the taking by the minister of administrative powers. Even with the timetable adjusted, discussion was uninspired. Mr Jenkins contended that the government backbenchers had a right to file dissenting amendments and that this had played a part in the government's decisions. But he reminded his listeners that for them the government must have the last word on what was possible.[65]

The Opposition attempted to reverse the procedure for disrepair on the detailing schedule. But, as Mr Brooke pointed out, the dichotomy in this instance between government and Opposition was complete. The Opposition would not give the rent increase until the last possible moment; the government believed only an immediate increase would produce repairs.[66]

Of all the amendments listed in the first table, only twelve were accepted for consideration. None was accepted in the form in which it was submitted. None of the amendments accepted at committee stage involved matters of great principle. Indeed, there were really only a half-dozen topics covered by these amendments. With two exceptions, these amendments were Opposition amendments. The exceptions were one amendment moved by Mr Jenkins and one moved by Mr Page (Conservative, Crosby), with Mr Sparks.

The Opposition attack had not been noteworthy. The number of amendments filed and presented was not of itself impressive. The amendments represented an agglomeration of individual efforts. They did not represent any collective wisdom, and in consequence were less effective than they might have been. Attacks were often misdirected, as in the failure to present a forceful case on the problem of decontrol by vacant possession. Instead, the Opposition concentrated on the ancient prejudices of the party. Many amendments were in consequence merely destructive. But the Opposition seemed particularly hampered in its efforts to oppose the Bill and in the publicity it tried to extract from them[67] by the lack of consistency and disorganisation which characterised the Opposition efforts.

The case for the Opposition had almost as few proponents as the government's. The development of the shadow ministry system meant that only two or three men who were *ministeriable* took serious interest. But the most successful amendments came not from these leaders but from their followers, especially if success is measured by acceptability to the government.

Though many amendments were tabled, though much forceful debating was indulged in by all participants, remarkably little of concrete importance resulted. Neither side obtained much good publicity out of the proceedings. The Bill was not substantially altered. Nor indeed, could Parliament have been said to give the Bill

G

the sort of scrutiny ancient constitutional doctrine had suggested was possible. This can be seen from the amendments tabled, the general directions of debate, and their consequence, which have been outlined in this section. Nor was the Opposition attack effective. By choosing to concentrate on good propaganda issues, such as rent increases, the Labour members failed to criticise effectively such matters as the unworkable nature of the disrepair procedure and especially the provisions for decontrol on vacant possession which were to be most criticised in the future.

## Report Stage

Report stage had many advantages, for both government and Opposition – a chance to consider, scrutinise and amend. The government might extract maximum publicity for concessions, the Opposition might claim the public's attention for its protests. Moreover, Report was a more disciplined occasion than Standing Committee. On the floor the Whips could maintain order, and speeches be of decent length and appropriate to the occasion. But how significant was Report stage as an opportunity to scrutinise?

Only two segments of the Rent Act came in for serious attack on Report: the decontrol provisions, formerly clause 9 (now renumbered clause 10) and the statutory instrument provisions it contained, and the disrepair procedure as defined by schedule 1. But if the number of divisions was, in absolute terms, smaller, their significance was increased. Divisions under a guillotine on the floor was a serious matter so far as the participants were concerned, for each division reduced the time for thorough debate on merits. The time had to be justified by the propaganda value that might be obtained. Amendments were not tabled by the Opposition on Report with the same casual air as those in committee. Care was taken that there were no conflicting proposals, and that most of the amendments had general party approval. This was reflected in the high proportion of Opposition amendments on which a division was forced. Indeed, almost every amendment presented by the Opposition in debate was divided upon.

Table 16 shows the amendments tabled on Report, subdivided by origin.

TABLE 16

*Amendments in the Order Paper on Report (clause numbers are altered)*[68]

| Section | Government Number | Government Division | Backbench Number | Backbench Division | Opposition Number | Opposition Division |
|---|---|---|---|---|---|---|
| Clause 1 | 3 | accepted | 1 | — | 1 | 1 |
| ,, 2 | 1 | — | — | — | 2 | 1 |
| ,, 3 | nothing | — | — | — | — | — |
| ,, 4 | 2 | — | — | — | — | — |
| ,, 5 | — | — | 1 | — | — | — |
| ,, 6 | nothing | — | — | — | — | — |
| ,, 7 | — | — | 1 | — | 3 | 1 |
| ,, 8 | nothing | — | — | — | — | — |
| ,, 9 | — | — | — | — | 1 | — |
| ,, 10 | 2 | 1 | 5 | 1 withdrawal | 8 | 5 |
| ,, 11 | 3 | — | — | — | 1 | — |
| ,, 12 | 4 | — | 1 | — | — | — |
| ,, 13 | nothing | — | — | — | — | — |
| ,, 14 | — | — | — | — | 2 | — |
| ,, 15 | 2 | — | 3 | — | 1 | — |
| ,, 16–18 | nothing | — | — | — | — | — |
| ,, 19 | 6 | — | — | — | 3 | — |
| ,, 20 | nothing | — | — | — | — | — |
| ,, 21 | 2 | — | — | — | — | — |
| New clauses | 3 | accepted | 1 | 1 | 3 | — |
| Schedule 1 | 4 | 1 | 4 | — | 11 | 7 |
| ,, 3 | nothing | — | — | — | — | — |
| ,, 4 | 3 | — | 2 | 1 withdrawal | 2 | 1 |
| ,, 5 | 7 | accepted | — | — | 1 | — |
| ,, 6 | 2 | — | 2 | — | 3 | 1 |
| ,, 7 | 1 | — | — | — | — | — |
| ,, 8 | — | — | — | — | 1 | — |
| New schedules | — | — | — | — | 2 | — |

TABLE 17

*Movers and Seconders of Motions for Amendments on Report to be Debated*[69]

| Government | Government Backbench | | Opposition Frontbench | | Opposition Backbench | |
|---|---|---|---|---|---|---|
| Brooke 11m | Cordeaux | 1s | Mitchison | 3m, 2s | Blenkinsop | 1m, 1s |
| Bevins 2m | Hay | 1m | Lindgren | 1m | Evans | none |
| Maclay 1m | Page | 1s | MacColl | none | Janner | 1m, 2s |
| Browne 1m | R. Jenkins | 1s | | | J. Hynd | 1m |
| | Rees-Davies | 1m | | | Key | 1m |
| | Horobin | 1s | | | MacDermot | 1s |
| | Lagden | 1m | | | McInnes | 1m |
| | | | | | Silverman (J.) | 1m |
| m = moved; s = seconded | | | | | Sparkes | 2s |
| | | | | | Willis | 1s |

The Opposition divided against only two government amendments. A considerable number were accepted without division after an explanation. Most remained undiscussed and were merely put *en bloc* at the time specified in the guillotine. One of the two divisions was almost procedural, the excising of Sir Ian Horobin's amendment. The other was a technicality; the Opposition claimed that the local authorities were not given sufficient discretion to reject undertakings by the landlord on the disrepair procedure.

Of the government backbench amendments only one was of real importance: the Rees-Davies amendment in the form of a new clause to limit the rents which could be charged on decontrolled premises (See chapter 6 for a discussion of the debate on this issue). It was the only clause in which a noticeable number of government supporters abstained. The other amendment proposed by a government back-bencher was Mr Lagden's (Conservative, Hornchurch) attempt to have his own constituency, Hornchurch, just on the border of the Metropolitan Police District, included within the definition 'London' on the ground that the sort of property in Hornchurch was not dis-similar from that on the other side. He withdrew the amendment. This sort of amendment was not, strangely enough, used by the Opposition and they did not take steps to force a division. This would have seemed an ideal issue to win public support. Another government backbench amendment to prevent compensation being given for tenant's improvements when not actually made by the sitting tenant was moved, but later withdrawn, by Mr Hay and Mr Page.[70]

Mr Mitchison himself was largely responsible for moving Opposition amendments. This paralleled the tradition of the majority-party-as-the-government that parliamentary time should be taken for collective rather than individual efforts. The major opportunity for the government to make changes in a Bill occurs not in Standing Committee but on Report, especially in the case of the Rent Bill. The time lapse between the new minister's arrival and the debate of significant clauses of the Bill did not really allow for effective con-sideration in committee. The outline of the concessions to be made, where these were in response to general political demands, could be given in committee but the details had to await more mature con-sideration. The duration of the Standing Committee provided time to think. These concessions have been considered in chapter 6. A fair amount of time was taken up by explanations of government amendments and backbench and Opposition congratulations to the minister on them. Some, like Mr Ray, occasionally demurred in their approval.[71]

There were none of the flamboyant speeches on Report that had been delivered at second or would be delivered at third reading. The Report stage resembled committee plus the discipline of Commons' standing orders. Only briefly could backbenchers of either side display their metal or their concern at the changes made. Even frontbench speeches tended to be rather formal. The minister put the change as quickly as possible; at the end of the debate the leader on the clause for the Opposition put his acceptance or rejection. If the proposal came from the Opposition the order was reversed. The debates were largely a rehash of discussions that had already taken place in committee. But now, more often than not, the final form of amendments was being debated. At this stage Opposition amendments found favour only in principle: the chance to incorporate them was in the Lords. In most cases their purpose was propaganda, not enlightenment or reform.

## The House of Lords

The continued existence of the House of Lords has been rationalised by the failings of government and Commons. Errors, omissions, indiscretions can be put right. The standard works have suggested that the Lords has performed an important function in allowing the government a final opportunity to put into a Bill concessions made at the Report stage but which it had not then had a chance to incorporate, making necessary changes in the draft, and to move a step further in the direction of consensus. Standard authorities have further suggested that the principles of a Bill could be given yet another serious review.[72] If any of these claims have had validity in general, they were certainly not applicable to the Lords' consideration of the 1957 Rent Act.

The second reading speeches in the Lords added nothing to what had already been said. Indeed, none of the government spokesmen offered any new insight into the drafting of the Bill. None represented the Minister of Housing, the Earl of Munster was Minister-without-Portfolio, Viscount Kilmuir was Lord Chancellor. On the Labour side there was an equal paucity of talent – or perhaps lack of interest. None of the Labour peers had any real expertise on housing. They were there by the accident of birth or their old age. None had any recent local government experience which might have compensated for ignorance of the general problems, based on their ministerial specialisation. Labour's principal spokesman, Lord Silkin, was ill throughout the committee and Report stages. Thus the primary burden of attack was carried by persons who in fact had not even done the minimal amount of homework which the Lords have been known to do. Even Lord Silkin in his second reading speech had nothing to add.[73]

Debates on committee and Report in the Lords are stage-managed. Partly the process is constitutional, but only partly. Officially, the Lords indicate in advance their intention to speak and the Lord Chancellor or his staff, knowing perfectly well what will be said, try to strike a balance between opposing sides and parties. The unofficial organisation consisted in the planning of strategy by those peers favourable to the landlords' interest was prearranged. The peers met in advance with an official or officials of the NFPO to apportion the parts of the case which they would discuss. The only addition to this was the insistence of Lord Meston on pushing his own pet amendment on street repairs.[74]

The pressure applied to the Lords by tenants' groups was almost nonexistent. They had no representation other than the Labour peers. For whatever else might be said, peers have not been noted for their intimate knowledge of rents or the middle classes, much less the working class.

The customary drafting amendments were of no interest except to the extent that they revealed the failure of the Ministry to cope successfully with necessarily complex legislation. There were many such amendments, but only a few of significance; most were consequential.[75] The interesting amendments were those from the 'backbenchers', for these showed the sympathy of the House. Such amendments were moved by Lords Broughshane, Grantchester, Meston and Ridley. Lord Listowel's might be regarded as representing the Opposition frontbench.

Lord Broughshane suggested that the return on improvements made by the landlord be increased to 10 per cent.[76] He also wanted to make sure that the rise in rates during the transition period was passed on to the tenant. This was accepted.[77] Lord Grantchester proposed to give leases to those excluded from control.[78] As this would merely extend control, it was rejected.[79] Another Liberal, Lord

Meston, moved two amendments. One attempted to exclude houses declared unfit for habitation from protection in clearance areas.[80] The other attempted to withdraw the permission granted to local authorities to grant certificates of disrepair against landlords who gave promises to do repairs if these landlords had previously broken such promises.[81] Viscount Ridley, who had served as chairman of two departmental inquiries into rents, moved amendments to give local authorities some control over rents of properties which they subsidised.[82] He succeeded in persuading the government to consider on Report an amendment to forestall compensation to the tenant where the landlord at the time of the 1957 Rent Act did not agree to the improvements made by the tenant.[83] The last three peers were N F P O spokesmen. On Report Lord Meston moved his amendment: to pass street repairs on to the tenant in the same way as structural repairs. It was accepted.[84]

The Labour Party's efforts in the Lords was summed up by their comments in the Report to the 1957 Annual Conference, 'We tried'.[85]

They had absolutely no impact either on the outcome or on the public. They raised the same arguments used in the Commons without any more conviction. Lord Silkin, who led for the Opposition, concentrated on security of tenure. But he did make a point of attacking the affirmative resolution provisions.[86] On committee stage the leaders moved all the formal amendments, without reason or justification. They tried to amend clause 10 (formerly clause 9) to set the decontrol limits at £60 in London. They offered neither significant reasons nor evidence for this arbitrary figure.[87] Similar amendments were moved by Lords Lucan and Ogmore.[88] The procedure was repeated on Report.[89] Attempts to strike at the statutory instrument provision which allowed the minister to use further slice decontrol by affirmative resolution seemed to carry more fervour but no more success.[90] Lord Ogmore moved to facilitate the exchange of tenancies, which was to become a hotly contested issue in later stages.[91] But as the minister had already rejected similar proposals it was hard to see why the amendment was offered. No effort whatever was made to defend the party's municipalisation policy when it came under attack. Lord Ogmore announced the sections which would be challenged by division as though listing a set of mandatory prayers rather than sincere devotions.[92] Nothing could be more out of keeping with the state of the case than his assertion: 'After all, this House is not a rubber stamp – at least, it should not be – and it is for us to consider these matters, whether the government are in favour of them or not, on their merits.'[93]

One serious question was raised but not answered. This was the issue of regional as opposed to value decontrol, raised by backbench Tories as well as Labour. But there was no substantial debate.[94]

The confrontation in the Lords could hardly have been serious, given the dominance of Conservative peers. How could Labour peers be expected to show vigour when they were aware that on a normal division the total number of Tory peers above the rank of baron surpassed the total number of Labour peers?[95] The substance, if any, in a House of Lords consideration was not present on this Bill. A party measure was carried through by precisely the same techniques used in Commons. There was no special consideration and only superficial concern with 'the national interest'. Certainly there was none of the insight into the future of which the House of Lords has been said to have had a special supply.

In the preceding sections the scope and character of consideration that the Commons and the Lords gave to the Rent Bill was indicated. Though consideration in the Commons was of some aid in providing the public with information, there was no evidence at any stage of consideration, in either House, of the scrutiny and criticism any legislation requires. Consideration seemed haphazard and uncertain. Neither side seemed able to provide a basis for either effective scrutiny or publicity.

In the next sections attention is turned away from the Rent Bill in particular towards three niceties of parliamentary activity. The guillotine and petition are parliamentary devices used in the House of Commons. Their application to the particular circumstances of the Rent Bill is indicated. Finally, some attention is directed to the place of the Rent Act in the debate on delegated legislation.

## Guillotine

Allocation of Time (Guillotine) Resolutions have had a history of disrepute from their inception to their contemporary usage. Only outworn standing orders make the guillotine necessary. All guillotine resolutions indicate is that the majority (the government) will not permit obstruction in the inevitable process of legislation for an 'unreasonable' length of time. For this privilege, in the case of the Rent Bill, the government gave the Opposition one day's parliamentary time, and the whole house took a rest. As Mr Macmillan said:

> A debate such as we shall have today should be regarded as a genial interlude in a long series of dull discussions – rather like the playtime interlude at school. . . . There is a great deal to be said for sham battles. They are much more agreeable than real ones, and political battles in relation to real ones are something like Mr Jorrock's famous definition of hunting: 'The image of war – without the guilt and only five and twenty per cent of the danger'.[96]

But members, especially backbenchers, have taken such opportunities quite seriously,[97] although it has been extremely difficult for 'responsible' persons on either side to regard such debates other than sound and fury.

> The Rt Hon. and Hon. Members who find themselves for the moment in Opposition are filled with an extraordinary devotion to the principles of constitutional government, to the free right of Members, to the long historic struggle of Parliament against the executive, to the cause for which Hampden died in the field and Sidney on the scaffold. But upon the government benches, they become comparatively immune to these high flown sentiments. They are influenced by the urgent necessity which every government feels to carry through their parliamentary business. . . .[98]

For only indirectly might the subject of the Bill being guillotined be discussed. The focus of the debate has been the right of the government to insist on a speed-up of business.[99]

The guillotine procedure has often been unnecessary. Voluntary arrangements 'through the usual channels' have been common. But on a variety of issues, ranging from Town and Country Planning (1946), Iron and Steel (1948), Television (1954), and Housing (1954, 1957), the Opposition of the day has demanded a public conflict, and consequently had to accept a guillotine far less satisfactory than might have been negotiated.[100] Partly this reflected the desire of the Opposition to 'make a show' for future electoral purposes. But also, it reflected an emotional involvement with 'the Parliamentary Club' which turned form into substance. The forms of resistance became the main purpose.

Opposition, *à outrance*, was the standard explanation supplied by Labour leaders for resisting the guillotine on the Rent Bill. Yet in 1954 the Housing Repairs and Rents Act was also fought, though, in principle, Labour favoured the Bill. The difference seems to have been the state of the Labour Party in the country. In 1954 Labour

G*

had not a hope of winning a general election, which at best might be some time away. By contrast, in February 1957 when the guillotine was proposed, Labour was leading in the opinion polls; the Conservative government was shaken (it had only recently been reshuffled); electoral victory was a real possibility if the prediction of the polls were a true indication. A few more days in Standing Committee would, of course, not gain material alterations in the Bill. On the other hand, the publicity from a guillotine debate might well hasten the day on which the Bill could be repealed. Public duty and political advantage coincided.

For the government, unable to alter parliamentary procedures, the guillotine offered a considerable advantage. While 'to the Opposition side of the House time means nothing',[101] to governments it is an imperative. Commanding reasons in the national interest might suggest immediate implementation of legislation. This was the government's case in 1957.[102] As Mr Sandys' former PPS (Sir H. D'Avigdor-Goldsmid) pointed out, the Opposition had, by the time the guillotine resolution was used, taken one hundred and forty-five and one-half columns as against a total of twenty-six and one-half for the government in Standing Committee Hansard.[103] Mr Mitchison attacked this charge as groundless but there could be no doubt that the Labour working party were prepared to talk the Bill to death if they could.[104]

The guillotine offered no guarantee of better legislation. Mr Chuter Ede argued that in present circumstances Parliament could not afford the habits of leisurely consideration possible in the past.

My experience of the House has been that under no government of modern times has legislation been too swift. The danger to Parliamentary democracy in this country is not from the speed but from the slowness of the forms that were used when this country was less populous than it is, and when the range of government activities was far less than it is today.[105]

And there were cogent objections to the guillotine imposed at an intermediate stage. One consequence could be that earlier clauses got overcomplete attention while later clauses got little or none.

But whether the government's timetable now allows sufficient time for the rest of the Bill to be scrutinised is more debatable. . . . But the moral seems to be that the government's best course would have been to introduce a timetable right from the start, as the Labour government did. . . . Delay in applying one merely means . . . that the first few clauses are discussed at inordinate length and the remainder tend to be skimped.[106]

The Labour Party in the 1957 debate sought to evolve a constitutional principle: that matters which involve a large number of people as individuals ought to be exempt from guillotine.[107] Though this argument might be 'serious' in a parliamentary sense, its primary purpose was technical. Under the cover of this 'constitutional question', a whole series of questions related to the substance of the Rent Bill itself could be raised. This was the whole point of contesting the guillotine. Having found some constitutional pole from which to hang a flag, the Opposition usually used the day's proceedings as an opportunity to further harangue the public on the sins of the wicked government. This tended to be repetitious and lacked new content, a characteristic more noticeable in 1957 than previously.[108]

The only significant point raised during the guillotine was that the clauses relating to Scotland should be referred to the Scottish Grand Committee. This would give the Scots a chance to scrutinise clauses relating exclusively to them and also to give the English more time to evaluate the clauses which concerned England. Although proposed by Mr Fraser (Labour, Hamilton) at various stages along the way, Mr McLay, acting for the government, had consistently rejected this procedure.[109] He contended that the clauses involving Scotland were inextricably bound up with other clauses which affected Britain as a whole.

Labour's case – that matters affecting the British as individuals ought to be debated completely – was strengthened by the supply of quotes from Tory ministers during their spell on the Opposition benches.[110] But the Labour case was not rational. It presupposed that Commons debates got sufficient publicity to properly inform the public of the details of new legislation. On the contrary, scornful treatment by the press of the day's proceedings probably gave mare favourable publicity to the government than the Opposition. As on Opposition device the guillotine debate had failed in its purpose.

## Petitioning, Questions and Early Day Motions

### *Petitions*

Petitioning, Jennings has said 'is of no use whatever'.[111] The description of the petitioning process given by Sir A. P. Herbert struck the right note:

It must be written (not printed or typed). It must be free of 'interlineations or erasures'. Every signature must be followed by an address,

It must conclude with a 'prayer' and the prayer must be repeated at the head of each sheet. The petition must be respectful, decorous, and temperate in language. Our language passed the officials' kindly scrutiny.... Our script was beautifully done: but some small error had been found in a date ... and if this was corrected the whole thing might have to be done again. (I forget how we got over that—either we were let off or we left the error in.)

When you present your petition you can either make a brief speech of explanation or, 'if required', the Speaker can instruct the Clerk to read the petition to the House. One point is that it is then printed in *Hansard*, but, as this business takes place in Question Time, you gain no great applause from the Speaker, or anyone else. But there were my 'Three Musketeers' goggling from the gallery, and I thought, having come so far they deserved it. The Speaker said: 'I know that it is a short one; but not only that I realise that there is some importance attached to it....

How proud, how thrilled, they were, to set their names to the historic scroll in the panelled room off Westminster Hall, to hear the words of Mr Speaker, and to see me carrying their petition to the Table. I was proud too. It showed once more what strength and soundness there is in some of the ancient customs we take for granted, or disregard, or even belittle.... It should, I think, have had a powerful effect. But as I dropped the petition into the bag behind the Speaker's chair, I was sadly aware that very few would be likely to think of it again. Still, it had advertised their presence and their plea, and there it is for history to read, in *Hansard*.[112]

Advertisement was the purpose of Labour's petition campaign. The purpose of obtaining signatures was not necessarily to present the petitions, or to influence the course of legislation. The P L P started the process too late and attempted too little for that. Initially, they sought to gain publicity for the extensive silent opposition to the Bill. In addition, it was hoped to alert a large number of people that a Bill 'harmful' to their interests was being put through Parliament by the government. The supposed advantage of making people aware of their rights under the Bill proved negligible.

The standard conclusion for these petitions was:

Wherefore your petitioners pray that the Bill be so amended that tenants shall not be evicted from their homes unless equivalent alternative accommodation is provided; that rents shall not be increased unless dwellings are in good habitable repair with reasonable amenities; and that in default of these amendments the Bill shall be rejected.[113]

The first presenter of the day, and sometimes others as well, made a short speech denouncing the Rent Bill and recalling the difficulties their own constituents would face were it to become law. They all demanded that their petitions be read.

Table 18 should give a fair profile of the petitions presented:

TABLE 18

*Petitions Presented to the House of Commons*[115]

| MP | Constituency (or area of petition) | No. of Signatures | Date | Vol. | Citation Column |
|---|---|---|---|---|---|
| Collins | Shoreditch | 16,000 | 7 March | 566 | 505–6 |
| Hastings | Barking | 6,000 | 19 March | 567 | 181 |
| Craddock | York | 21,000 | 27 March | — | 1119 |
| W. Edwards | Surrey (Federated Trades Council) | not stated | 9 April | 568 | 935–7 |
| Gibson | Clapham | 55,000 | 9 April | — | 935–7 |
| Corbet | Camberwell | not stated | — | — | — |
| Lipman | Brixton | 2,000 | — | — | — |
| Stewart | Fulham | not stated | 10 April | — | 1101–3 |
| Parkin | Feltham | — | — | — | — |
| Mellish | Bermondsey | 3,600 | 11 April | — | 1269–70 |
| Isaacs | Southwark | not stated | — | — | — |
| Albu | Edmonton | — | — | — | — |
| W. Edwards | Stepney | 8,000 | 15 April | — | 1521 |
| D. Jay | Battersea | 1,000 | — | — | — |
| Weitzman | Stoke Newington and Hackney | not stated | — | — | — |
| Mrs J. Butler | Wood Green | 3,000 | 17 April | — | 1892–3 |
| Mrs L. Jeger | St. Pancras | 700 | — | — | — |
| Sir L. Plummer | Deptford | 2,000 | 18 April | — | 2071 |
| Key | Poplar | not stated | 1 May | 569 | 171 |
| Hewitson | Hull | — | 7 May | — | 769 |
| A. Evans | Angel | 2,400 | 16 May | 570 | 543 |
| Dugdale | Brentford and Chiswick | 6,000 | 21 May | — | 1105 |
| Hayman | Exeter (own member refuses) | 1,171 | 4 June | 571 | 1048 |
| Orbach | Hampstead (Brooke's) Willesden | not stated | 5 June | — | 1223–4 |
| Lewis | Luton (Dr Hill's) | not stated | — | — | — |

Why the petition was chosen as a method has remained an enigma. The petitions came in far too late to be of any real value in parliamentary terms. If they received sufficient attention they might be of some value in local elections. But they did not seem to attract very much notice. Not since the Finance Bill of 1909 had petitions been presented, as these were after a Bill had completed its third reading. Two Tory backbenchers, Major Legge-Bourke and Mr Agnew protested at this Labour practice, but the Speaker held it to be quite proper.[114] Nor was it possible to understand why the particular petitions were chosen. Some were sent to the minister and hence buried in oblivion. Others were presented to the House. But surely there ought to have been some petitions from the provincial urban areas and rather more impressive petitions from London?

## Questions

Only two parliamentary questions of any merit were asked during the debate. One, by Mr Eric Fletcher, pointed to the Islington Borough Council resolution of 21 December 1956. In his view the minister's reply was most unsatisfactory. Despite a supplementary by Mr Mitchison, he got no further satisfaction.[116] At the end of April, just before the Lords' amendments were considered, Mrs Butler asked a question with supplementaries as to whether consultation on the state of the facilities for homeless families which would be needed when the Bill became law had begun. The minister, naturally, denied that such consultations would be necessary or that homelessness would be a problem.[117]

## Early Day Motions

There were no Early Day Motions while the Bill was going through Parliament. Why this particularly attractive procedure was not used has remained obscure; no one has supplied a reasonable explanation. Professor S. E. Finer, whose book covered the 1955 Parliament never explained why, out of three hundred and eighty-eight motions, none dealt with the Rent Bill. A possible explanation lay in the nature of the E D M: the E D M was intended to express backbench sympathy. They were not during the 1955 Parliament, as they became in later Parliaments, a general technique used to gain press notices. Since there was no division among Labour MPs, no E D M s arose from the Labour backbench. Conservative backbenchers did not use E D Ms because they would generate more publicity than was desirable for the party image.[118]

None of these techniques proved effective. The petition was buried, whether sent to the minister or the Commons. The questioner was stymied by the stolid fashion in which Mr Brooke and Mr Bevins answered. The E D M was never attempted. It would appear that the most successful approaches were also the most silent: the private contact with the minister or his staff.

## Delegated Legislation

The subject of delegated legislation, that is, the granting to the government of the right to make further legislation by Order-in-Council or other statutory instruments, is close to the heart of parliamentarians. The subject led through nice questions of procedure and philosophy. Like the 'shall-may' debate, a discussion of statutory instruments and delegated legislation gave members a chance to rehash a familiar question in a new setting.

By 1957 parliamentary scrutiny was not as important as it had been. Even Dicey, not normally an advocate of any challenge to parliamentary consideration, was enthusiastic about the advantages of delegated legislation.[119] Since the first world war the panoply of emergency regulations has made statutory instruments common. In 1906 there were only 165 general purpose statutory instruments clauses. By 1946 1,219 had been enacted in a single year.[120] Statutory instruments were the result of delegation of legislative power to the government. By Order-in-Council, or by instruments to be laid on the table of one or both Houses, for affirmation or not, the government was to be able to vary law or make new law in particular circumstances. Even before the mass of peacetime delegation of power, scholars noted that the expanding concerns of government made the extensive use of statutory instruments essential.[121] Ever since Chadwickian principles of local government administration had been abandoned there had been extensive local use of delegated power. But neither the Donoughmore Committee of 1929 nor the Select Committee of 1953 had put to rest parliamentary concern.[122]

In the Rent Act, clause 10(3) was of some concern. This resembled a 'Henry VIII Clause' (of this name Jennings has said: 'it has about as much relation to . . . the Statute of Proclamation as a Dogs Act has to Magna Carta'), which gave ministers the right to modify Acts of Parliament.[123] The minister was given the right to vary the limits of decontrol by affirmative resolution. The Donoughmore Committee had advised against this form of power.[124] Less than ten years later the first Ridley Committee on rent restriction recommended that precisely this form be used. At the time, it was hoped to decontrol on a regional basis.[125] This procedure was not, by the middle 1950s, regarded as unusual, though it was still the subject for debate.[126]

The Opposition attack on this section was divided into two parts. Mr Lindgren presented a case which illustrated the consequences of the reductions of the limits which the minister was expected to make. Assuming that the tenants could decipher the provisions, it would still be impossible for them to know when, or whether, they were subject to decontrol. Mr Bevins tried to be reassuring without committing the government indefinitely: the government had no intention of using its powers in the immediate future.[127] In the end, Mr Brooke explained (on third reading) that the government would under no circumstances bring in an affirmative resolution within the next twelve months following enactment.[128]

The other part of the Labour case was based on the Donoughmore Report. Mr Niall MacDermot, a new MP who had just won a formerly Conservative seat in a by-election at North Lewisham, presented the Labour view that none of the reasons normally ascribed for using delegated powers were applicable in the case of the Rent Bill.[129] It meant that the minister could make a major revision in the Bill without further parliamentary consideration as to the need or desirability for the change being made.[130]

Mr Geoffrey Rippon, a senior Conservative backbencher, was perhaps the most sensible. He reasoned that the form which the delegation took in this instance an affirmative resolution, was the most conservative and least offensive to parliamentary sovereignty.[131] The emergency war and postwar measures had supplied ample precedents for this procedure.[132] Although not originally so intended, this procedure, Mr Rippon insisted, offered the advantage of being able to deal with the problem on a regional basis.[133] Mr Mitchison's view that the affirmative resolution might not always serve as a sufficient guarantee might well be true, but it did not answer the question as to how sufficient flexibility for action would be provided.[134]

The debate continued throughout all the stages in the legislative process. But only on Report was the debate in focus. Concern was general among the members of all parties. But Tories were right when they complained that Labour put the case more strongly than seemed justified by the circumstances.[135]

Both Sir C. K. Allen's *Laws and Orders*, the second edition of which appeared in 1956, and Jennings' *Parliament*, which appeared the next year, maintained that delegated legislation of the sort used in the 1957 Rent Act was legitimate. Certainly Allen's chapters on delegation must have encouraged draftsmen and lawyers in its formulation.[136] The 1953 Report of the Select Committee on Delegated Legislation also encouraged the contemporary practice.[137] The fact that a Labour government passed the enabling statutes which defined statutory orders of the sort used in the Bill ought to have discouraged Labour Opposition.[138]

But Mr Rippon extended the meaning of the constitution too far by his implicit contention that an affirmative order could be reversed. The whole value of such orders, as Kersell made clear, was not to give Parliament a chance to veto but rather to give Parliament a chance to say what it would like to see done.[139] Why was the promised delay in the use of delegated power so long in coming? Certainly the delay was in direct contradiction to the principle set forth in the Donoughmore Report as to the manner in which such clauses ought to operate. To the Opposition the affirmative resolution provision was a positive gain. For approval the government had to find parliamentary time, whereas under any other form it was the Opposition who had to make time.[140]

Because the statutory instruments provision was only one of many controversial provisions, only limited contribution was made to the debate on the philosophy of the matter. Whatever the gains to the study of politics, greater were the gains to the politician who had a chance to display their skill on an old favourite for debate.

## Summary

The parliamentary stages of the legislative process on the Rent Act moved slowly to an end. Neither in the debates on the Bill itself, nor in the special devices and forms of consideration common to such legislation, did Parliament show itself particularly adept at publicity or scrutiny. The legislators showed themselves unable to come to grips with the essential problems posed by the Rent Act. In part, this reflected the diametrically opposite views taken by the two parties. In part, Parliament was caught up in the continual struggle for power between government and Opposition. In this, publicity, not scrutiny, was the main theme. This was abundantly clear from the use made by the Opposition of the amending process both in Standing Committe and on Report. But even these activities were not noticeably successful. Neither the guillotine debate nor the petitions produced anything like the publicity that might have been expected; certainly, no political rewards emerged. In this setting, the real conflicts, the real attempts at policy formulation could take place only within the parties themselves, Whether this, in fact, occurred can be seen from the studies of the two principal parties which follow.

NOTES

1 Sir W. Ivor Jennings, *Cabinet Government*, Cambridge University Press, Cambridge, 1961, p. 510.
2 1956–7 H C S C Deb.,I, cols 837–8.
3 567 H C Deb.5s., col. 1435.
4 1956–7 H C S C Deb.,I, col. 163.
5 *Ibid.*, cols 54–5.
6 567 H C Deb.5s., col. 1432.
7 *Ibid.*, col. 980.
8 See chapter 7.
9 560 H C Deb.5s., cols 1762–3.
10 *Ibid.*, col. 1787.
11 *Ibid.*, col. 1804.
12 *Ibid.*, cols 1799–1800.
13 *Ibid.*, col. 1861.
14 *Ibid.*, col. 2004.
15 *Ibid.*, cols 1987–96.
16 *Ibid.*, cols 1959–61.
17 *Ibid.*, col. 2043.
18 *Ibid.*, col. 2054.
19 *Ibid.*, cols 2009, 2059.
20 *Ibid.*, col. 2059.
21 *Ibid.*, col. 2053.
22 567 H C Deb.5s., col. 1363.
23 *Ibid.*, cols 1402, 1412.
24 *Ibid.*, col. 1383.
25 *Ibid.*, cols 1470 ff.
26 B. Crick, *Reform of Parliament*, London, 1964, pp. 82 ff.
27 *Minutes of Standing Committee A.*, 1956–7.
28 *Ibid.*, drawn by the author.
29 1956–7 HCSC,I, col. 7.
30 *Ibid.*, col. 194.
31 *Ibid.*, col. 202. Both Mr Hay and Sir E. Errington got themselves added, as did Mr R. Jenkins. Sir Ian was assigned to the committee for the entire session.

32 *Ibid.*, col. 4.
33 *Ibid.*, cols 5, 192.
34 *Ibid.*, cols 5–6.
35 *Ibid.*, col. 272.
36 *Ibid.*, cols 33 ff.
37 *Ibid.*, cols 77 ff.
38 *Ibid.*, cols 146 ff.
39 *Ibid.*, col. 111.
40 *Ibid.*, cols 339–40.
41 *The Economist*, vol. 170, p. 793.
42 1956–7 H C S C Deb.,I, cols 307 ff.
43 *Ibid.*, col. 500.
44 *Ibid.*, cols 314–5.
45 *Ibid.*, col. 448.
46 *Ibid.*, cols 450 ff.
47 *Ibid.*, col. 553.
48 *Ibid.*, cols 566 ff.
49 *Ibid.*, col. 570.
50 *Ibid.*, col. 584.
51 *Ibid.*, cols 660, 593, among others.
52 *Ibid.*, col. 593.
53 *Ibid.*, cols 762, 584.
54 *Ibid.*, cols 630, 555, 609, 631–2.
55 *Ibid.*, cols 711, 765.
56 *Ibid.*, col. 791.
57 *Ibid.*, col. 776 (Mr Mitchison).
58 I.e. Sparks-Page amendment, *Ibid.*, cols 901, 895.
59 Discussed in chapter 6.
60 1956–7 H C S C Deb.,I, cols 793, 948, 834.
61 *Ibid.*, cols 910, 793.
62 *Ibid.*, cols 810, 794, 907–8, 973.
63 *Ibid.*, col. 815.
64 *Ibid.*, col. 1056.
65 *Ibid.*, cols 981, 977.
66 *Ibid.*, cols 1225–6.
67 See chapter 7.
68 567 H C Deb.5s. Drawn by the author.
69 Drawn by the author.
70 567 H C Deb.5s., cols 1266 ff.
71 *Ibid.*, col. 975.
72 Jennings, *Parliament*, Cambridge University Press, Cambridge, 1961, pp. 398 ff.
73 203 H L Deb.5s., cols 14–22.
74 *Property*, May 1956, p. 14.
75 203 H L Deb.5s., col. 1053.
76 *Ibid.*, col. 737.
77 *Ibid.*, col. 761.
78 *Ibid.*, col. 713.
79 *Ibid.*, col. 715.

80 *Ibid.*, col. 656.
81 *Ibid.*, col. 750.
82 *Ibid.*, col. 733.
83 *Ibid.*, col. 764.
84 *Ibid.*, cols 1034–5.
85 Labour Party *Report on the Fifty-Seventh Annual Conference*, Labour Party, London, 1957, p. 68.
86 203 H L Deb.5s., col. 22.
87 *Ibid.*, col. 672.
88 *Ibid.*, cols 683, 697.
89 *Ibid.*, col. 1015.
90 *Ibid.*, col. 709.
91 *Ibid.*, col. 725.
92 *Ibid.*, col. 1014.
93 204 H L Deb.5s., col. 725.
94 203 H L Deb.5s., cols 37, 683, 707.
95 *Ibid.*, col. 654.
96 524 H C Deb.5s., col. 43.
97 A. P. Herbert, *Independent Member*, Methuen, London, 1950, pp. 379–80.
98 524 H C Deb.5s., col. 42 (Mr Macmillan).
99 *Ibid.*, col. 44.
100 1956–7, H C S C,I, cols 159–60.
101 524 H C Deb.5s., col. 43.
102 564 H C Deb.5s., cols 43–4.
103 *Ibid.*, col. 74.
104 *Ibid.*, col. 55.
105 434 H C Deb.5s., col. 125.
106 *The Economist*, vol. 170, pp. 596–7.
107 564 H C Deb.5s., col. 48.
108 *The Manchester Guardian*, 5 November 1957.
109 564 H C Deb.5s., cols 81–5.
110 *Ibid.*, col. 55.
111 Jennings, *Parliament*, p. 28.
112 Herbert, *Independent Member*, p. 419.
113 567 H C Deb.5s., col. 1119.
114 568 H C Deb.5s., cols 935–7.
115 Citations attached, see table, column 3.
116 563 H C Deb.5s., cols 9–10.
117 569 H C Deb.5s., cols 15–16.
118 S. E. Finer *et al*, *Backbench Opinion in the House of Commons*, Pergamon, London, 1962, pp. 8 ff.
119 A. V. Dicey, *Introduction to the Study of the Law of the Constitution*, St. Martin's Press, New York, 1961, p. 52.
120 S. D. Bailey, *British Parliamentary Democracy*, Harrap, London, 1962, p. 213.
121 Paul de Visscher, *Democratie Anglaise . . .*, Casterman, Paris, pp. 190 ff.
122 Chih-Mai Chen, *Parliamentary Opinion of Delegated Legislation*, Columbia University Press, New York, 1933, and de Visscher, *Democratie Anglaise*, pp. 248 ff.

123 Jennings, *Parliament*, p. 500.
124 Cmnd 4060, p. 66.
125 567 HCDeb.5s., col. 1192.
126 Jennings, *Parliament*, p. 516.
127 1956–7, HCSCDeb.,1, cols 1195–6.
128 567 HCDeb.5s., col. 1476.
129 *Ibid.*, cols 1177–8
130 *Ibid.*, col. 1101.
131 *Ibid.*, col. 1184.
132 *Ibid.*, cols 1184–5.
133 *Ibid.*, col. 1186.
134 1956–7, HCSCDeb.,I, col. 959.
135 560 HCDeb.5s., col. 1791; 567 HCDeb.5s., cols 1376, 1415.
136 Jennings, *Parliament*; C. K. Allen, *Law and Orders*, Stevens, London, 1956, p. 198.
137 Para. 65.
138 Statutory Orders Act (1946).
139 J. E. Kersell, *Parliamentary Supervision of Delegated Legislation*, Stevens, London, 1960.
140 Allen, *Law and Orders*, pp. 143 ff.

# 10
# Party Politics: The Conservatives

The ministers, the cabinet, and Conservative MPs were not merely the government and its supporters, they were also a part of a mass party. To what exent was the Rent Act a product of party as well as governmental decision-making? How well could the party deal with research problems? What was the role of the central organs of the party and the central office? What was the role of Conference and the local associations? How did this affect the activities of the MPs as Conservatives? What impact did this activity have? To what extent were the ministers playing party as well as governmental roles? The answers will help to measure the role of the party decision-making process in the legislative process.

Information was a necessary prerequisite for decision-making. It was of considerable advantage to the Conservative Party to have an organisation capable of doing the research upon which decisions might be based and justified. The principal parts of this research organisation were the Conservative Research Department, which is under the direct authority of the leader of the party, the Central Office machinery, and the Bow Group, a quasi-independent body.

The Conservative Research Department was set up under the direction of Mr R. A. Butler in the years of postwar Opposition to provide facts and notes of day to day interest as well as to staff-parliamentary committees and undertake long-term research to assist in the formulation of party policy.[1] Even after 1951, with the entry of many of CRD's brightest members into Parliament, the department was an important source of research and policy suggestions, if somewhat overshadowed by the Ministries. The department was particularly lucky in housing and rent control. The official in charge of these topics, Mr G. D. M. Block was a recognised expert. Though his party writing style often recalled the manner of the Primrose League, he could have given good advice. In fact, he was not consulted during the formulation or amendment of the Bill. His role was purely to advise the National Union and MPs. Though he disapproved at the time of decontrol on vacant possession, he thought in general that something needed to be done.[2]

In 1955 C R D produced a mimeographed circular on the problems of rent control in their historical perspective. The significant items included were a statement on the failure of decontrol by vacant possession and comments on the Morley Commission. The Report commented favourably, however, on the consequences arising from the 1938 Act where a form of slice decontrol was used.[3] Shortly after the Rent Bill was published, Mr Block produced another mimeographed statement upon it.[4] This was followed by a statement on the decontrol provisions.[5]

The general tenor of the statement explaining the Rent Bill was unquestionably conservative. The principal issue was cast as freedom v. control. Decontrol would not mean, automatically, increases in rent but might ultimately mean reduced rents.[6] This was reasserted in the special handout on decontrol.[7] To establish a relationship between rents and personal income was inappropriate, according to the general statement on the Bill. In 1946 rents had taken 7·65 per cent of income. By 1955 they still accounted for only 6·55 per cent.[8] During the same period salaries rose by 106 per cent, wages by 104 per cent, but rents by only 42 per cent. Shortage of repair funds was evident and dangerous. Restoration had been postponed needlessly.[9] The Act was now possible because Mr Macmillan's effort had reduced the shortage of housing and Mr Sandys had made a start at slum clearance.[10] The Rent Bill, Mr Block wrote, should have considerable impact. Nearly half the total housing in the United Kingdom, according to Mr Block's figures, was privately rented: 5·7 million in England and Wales, 6·5 million in Britain as a whole. Of these 5 million and 5·7 million respectively were controlled.

The main vehicle for C R D publicity was *Notes on Current Politics*. In one issue, written by Mr Block,[11] a very good presentation of the Bill which answered the principal objections was presented, along with a careful analysis of the reasons for the Bill.[12] Continued coverage of the Bill, however desirable, was precluded by the limits placed on publications.

By 1961 the C R D view had become less enamoured of the free market and it made a clear admission that the decontrol policy could not work. Whether this was in fact a reversal of past opinion or the publication of views withheld at the time, must remain of course conjectural.[13]

The other major part of the 'think factory' within the party was the Bow Group. This was semi-independent, in the sense that it was composed of individual M Ps and had no direct connection to the party or the leadership. But its connections were none the less intimate because of its identity of interest with the party, however independent it appeared. In August 1956, two members of the Bow Group, Mr Geoffrey Howe and Mr Colin Jones, published *Houses to Let* under the group's imprimatur. They concluded that '. . . It is difficult to see what general hardship or harm could arise from the operation of the free market in rents – once present rentals had been restored to market levels'. They recognised that hardship might ensue, but this could be dealt with on a welfare basis.[14] The system up to 1956 was rejected for two reasons. It did not make repairs possible while disrepair procedures deterred applications for increases,[15] and the system of control stabilised rents below the market level, a subsidy from land-lord to tenant, and created distortions in the housing market, especially as between council and private tenants. Private enterprise was discouraged.[16] Howe and Jones contended that a rise in rents of between 190 and 285 per cent was necessary,[17] that a start towards fixing rents at something approximating a 'reasonable rent' was long overdue, and urged the use of rateable value.[18] They proposed to continue security of tenure and to extend rights of possession.[19]

Some fundamental objections were raised to the proposals in the pamphlet. The *Estates Gazette*, the trade newspaper, pointed out that the calculations were highly conjectural, due to a lack of proper statistical information. It argued that while the overall situation had improved, local shortages were still acute. They contended that only the middle classes would be 'penalised' by the proposal of Mr Howe and Mr Jones.[20] But Mr Howe persisted with one of the principal Tory themes, the excessive subsidisation of the tenant, in an article for *Estates Gazette* in October 1956. Not only did Mr Howe argue that there was considerable wastage of accommodation but also that landlords were subsidising tenants to the extent of £160 million, as compared with £120 million by local authorities for council houses.[21] By January 1957, faced with the reality of the government's Bill, Mr Howe modified his position somewhat in a letter to *The Times*. De-control leading to a free market, he now decided, was possible only if there were sufficient supply. He suggested that while only twelve months' notice to quit should be given on transition, with an additional six months for any rent increase, sitting tenants should not pay rent in advance or a premium for a first lease. For the long run, he urged that six weeks' notice become standard.[22]

There was some effort by the Central Office to influence activity on the Rent Act both before and during the legislative process. Central Office certainly had a definite view on the matter. This was reflected in the 1959 Campaign Guide which argued that there were only two reasons for decontrol: to assure that houses were let at an economic rent, and to relieve the housing shortage by 'progressively recreating a free market in unfurnished lettings and so bringing about a more economic use of accommodation'.[23] During the early stages of the debate, Central Office produced a single pamphlet, 'The Rent Bill – what it means to you'.[24] It made good use of cases, within a handsome format, but was not otherwise significant. Central Office was also responsible for 'Twenty Questions on the Rent Bill', which appeared in several party and pressure goup publications, including the *Londoner*.[25] Yet its views on the advantages of the free market were never made clear. In the 1957 model election addresses it had taken a very cautious view:

Now the government has had the courage to tackle the injustices of the Rent Acts. It is wrong that many house rents are lower than rents of weekly instalments on TV sets, and that landlords should be forced to subsidise tenants indiscriminately. It is wrong that old houses should be allowed to decay for want of money to keep them repaired. It is wrong that many dwellings should be half used or empty because of unfair rents. The right policy now that acute housing shortage has been relieved is progressively to remove houses from the Rent Acts as the housing situation improves.

The Rent Bill, therefore, will decontrol the higher valued dwellings, just as was done in 1933 and 1938, subject to real and full safeguards to tenants in the transition period. Decontrol will mean less waste and underoccupation and therefore more accommodation for all. Six out of seven tenants will, however, remain controlled, with new rent limits that reflect present day repair costs.[26]

This was far different from the line it was subsequently to take and the line known to have been popular with Conference, and indeed some party officials themselves.

The party's most important organ for publicity was *The Spectator*, despite the vague and informal nature of the party's control. It gave remarkably little coverage to the 1957 Rent Act debates. A single leader admitted that the 1954 Act was too timid, but complained that the government in the 1957 Bill was going too far. *The Spectator* contended that 'no government can afford to base its legislation on sound theoretical premises alone'.[27] The political commentary columns of Mr Charles Curran noted with admiration the success of Mr Sandys' political strategy.[28] But Mr Curran was obviously not very well informed on decision-making in the government. In an earlier article his ignorance of the government's policy was all too evident.[29]

By comparison with the efforts now devoted to party policy and publicity, and propaganda associated with general elections, the efforts of the research and publicity sides of the 1957 Rent Act debate seemed small. But in the context of their time and occasion they were significant. The reports of the CRD represented the opinions of a party official with considerable expertise. Those of the Bow Group, if more amateur in origin, were sincere efforts to base viewpoints on research. The publicity given to the Bill by Central Office, though it deliberately emphasised non-policy aspects of the legislation, was of a reasonable standard and was widely disseminated. But certainly neither the Bow Group nor the *Spectator*, which might have been expected to stimulate debate in the constituencies, prior to discussion of the legislation, did very much. Nor did the official party organs, the CRD or Central Office, provide wide dissemination for such internal discussion of policy as was taking place.

Both Professors Beer and McKenzie have discounted the importance of the Conservative Annual Conference as a forum for policy discussion, much less for influence.[30] Yet its policy formulations have on rare occasions, such as in the Housing Debate of 1951, proved a vital factor in government policy. This was not possible on rent control. The conference meets for a short period each year during which time it has to consider a wide variety of topics. Despite the system whereby a single resolution is discussed, rather than the composite system used by Labour, rent control as an aspect of the housing problem could seldom get more than passing attention. These debates did not direct policy. They certainly gave the party officials and the government a forum in which to take the pulse of constituency opinion and thus give shape to the outlines of policy.

In 1953 the conference received a total of thirty-three resolutions on housing. All but one of them came from constituencies within the Greater London Conurbation. Many could not be debated. Among those not considered were nine resolutions on housing subsidies.[31] Assorted other resolutions urged a declaration of faith in 'property owning democracy'[32] and suggested various arrangements for the sale of council houses or the provision of housing for the aged. In this year the resolution chosen for debate was by Graham Page from North Islington. It congratulated the government on the achievement of three hundred thousand houses per annum but urged that attention now be focused on repairs.[33] This year there were a total of fourteen resolutions which called for some change in the system of rent control. Mr Angus Maude, representing Ealing South, urged the 'amendment of parts of the Rent Restriction Acts which have led to deterioration of so many properties'.[34] Comparable positions were taken by Mr R. Bulbrook of North Kensington, Mr R. Hinton of Watford, Mr F. W. Askew of South-West Hertfordshire, and Mr Bromfield of Harrow East.[35] The University of London resolution attacked the Rent Acts most strongly. It:

> deplores the monstrous injustice of the Rent Restriction Acts which, in effect, heavily subsidise one section of the community at the expense of another and inflict much hardship upon property owners, particularly elderly people with small incomes. For this reason and also because the Acts are responsible for rendering much property uninhabitable through inability of owners to carry out essential repairs. . . .[36]

In 1954 although almost all of the resolutions on housing were concerned with the subsidies question, these were not debated. From among the relatively small total of housing resolutions a resolution by Mr G. F. Walker of Newcastle East, urging that greater emphasis be placed on home ownership, was selected. There were no resolutions on rent control and very few from the Greater London area.[37]

In 1955 Ipswich, Enfield, Romford, North-East Kent, Southall and North Paddington sent resolutions to the conference urging that councils be required to charge an economic rent.[38] The resolution debated was P. M. Bromhead's attacking council house subsidies.[39] There were several resolutions urging increased speed in slum clearance but only two resolutions which sought changes in the Rent Restriction Acts.[40]

Of the fifteen resolutions on housing at the 1956 conference, six called for the amendment of the Rent Restriction Acts. Reminiscent of the 1953 conference was the resolution chosen for debate, Mrs Hoare's (of the London Conservative Union):

> That this conference notes with approval the elimination of obsolete property that is taking place under the slum clearance drive, but observes

with regret that a substantial portion of the nation's stock of houses is exposed to deterioration, owing to the operation of the Rent Restriction Acts, and calls upon the government to bring a just and urgent remedy to this aspect of the housing problem.[41]

Others, such as Mr Chapman Walker's, urged that distortions of the Acts be eliminated,[42] Mr L. M. Thomas from Canterbury urged decontrol on vacant possession.[43] The remaining resolutions on rent control, from Hampstead, Southall, Chichester, North-East Kent and Ealing South, all called for general reforms.[44]

That the 1957 conference was pleased with the Rent Act can be seen from the resolutions of congratulations that appeared in the programme; these came from South Lewisham, Newcastle West, Barons Court, North Islington, and Birmingham. But the conference then turned to other problems on housing policy facing the government.

Aside from the 1956 conference, the occasional references to the Rent Restriction Acts in debate did not really give much indication as to the sympathies of the party as a whole or any of its parts. Some have claimed that Mr Sandys made his announcement on rent control to this conference in response to the 'pressure' of resolutions. Others, equally authoritative, have asserted that the L C U resolution was 'inspired' to give Mr Sandys an opportunity to do so.[45] In any event, the debate in 1956 was a good deal sharper than the normal run of Tory debates on housing. To Mrs Hoare the principal social problems stemmed from housing. Continued control, she argued, precluded any improvement.[46] Another member of the union, in seconding Mrs Hoare, asked that 'we should set property free'.[47] Decanting was precisely what was needed, in his view, and surplus rents ought to go to the landlords.[48] Mr Smith of Stockport North would encourage home ownership by reducing the obligations of the building societies. Lieutenant-Commander Marten, a representative from North Dorset and a leading figure in the property world, noted that even if rent was doubled there would not be enough for repairs. He called for a full programme, including incentives, tax allowances and grants. He warned the government against raising rents and incurring odium without 'creating a climate in which the property owner can invest with confidence'. In the absence of this, he contended, the houses needed could not be provided.[49] It was in response to these speeches and resolution that Mr Sandys outlined his proposals for a new Rent Bill.[50]

There was no particular pattern of participation in these debates. Most of the constituencies represented did not have any special housing problems that would explain their concern. It may be guessed that their participation was the result of the interests of local activists.[51] But one organisation which did not participate in these debates had an immediate interest which it reflected in independent activity.

The local organisation most directly involved in the Rent Bill's political difficulties was the London Municipal Society, the central London Tory organisation. Remarkably little direct information on the activities of this organisation at the time have been unearthed. Two coincidences should be borne in mind. Mr Enoch Powell, parliamentary secretary at the Ministry during the drafting and second reading, was a past secretary. Its secretary from May 1956 was Mr John Hay, also chairman of the Backbenchers' Committee on Housing and an employee of the NFPO. The only available source on LMS activity was *The Londoner*, its monthly journal. In April 1956 the magazine noted that increasing the total stock of houses would not necessarily solve the housing problem and announced that the government was looking into alternatives.[52] In October it attacked quite strongly the proposals made by Labour for municipalisation. The arguments were standard: it would be too expensive and local authorities could not cope effectively with the problems.[53] It speculated on the extent to which 'Mr Gaitskell and his right wing supporters' had been at variance with the proposals. But as to the Rent Bill itself, there was virtually no discussion in print.[54] This, despite the pivotal role of London.

Indeed, it was London that prevented unity within the Conservative Party in the House of Commons. There was a substantial group of London and suburban MPs, together with a few others, who opposed much of the legislation and certainly sought to get the operative provisions modified or their impact delayed. The entire potential membership was: R. Jenkins, I. Ward, A. Braithwaite, A. Marlow, D. Orr-Wing, R. Allan, Cdr Noble, J. Cordeaux, A. Price, F. Harris, Reader-Harris, J. Crowder, J. Smyth, T. Clarke, G. Cooke, Mrs Hill, Sir W. Wakefield, S. MacAdden, H. Webbe, F. Burden, F. W. Farey-Jones, P. Wall, R. Jennings, H. Kerby, G. Lagden, H. Linstead, J. Vickers, W. Rees-Davies.[55] In fact it was usually limited to the 'Margate mutineers': Reader-Harris, R. Jenkins, J. Cordeaux, G. Lagden, T. Clarke, G. Cooke, Mrs Hill, Sir W. Wakefield, S. MacAdden, W. R. Rees-Davies, and I. Ward.[56]

The leader of these militant backbenchers was Mr Robert Jenkins, M P for Dulwich. Unfortunately, his credibility as leader was reduced by two factors: he did not get on well with Mr Brooke and he had a history as a rebel (on superannuation for teachers' and nurses' pay).[57] This did not prevent him from serving successfully as a propagandist. In his view only his good relations with the press prompted the publicity of the 'mutiny' to a far greater extent than it deserved.[58] In addition to tabling amendments on both Committee and Report, and participating in delegations to the Minister, Mr Jenkins also made an appearance before the central council of the Conservative and Unionist Associations to urge (without success) that the council support modification of the Bill.[59] By his own account, the record of futility was a poor reward for the effort expended.

Another major figure among the rebels was Mr W. R. Rees-Davies, MP for Isle of Thanet. His most significant gesture was an amendment, tabled on Report, to limit increases in decontrolled property to 2·5 G R V.[60] In two articles published in *The Daily Telegraph* he asserted that although 'the Rent Bill is courageous and thorough' the real and imaginary fears of the middle-class tenants ought to be assuaged. Tenants were, he thought, willing to pay fair rent. But in London the opportunities for extortion were likely to be quite considerable. Initially, he proposed to limit first tenancies to 2·5 G R V increases and give extensive rights of possession to tenant and landlord.[61] Later he repeated his suggested limit on increases but pointed out that restrictions on premiums could substitute for tenants' rights of possession.[62] Mr Rees-Davies spoke extensively at protest meetings. Like Mr Jenkins, he was in a dangerous political situation as a marginal M P from an area likely to be hit by the decontrol provisions.[63]

Typical of the more silent opposition was Mr Robert Gresham-Cooke, M P for Twickenham. Though he agreed with the 'rebels', he nonetheless held that the Bill had to be carried through as part of party policy. He therefore contented himself with abstaining on the Rees-Davies amendment. Although under considerable pressure to oppose the government from both the local press and his constituents, he concentrated on trying to persuade the landlords to 'go easy' on tenants. His advice, apparently, was confined to consultation with a young solicitor in the constituency, a party volunteer.[64]

The parliamentary activity of these protesting Conservatives was concentrated upon the original clause 9 (the decontrol provisions).

Mr Anthony Marlow tabled an amendment, as early as 4 December 1956, that would extend the transition period to three years on a lease fixed by the county court. But the principal amendment came in the form of a proposed new schedule. This was tabled on 13 February 1957 by Mr Rees-Davies, Mr Jenkins, Sir W. Wakefield, Dame I. Ward, Dame J. Vickers, Mr MacAdden, Mr Burden, Mr Kerby, Mr P. Wall, Mr Reader-Harris, Sir H. Webbe, Mr Cordeaux, Mr T. Clarke, Mr J. Temple, and Mrs Hill, of whom three were actually on the Standing Committee. They proposed that five year leases be given, on the same basis as proposed by Mr Marlow. Further, they proposed that premiums be prohibited with penalties, a limitation on excessive rents, and that tenants be given first option to purchase. This latter proposal was tabled on 8 March. These were the only 'rebel' efforts in committee. But on Report this same group, omitting Mr P. Wall, Sir H. Webbe, Dame J. Vickers and Mr J. Temple, proposed an amendment to limit increases to the limits the property would bear if controlled and another, which was debated, to limit increases to 2·5 G R V. These amendments were tabled on the same day (18 March), presumably to assure that one or the other would be selected for debate. Eventually, the proposers abstained, along with the others who had supported action in committee. No stronger action was taken because of pressure of the Whips, a fact which reduced the numbers and diversity of the group so as to render a negative vote ineffectual. Strong pressure had been used by the government Whips on potentially dissident members even though there was only a two-line Whip and some ministers were absent unpaired.

In addition to parliamentary activity, a delegation of the Conservative Party London Members' Committee led by Mr Henry Price (Lewisham South) and Mr R. Jenkins saw the minister in January 1957 about the provisions of clause 9. They got no satisfaction.[65]

The focus of Conservative backbenchers' activity ought to have been the backbench Housing Committee. But its chairman has contended that the committee 'had no role to play at all' prior to the introduction of the Bill. There had been many meetings of the committee prior to introduction, at which the ministers were present, when members argued 'for a more logical and consistent rent structure to be created in aid of the general housing problems of the time'. London M Ps and those from other populated areas, the chairman observed, 'were very doubtful as to the wisdom of tackling the rent problem in the light of the personal political repercussions which they could expect from people who would either have to pay higher rents or possibly vacate . . .'. It was these, it would seem, who frustrated the normal drive of the committee.[66]

Not much has been revealed about the meetings this committee held during the debate. Despite the efforts of its officers, many members might need to be assuaged. Its officers at the time were: the chairman, Mr John Hay; the vice-chairman, Sir I. Horobin and Mr Graeme Finlay; and secretary, Mr Graham Page. Certainly the principal meetings of the committee were held from January to March when crucial decisions on strategy would be debated.[67] On 30 January Mr Brooke and Mr Bevins met with the committee to discuss the various proposals of delay made by Mr Marlow and Mr Rees-Davies. The Times reported that the eighteen-month delay was viewed as the least acceptable because it would come up just before the general election.[68] Though the chairman has claimed that he assured everyone of a full hearing, and would communicate their views to the minister, it has been pointed out that the 'revolt' from the rank and file of the committee over decontrol was characterised by the absence of association with the Housing Committee as such and distinct from the regular pattern of negotiation through the committee's officers.[69]

The chairman has commented that the unusually large attendance at the committee's meetings on the Bill precluded efforts by the committee itself to undertake conciliation. But, he said, the officers 'did the best we could to satisfy those who were doubtful of government policy and the provisions of the Bill, for the officers of the committee were themselves unanimous that the approach was the right one'.[70]

The chairman, Mr John Hay, was the member for Henley, a county seat in Oxfordshire. His majority was substantial, in one of those constituencies where the voters would vote 'for a pig' if the Conservatives put one up. Thus he would be politically unaffected by the Bill. Mr Hay has admitted his interest:

I represented no special interests except those of my constituents generally. I was, however, closely in touch with various property owning organisations who supplied me (and other members) with information and observations from time to time, but I cannot be said to have represented their particular interests.[71]

At the time of the Rent Bill, Mr Hay was the paid legal advisor to the National Federation of Property Owners, with office space in their headquarters. He received considerable sums for articles written by him and published in their journal. They had reason to consider him one of their chief parliamentary representatives in the Commons. Certainly he took an active part in the planning of their campaigns.[72] Of at least one interest group, the R I C S, he asked what points they proposed to make on the committee stage and how he could be of assistance to them.[73]

The activities of the committee's officers revealed their inability to win Mr Brooke's confidence. In company with Sir I. Horobin, Mr Finlay and Mr Page, Mr Hay placed on the order paper amendments to clause 9 which attacked profiteering and raised the limits for increases of rent to statutory tenancies.[74] To schedule 4, on transition provisions, this same group moved an amendment to prohibit premiums. The group moved an amendment to clause 12 as well. They knew they had made a strategic mistake when Labour took over the amendment and forced a division upon it. Amendments to clauses 13 and 16 were largely technical. The group put down amendments asking for a clarification of the landlord's responsibility for disrepair and to limit the right of tenants' compensation which the minister had already conceded in principle. They, along with Dame Joan Vickers, proposed the extension of 'notice to quit' to four weeks. In all the foursome put down nine amendments on the order paper at Report but only one was actually moved. Even this one, by Mr Hay, was withdrawn when Mr Mitchison showed that Mr Hay was mistaken as to the consequence of his amendment. The inconsistency in the amendments which appear in Mr Hay's and other officers' names indicate that they did not all agree with every amendment but that all agreed to sign any amendment put down by any one of the others, as in the Horobin amendment to avoid profiteering. Though Mr Hay was consulted by the minister, the need to put down amendments at this stage would indicate his lack of influence with Mr Brooke. Certainly there was no indication that Mr Brooke took Mr Hay particularly seriously in decision-making.[75]

Among the other officers, Sir I. Horobin's position more nearly paralleled that of the London M Ps. In his view, while in most of the north total decontrol was possible, what was proposed would prove insufficient to provide a free market.[76] He did move an amendment in committee against the advice of the minister, and successfully; his

H

proposal to prevent profiteering. Aside from a letter to *The Times* and this amendment, however, he remained docile and made only a gesture of attacking the government. In debate he defended the free market principle. Aside from their cooperation with Mr Hay at the committee and Report stages, the other officers remained quiescent.

The pro-landlord Conservative MPs sat on Standing Committee but had no official position within the party: Mr C. N. Thornton-Kemsley and Sir Eric Errington, both connected with the NFPO. Though both of these were good party men who seldom participated, their presence served to stiffen the government's determination to be firm on the Rent Bill.

Such stiffening of Tory ranks would not normally be required. But the preparation of the party for the revision of the Acts, and the indoctrination of the party once the decision to go was taken, were remarkable for their failure on what has usually been a Tory strong point. It was a ministerial failure.

The first warning of a decision to act came in 1955 when Mr Sandys said: 'The review of the structure of rent control . . . is a further step in that direction – the provision of a separate home for every family, clearing slums, preserving existing stock – in short we are tackling the housing problem on all fronts. We are pursuing a comprehensive and coherent policy'.[77] Without further warning until the 1956 conference, Mr Sandys then stressed the haphazard nature of control and the resulting anomalies; the 'subsidy' that landlords paid to a tenant 'who may be better off than he is'; security of tenure and the consequent wastage of accommodation. Earlier change had not been possible, he insisted. Houses with vacant possession could now be decontrolled without risk. Those in owner-occupation could be excluded with similar ease. Slice decontrol, an addition, had become feasible and necessary as well as a rent increase for those properties which remained in control. 'The Socialists are certain to misrepresent our motives, but that will not deter us from an act of justice and commonsense which is long overdue'.[78] Mr Sandys said nothing more until second reading in November. Publicity until January consisted only of the reports in the press of second reading speeches.

The tone changed in 1957 with the change of minister: Mr Brooke preferred to comfort rather than defy. In a series of speeches, the first of which was given at North Kensington on 28 January 1957,[79] he stressed what was subsequently repeated in committee that landlords would not 'make a good thing out of decontrol by demanding extortionate rents, or serving on everybody notices to quit in order to sell . . .'. The economics of the situation meant that such landlords would be left with the liability of vacant property. Sensible landlords, he reasoned, would keep their tenants on reasonable terms.[80] At the Royal Institution of Chartered Surveyors in March, Mr Brooke argued that the Bill would be 'either a triumph or a disaster'. So long as the landlords exercised good judgment there would be better housing for all.[81]

The prime minister, Mr Macmillan, was called upon to enter the debate. He made two speeches, one a general public speech in his constituency and one to the Association of Land and Property Owners. The reason for these interventions was the fear that Labour anti-Rent Bill activity had monopolised the press reports on the Bill and that the Conservatives' image with the public was further tarnished. To the public, Mr Macmillan spoke of the promise for the future with almost messianic fervour:

As a result of our housing drive you see quite a number of 'For Sale' boards today. You did not see many six years ago. Well, I want to see 'To Let' boards up again. We must bring back private investment into this type of property, both by conversions and by new building. A great deal of this sort of building was done before the war; I want to see it done again. In short, so long as full control continues there is no chance that there will be enough of this kind of accommodation to let to meet the demand.[82]

To the A L P O he pursued the theme that 'scarcity can only be overcome by removing restrictions'.[83] Neither of these speeches bore any relation to the ministers' line on what the consequences of the Act might be. Surely few in the Ministry expected to achieve anything like the results which Mr Macmillan foresaw. One should ask, then, who composed these speeches and to what end?

The party's propaganda also had to counter a slight electoral blunder. During the discussions on the Act, the Labour Party alleged that in the 1955 election the Tories had pledged themselves not to seriously alter the pattern of rent restriction in the interchange provoked by Bevan.[84] On May 11 1955 Bevan had said that 'if the Tories get back with a majority all rent controlled houses will have an increase in rent'. It seems that the party over-responded to this attack.[85] It was never, in any case, an effective weapon against the Tories.

Though the Conservative Party possessed an excellent research apparatus, which produced several documents on rent control, there was no indication that these had any impact upon government or Ministry policy. Nor, indeed, was the propaganda effort ever completed. The research done had no real connection with the views being formulated in the constituencies or in the party conference. The conference views lacked the dignity of considered policy and the coherence of continuous debate. Such was the nature of the conference debates on housing that no significant doctrine could ever emerge from it. It was too disjointed, each year the focus was altered. The lack of cohesive party policy on rent control was reflected in the parliamentary party. There could be found the officers of the backbench members' committee defending the landlord's interest and a group of Greater London M Ps defending the middle-class tenant. But, despite claims, none seemed to speak for the national interest with an overall view of housing problems. The consequence of this was that both the Minister of Housing and the prime minister had to enter the debate to stiffen support in the party and Parliament for the Rent Act. Although it is impossible to measure the extent to which party disunity affected the modifications in the Rent Bill, the protests indicated that some consideration of competing party views took place. But the backbench committee hardly proved the channel of communication that it is often thought to be. The Conservative Party had won victories primarily to obtain the right to govern. It was pleased so long as its leaders did just that. How this differed from the posture of Labour, both as an Opposition party and an 'ideological' party can be seen in the following chapter.

NOTES

1 R. T. McKenzie, *British Political Parties*, Mercury, London, 1964, p. 285.
2 G. D. M. Block, *Developments in Rent Control Between 1915 and 1955*, Conservative Research Department (Mimeographed), P H C 55C2.
3 *Ibid.*
4 Conservative Research Department, *Rent Control, Housing Policy and the New Rent Bill*, C R D, 9 November 1956, P H C (56) (4).
5 C R D, *Rent Bill 1956 – Decontrol Provisions*, C R D *circa*. January 1957?, no marks.
6 G. D. M. Block, *Developments in Rent Control . . .*, para. 12.
7 *Ibid.*, para. 2.
8 C R D, *Rent Control, Housing Policy and the New Rent Bill*, p. 18.
9 *Ibid.*, pp. 15–16.
10 *Ibid.*, pp. 3–4.

11 Letter of G. D. M. Block to the author, 1 July 1967.
12 C R D, *Notes on Current Politics*, No. 25, 10 December 1956.
13 G. D. M. Block, *Rents in Perspective*, Conservative Political Centre, London, 1961.
14 G. Howe and C. Jones, *Houses to Let*, C P C (for the Bow Group), London, 1956, p. 38.
15 *Ibid.*, p. 15.
16 *Ibid.*, pp. 29–30.
17 *Ibid.*, p. 39.
18 *Ibid.*, p. 60.
19 *Ibid.*
20 *The Estates Gazette*, vol. 168, p. 137.
21 *Ibid.*, 30 October 1956, vol. 168, p. 401.
22 *The Times*, 15 January 1957, p. 7.
23 C R D, *The Campaign Guide* (1959 General Election), C R D, London, 1959, p. 220.
24 Conservative and Unionist Central Office, 'The Rent Bill – What it Means to You', C U C O, London, no date.
25 *Londoner*, no. 228 (January 1957), pp. 37 ff. (the magazine of the London Municipal Society).
26 Conservative and Unionist Central Office, 'Background Material for Election Addresses', C U C O, 1957.
27 *The Spectator*, vol. 198, p. 164.
28 *Ibid.*, vol. 197, pp. 526, 703.
29 *Ibid.*, vol. 196, pp. 848 ff.
30 See McKenzie, *British Political Parties*, pp. 188 ff., and S. H. Beer, *British Politics in the Collectivist Age*, Knopf, New York, 1965, pp. 370 ff.
31 National Union of Conservative and Unionist Associations, 'Seventy-Third Annual Conference, Programme of Proceedings', 1953, pp. 56 ff., res. nos. 84, 89, 93, 95.
32 *Ibid.*, Isle of Wight, res. no. 97.
33 *Ibid.*, res. no. 82.
34 *Ibid.*, res. no. 85.
35 *Ibid.*, res. nos. 103, 106, 107, 112.
36 *Ibid.*, res. no. 110.
37 N U C U A, 'Seventy-Fourth Annual Conference, Programme of Proceedings', 1954, pp. 68 ff.
38 *Ibid.*, res. nos. 192, 193, 194, 195, 196.
39 *Ibid.*, res. no. 191.
40 *Ibid.*, res. nos. 203, 205.
41 N U C U A, 'Seventy-Sixth Annual Conference, Programme of Proceedings', 1956, res. no. 42.
42 *Ibid.*, res. no. 43.
43 *Ibid.*, res. no. 44.
44 *Ibid.*, res. nos. 45, 46, 47, 48, 50.
45 It would not be the first time, see McKenzie, *British Political Parties*, p. 190.
46 N U C U A, 'Report of the Seventy-Sixth Annual Conference', 1956, pp. 51 ff.
47 *Ibid.*, p. 53.

48 *Ibid.*
49 *Ibid.*, p. 54. Indeed his warning proved prophetic of what was to come to pass.
50 *Ibid.*, pp. 54–5.
51 Comment of Professor D. V. Donnison to the author. See D. Donnison and
    D. E. C. Plowman, 'Functions of Local Labour Parties', *Political Studies*,
    1954, pp. 154–67.
52 *Londoner*, no. 225 (April 1955), p. 55.
53 *Ibid.*, no. 227 (October 1956), p. 113.
54 See above,
55 *The Daily Telegraph*, 26 February 1958.
56 *The Times*, 27 March 1957.
57 Interview with Mr Robert Jenkins, J P.
58 His source of information was an organisation called the Tenants Protection
    Council whose papers have been destroyed.
59 *The Daily Herald*, 22 March 1957.
60 See chapter 6, where this is discussed.
61 *The Daily Telegraph*, 17 January 1957.
62 *Ibid.*, 4 March 1957.
63 *The Daily Mirror*, 3 December 1956, p. 3.
64 Interview with Mr R. Gresham Cooke, M P.
65 *The Times*, 18 January 1957, p. 4.
66 Letter of Mr John Hay, M P to the author, dated 24 January 1966.
67 *The Manchester Guardian*, 26 March 1957.
68 *The Times*, 31 March 1957, p. 8.
69 *The Real Estate Journal*, no. 4, p. 126; quotes from letter of Mr John Hay to
    the author dated 24 January 1966.
70 Letter of John Hay, 24 January 1966.
71 *Ibid.*
72 See chapter 8.
73 R I C S MSS: Hay to Hawkes, dated 13 November 1956.
74 13 and 15 Eliz 2., p. 7; *1s.* 29 and 30, *p. 81s* (in *Supplement to the Vote, 1956–
    1957 Session*).
75 Letter of John Hay, 24 January 1966.
76 Letter to *The Times*, 25 January 1957, p. 9.
77 546 H C Deb.5s., cols 258, 813.
78 N U C U A, 'Proceedings of the . . . Annual Conference', p. 55.
79 C R D, 'The Rent Bill', 10 April 1957.
80 *The Municipal Journal*, vol. 65 ii, p. 217.
81 *The Daily Herald*, 6 March 1957: *The Primrose League Gazette*, May 1957.
82 *The Times*, 19 March 1957, p. 4.
83 *The Estates Gazette*, vol. clxiii, p. 485.
84 560 H C Deb.5s., col. 1779.
85 C R D, *1955 Daily Notes*, nos. 7, p. 9 and 8, p. 15.

# 11
# Party Politics: Labour

The main purpose of party is power.[1] In twentieth-century Britain this can be obtained only by success at a general election. The Opposition, in search of power, has relatively few opportunities to present itself to the electorate. Whether or not one accepts the 'Crick' view of parliamentary activity as a never-ending electoral campaign, no matter whom the Opposition has to impress it has to be effective opposition.[2] The success of the Opposition in winning public opinion or convincing the government depends upon the success of the Opposition's policy formulations. Colonel Varley has pointed out that 'it's tricky trying to advertise a product if you don't really know what the product is'.[3] In 1957 not only did the Labour Party need policy for itself, but also for the success of Opposition parliamentary tactics. Even the Conservatives have found that without a clear policy they cannot be a successful Opposition.[4] This was all the more true of Labour, who claimed to be an ideologically based party.[5] In this chapter, therefore, the development of Labour's policy on rented housing is shown as the preliminary to its Opposition to the 1957 Rent Act. The failure of the latter is connected to the failure of the former.

Labour's thoughts on housing changed very slowly. Indeed, John Wheatley's complaints about bankers' profits in the 1920s sounded not too different from G. D. H. Cole's complaints of the 1940s.[6] Municipalisation became party policy in 1956 and departed unlamented in 1961 – a good case study of intellectual failure.* But the policy did not emerge from the fertile minds of a policy committee alone. Its origins could be seen in a series of pamphlets and Reports prepared for the intellectual side of the Labour movement throughout the early 1950s.

The intellectual machine of the Labour Party has three principal parts: the Fabian Society, the Cooperative Party, and the Research Department of the NEC. Though both the Fabian Society and the

* This, i.e. municipalisation, was not quite the same as the proposals of the Milner Holland Committee and others in more recent times.

Cooperative Party had links with the Labour Party in a formal way, their intellectual contributions were not formally received or noted. These were thrown into the intellectual pot of the 'labour movement' from whence they might or might not emerge as party policy. It was the Research Department, which staffs N E C and policy committees, which could directly influence party policy. All of these groups, and the N E C, had a share in the formulation of party policy for the municipalisation of all rented accommodation. In consequence, the intellectual evolution ought to be seen not as the product of several organisations to be integrated in 1956, but as a continuous debate which was resolved by the N E C and Annual Conference in 1956.

Though a pamphlet proposing municipalisation was prepared by B. Rodgers for the Manchester Council of Social Service as early as 1950, the first contribution which received attention was D. L. Munby's Fabian pamphlet, 'The Rent Problem'.[7] The government had failed to deal with the problem of rent as a whole.[8] Current production of housing was only a small fraction of total supply and future planning did not seem adequate.[9] Mr Munby concluded that housing was 'in general a case where public control works fairly well, and the price system not so well'.[10] To fix the demand for housing was easy, only the standard at which it should be supplied was debatable.[11] The working class did not want to own its own houses, and private enterprise was not feasible in a market where initiative or risk were not rewarded.[12] The specific problems of the contemporary situation were: 1. Rents, too low to make repairs; 2. Anomalies which produced different prices for similar accommodation; 3. A tendency to immobility; 4. The role of Council houses as a deterrent to mobility; 5. The arbitrary nature of the redistribution of income by housing taxation (Schedule A, etc.).[13] To effect change, Mr Munby demanded courage: 'Rents are inescapably political; no solution will satisfy everyone, while inaction will merely perpetuate waste and injustice'.[14] He rejected the free market as unworkable. The increase in supply would prove insufficient to keep rents within bounds. In a free market the capital cost of the current stock was not discounted by suppliers, as it should have been. Monopoly rents were encouraged.[15] To eliminate the private landlord, he proposed, would get the necessary repairs done, rents equalized and occupation made more rational.[16] For compensation, he would merely capitalise current income.[17]

The Cooperative Society Conference in 1952 took up Mr Munby's proposal. A resolution opposed any amendment of the Rent Restriction Acts which favoured the landlord.[18] The National Executive of the Cooperative Party proposed that the 'local' authorities should be empowered either to acquire the ownership of suitable large groups of property within their area as was done in the Birmingham case, or to take over the management of rents and repairs of such 'properties'.[19] The central government, the Report recommended, should provide subsidies or low-interest loans to help with the cost of initial repairs. For houses still in private hands, rent tribunals would be constituted to adjudge demands for rent increases. These would be granted if landlords obtained certificates from the local authorities that the houses had been repaired satisfactorily.[20]

The committee placed itself on record to:

reject those policies which would give increases to all landlords. Such policies are based on the vain hope that if the provision of housing is made more profitable landlords will automatically decide to service the nation's social purpose. . . . The provision of houses to let is a public responsibility.

The only way to fulfil this was to take most of the rented accommodation into public ownership.[21]

This Report encountered considerable difficulties in conference. Every possible construction was placed upon it. Some thought it would help the landlords. Others preferred not to place so 'heavy a burden on local authorities'. Others objected to the presentation of the 'repairs only' alternative.[22] Various proposals were made by the National Committee and various branch organisations to improve the report.

The most extreme proposals were those of the London Political Committee of the Coop. These included the municipalisation of houses with compensation assessed by the district valuer and paid out of the Exchequer. This, the London Committee contended, would cut rents to one-third of the contemporary charge.[23] The National Committee considered the London proposals impractical, as both too stringent and too demanding of local authorities.[24] The proposals of the Hampshire and Sussex Federation would limit the takeover, initially, to property controlled between 1920–39. This, it was suggested, should be at site value only, since landlords would have recouped more than their investment.[25] Houses built after 1922 should remain in control at rents adjusted to original cost and site value.[26] On the other hand, the Portsmouth party submitted a

*H

memorandum 'opposing' the principle of bringing all rented houses under public ownership.[27]

The conference was unable, in the end, to adopt a Report in time to form the basis for policy on the 1954 Housing Repairs and Rents Act.[28] At the next conference the National Committee rebuked the conference for turning down a Report not for substantial reasons but for the procedural reason that most parties did not have enough time to consider the report in detail.[29] This time the Report was was accepted.

After this debate Mr David Eversley and Mr James MacColl published two additional Fabian pamphlets.[30] Mr Eversley's pamphlet emphasised that the 'provision of a home has become a social service' and that 'welfare criteria' should be used in distribution.[31] He pointed to general acceptance, even by Tories, of the role of local authorities and contended that the state could distribute houses more fairly than would the free market.[32] Mr MacColl demanded municipalisation:

> Public authorities must take over the very worst property: Mr Macmillan says so. They must take over the improvable property: *Challenge to Britain* says so. What about the middling stuff that calls for careful management in the evening of its days? ... If, as I expect, it [the Macmillan Housing Repairs and Rents Act] breaks down and causes a good deal of trouble to tenants without getting much serious repair work done, there will be a need to do something quickly and public ownership is the only acceptable alternative. If, on the other hand, I am wrong and the tenants become used to paying increased rents and the landlords to doing repairs, the priority will be less urgent. ... [33]

Mr MacColl argued that it was financially advantageous for the local authorities to get a mixed bag of properties to assure exchange between different types of dwellings in order to meet different needs.[34] The house's real value, not its necessary life, should be the basis for compensation.[35]

The debate was finally brought to bear on policy with the appointment of a policy subcommittee on housing, the NEC study-group on housing, chaired by Mr A. Greenwood. The NEC members on the subcommittee were Miss Bacon, Mrs Castle, Mr Gooch, Miss Herbison, Mrs Mann (all of whom were also members of the PLP) and Mr G. I. Brinham. Coopted onto the committee were Mr Janner, Mr Lindgren, Mr Mitchison, Sir L. Plummer, and Mr J. Silverman, all of the PLP. From the LCC came Mr W. G. Fiske. Others added were Mr J. T. Evans, Mrs A. Happold, Mr Wyndham Thomas and Mr Michael Young.[36] This group met three or four times to settle general principles. Its secretary, Mr G. Reynolds, then local government officer at Research Department, presented a draft for revision by the group. Before printing, the NEC had one more chance to revise.

Memories of the discussions in committee and with party leaders varied. Some contended that Mr Gaitskell opposed municipalisation root and branch.[37] This was denied by Lady Gaitskell and by Mr A. Skeffington, who would have been Gaitskell's line of communication to the committee.[38] The view of Mr Reynolds, and of many members of the group, was that municipalisation had to come. The issue was only whether Labour would do the job quickly, or let history take its inexorable course.

The radical influence on the committee probably came from the Research Department, which has always had a reputation for radicalism, via the committee secretary, Mr G. Reynolds (who did not). But in addition, Mr Greenwood, Mrs Castle, Mr Fiske, Mr Mitchison, Mr MacColl and Mr J. Silverman all had prior commitments of one sort or another to municipalisation.

The principal dispute about policy in committee arose over the question of a single or a floating vesting date, the date on which the local authorities would take title, as municipalisation progressed. A great deal of the property which would be taken over would be 'slum' property. Of the local authorities, only Birmingham would have had meaningful experience with this type of housing management. For months, and perhaps years, local authorities would find themselves in the unenviable position of charging rents for properties unfit by normal standards. Even more important, there could be little preparation, nor early achievement, of any substantial repairs programme. No local authority would want to be called a 'slumlord'. Administrative difficulties were equally insurmountable. If vesting were to take place on a single day, on that date the number of dwellings in local authority control would double at least. Nor would the impact fall evenly. A few large urban authorities would have many. Outside London these would come in unhandy packets of six or a dozen terraced dwellings. In London there would be fewer landlords but there would also be many more problems associated with the houses. The legal mechanics of arranging for the transfer of properties and the provision of rent collection alone were complex enough.

Most local authorities did not have the organisation readily suscep-
tible to the expansion required. The LCC people, though not Mr
Fiske himself, preferred a floating vesting date. They intended to take
over only the better quality property. Slum clearance programme
would dispose of the rest. The majority of the group considered a
fixed date feasible and preferable. Mr MacColl contended that once
the owners realised municipalisation was policy no repairs at all
would be undertaken. The difficulties, in his view, were within the
capacity of most authorities.[39] The crucial sentence in the June draft,
presented by the study group to the NEC, took the position that:
'The next Labour government will, therefore, consult with the local
authorities and will cooperate with them in the preparation of plans
which will provide for the acquisition of these houses by a fixed
date.'[40] But already at a 'Labour Party Housing Conference' early in
the year, a public preference had been expressed for 'gradual acquisition'.[41] The final published version did not refer to a fixed vesting
date.

The party publication *Homes of the Future*, was a comprehensive
discussion of the housing problem, including a section on private
rented accommodation with the rest of the plans for local authorities.
The remaining sections of the statement dealt with plans for easier
home ownership, the service house, the building industry, town planning, and the problems of financing the proposals made. In all, out
of some sixty pages, only ten were devoted to the privately rented
dwellings,[42] but these few are full of contempt for the private landlord. 'They are interested in property as an investment and, as such,
expect to get an income from it. The fewer repairs carried out the
larger their net income'.[43] To ensure adequate repairs and security
of tenure, with some ill-defined limit on increased rent, the recommendation was to municipalise most privately rented housing.

About the Rent Restriction Acts themselves, *Homes of the Future*
said little. They should be amended with respect to houses remaining
in private hands by making it harder for landlords to obtain certificates of disrepair (under the 1954 Act) and by making security of
tenure on succession easier.[44] The appendix carried a 'refutation' of
the argument that rent control discouraged repairs.[45] The Macmillan
Act, it was argued, did not work because increases did not balance
the cost of repairs.[46]

It was the conference, or so Labour officials formally argued, which
had to approve *Homes of the Future* before it became accepted party

policy.[47] But if the debate on rent control and municipalisation was not new to the Labour movement, it certainly did raise new questions in the conference. The agenda of conferences from 1953 through 1956 showed no great affinity by constituent bodies (of which the conference is composed: unions, socialist societies, constituency parties) for municipalisation, nor was there any indication in favour of changes in the Rent Restriction Acts. On the contrary, many resolutions demanded the preservation of the contemporary Acts; but even more demanded their extension to council houses as well. As late as 1956 when the conference proposed to municipalise housing, there were strong objections that local authorities raised rents unreasonably and did not give adequate security of tenure.[48] Emphasis on the subject of housing resolutions varied over the years. In 1953 and 1954 (at Margate and Scarborough) rent restriction attracted a number of resolutions. In 1955 and 1956 (Margate and Blackpool) the focus of resolutions turned away from rent control towards the increasing tendency of the government to withdraw subsidies and increase the cost of borrowing for new construction.[49] In addition, three resolutions to the 1956 conference attacked the differential rents scheme.[50] It was in this context that *Homes of the Future* was discussed.

'It is indisputable that in the realm of housing private landlordism has failed . . .', said Mr A. Greenwood when presenting *Homes of the Future* to the Annual Conference at Blackpool. 'There is only one answer to this problem and that is social ownership.'[51] But he meant by this, '. . . Not nationalisation, because housing is a very personal and very intimate thing which should not be subject to the authority of some remote board a long way away from the people who are living in the houses'.[52] He recognised that local authorities would need varying amounts of time to take over properties both because of administrative difficulties and the need to do repairs quickly.[53] These were the points on which critical resolutions had been submitted.

Mr Bevan pointed out that 'the executive has used language that can be used by a future opponent of the proposal to postpone its operation almost indefinitely'.[54] He foresaw no administrative difficulty in a single vesting date since the houses and their rents were already known. This contradicted his own assertion while minister, when he had ridiculed the notion of municipalisation as administratively impossible.[55] Repairs might be a problem, but he claimed that Resolution 231 would overcome this obstacle: 'I beg the conference,' he said, 'to believe that it will not be a practicable administrative proposal to start this operation piecemeal in different parts of the country. It will have to come into operation simultaneously at a given date, otherwise it will not start.'[56] He pointed to the obstacle of councillors who were 'councillors first and Socialists second' in explanation.[57] Mr Bevan was supported by resolutions of the Sheffield Trades Council and Labour Party which called for the 'socialisation of all housing', and the Liverpool, Edge Hill Constituency Party Amendment to limit the impact of the Sheffield resolution to rented housing 'and instructs the next Labour government to introduce legislation naming the day by which all such property shall have been taken over. . . .' Bevan's motion was remitted to the NEC, Sheffield's remained undiscussed.

Conference accepted *Homes of the Future* as presented by the NEC. It had little choice. Bevan pointed out '. . . in the exigencies of parliamentary debate, I have already committed the party to this principle [municipalisation] before conference met'.[59] But even had opposition developed, it would have been disorganised. The agenda of the conference was printed before *Homes of the Future* appeared. Thus, none of the potential dissidents could attack the document directly in resolutions. And in any case the bulk of the resolutions on housing were concerned with the impact of the new government policy which called for differential rent schemes in council houses. Resolutions also asked for the provision of sufficient loan funds to local authorities to make construction possible. There was neither opportunity nor interest in a full policy debate on municipalisation.

Thus municipalisation became Labour's policy for rented housing. In fact of course this settled nothing. For Labour had adopted a name, not a policy. The implications of municipalisation, especially how much housing was to be taken over, when, and with what compensation, were never resolved. It was, as politicians discovered, not an effective answer to the Conservative's proposals even had its implementation in the foreseeable future been possible.

Labour opposed Rent Bills which would increase rent as a matter of reflex. Certainly they lacked information either in taking the decision to oppose, or in the actual Opposition process. The bodies able to undertake research, even of this most practical nature, were limited. There was the Research Department, the leaders of the working party on the Bill, and the Housing Subject Committee of the PLP. None did very much.

At Transport House, the Research Department assigned the problem of rent control to the local government officer. Since he and two assistants were at that time responsible not only for local government and housing but also for the entire range of social policy, understandably he confined himself to the preparation of a short memorandum for use by members of the Standing Committee. There was no time for more. In addition to the publication of a series of regular publications, the local government officer and staff had to write about thirty letters a day in answer to questions from local organisations. Though the department did send out about one hundred questionnaires on the housing problem, to Labour local authorities, of which seventy were returned, no further effort at information collection, much less the provision of research for members was attempted.

Resources for the more practical task of opposition to the particular legislation would have seemed more adequate. Those members of the working party with local government experience and connections could collect data on the 'human' and social questions raised. Legal aspects of the new Bill could be dealt with by those solicitors in the party with Rent Act experience. Of course, some barristers also had extensive Rent Act practices. Mr Mitchison, who led for Labour, and Mr Barnett Janner were among those in the Labour working party. In addition, the party could call upon the services of Mr Ashley Bramall of the City of London Labour Society, one of three principal writers on Rent Restriction law.

But most of the talent available seems not to have been used. The local authority data, such as it was, did not appear in the debates. Nor was there any indication that the various expert individuals were consulted. Key individuals such as Mr Fiske, then chairman of the LCC Housing Committee were not called into the working party, though normally outsiders could be and often were consulted. Mr Ashley Bramall was the author of several books on rent control and the editor of the ninth edition of the authoritative *Megarry on the Rent Acts*. Though a former Labour MP, and in 1957 still a prospective parliamentary candidate, and a member of the same Inn as Mr Mitchison, he was 'neither asked for nor gave any help to the Labour Party during the passage of the Bill through Parliament'.[60] His services were used, however, by the constituency parties.

Despite these failures, members of the working party found the system of preparation, or its absence, satisfactory. Some members complained that they were occasionally 'caught out' in a mistake of fact or conclusion. But this happened even to experts, as in the case of Mr Mitchison on second reading. No amount of 'information' could prevent misstatements completely.

Some information was collected, and used. London members produced a fair amount of detailed information in the form of samplings drawn up by local authority officers to show rents now and what they would be when the Act would come into force. The Local Government Subject Group, however, whose subject including housing, was not able to furnish very much assistance. The Local Government Group vice-chairman, Mr MacColl, did attempt to brief his members. The activities of the group resembled the W E A study group rather than a serious study effort.[61] Once the Bill started on its way there was no attempt to aid the working party with research.

There is no indication that any information was needed to determine the PLP's opposition to the Rent Bill. But the precise nature of the decision-making process was never clear. Some claim the decision was taken by the Parliamentary Party's Local Government Group and accepted by the party as a whole.[62] Others excluded the role of the Local Government Group and traced the decision to an N E C resolution. Still others claimed that the P L P as a whole, with its leadership, made the relevant decision. But however unclear the evolution of the decision to oppose, Labour proposed to wage an orthodox opposition.

The Labour leader on the Bill in a retrospective analysis pointed out that a really successful parliamentary opposition was never considered possible:

> There's no chance nowadays for an Opposition to win a parliamentary battle: the Bill will go through unless the government resigns. The most the Parliamentary Labour Party could hope for on the Rent Bill was a demonstration in force and some concessions, or perhaps a temporary split among the Tories on certain indefensible points in the bill.[63]

This conservative philosophy of the role of the minority party in the legislative process, which claimed at least one distinguished opponent, was the reason for Labour's political failure in the middle 1950s.[64] Accordingly, Labour did not press their alternative plan in the debates. This, claimed the leadership, was not the duty of the Opposition. But this attitude was also the best policy in view of disagreements within the party about what municipalisation actually meant. On the other hand, lack of useful policy hampered Opposition strategy.

The policy of municipalisation was Mr Bevan's. But by the time the Rent Bill was debated he had moved over to foreign affairs, and Mr Mitchison had succeeded as spokesman on housing. Though in 1945 Mr Mitchison had written articles, in both *The Chronicle and Echo*[65] and *The Daily Telegraph*,[66] demanding that housing be treated as a public service and attacking the private landlord, his enthusiasm seemed to have waned by 1956–7. His defence of municipalisation in the Queen's Speech was thin, uninspired and unpersuasive.[67] Mr Mitchison's deputy was Mr G. Lindgren, parliamentary secretary to Hugh Dalton in the last days of the Ministry of Town and Country planning (transformed into Housing and Local Government), who was more firmly committed to municipalisation. But long tenure in Parliament led him to prefer 'true opposition'. To him, as to Mr Mitchison, opposition meant successful delay of what could not be prevented. These two, Mr Mitchison and Mr Lindgren, together with the Whip, Mr Wilkins, took the major decisions in consultation with one or two other interested M Ps, such as Mr MacColl, then chairman of the subject group on local government. They formed an inner group to govern the activity of the working party.

The Opposition to the Bill was organised upon the assumptions of the leaders. Everyone on the 'working party' (all M Ps on the Standing Committee, mainly) submitted amendments on topics of special interest to themselves. Mr Mitchison and Mr MacColl helped with the drafting. But the principal amendments came from Mr Mitchison himself. These he distributed in typescript, with a brief statement of the reasons for them. Sometimes, however, he decided a topic needed coverage and handed the amendment to one of his colleagues. In that case, the member was expected to do his own research and make the best possible case. However, members tended to pursue their own amendments. The extent of this can be seen from the number of cross amendments tabled, and debated, in Standing Committee.

Time has obscured or blurred memory of the strategy on the floor and in committee. To Mr Mitchison, the purpose of the Opposition was to secure maximum publicity for the cause. Some members of the working party preferred to pursue their role of 'Opposition to the end'. But most considered that their participation in a genuine legislative process was meaningful if they could win some concessions, at least in detail, from the government. Whether in the heat of battle the distinction between principle and detail could be discerned was often in doubt. The 1957 Parliamentary Report to the Annual Conference stressed the combative element. It, like Mr Mitchison's own statement at the end of the debates, stressed the concessions that were obtained on exchange of dwellings, leases, and tenants' improvements.[68]

In retrospect the members of the working party claimed that their principal concern was security of tenure. All agreed that some change and rent increase were long overdue. Those who had administered local authority houses were particularly aware of this problem. But there was also the broad social question that housing must be provided for everyone. However, the rent increase was a thorny issue. Certainly Mr Mitchison contested the desirability of giving one, despite his acceptance of the need for more money to do repairs.[69]

On the whole, the Labour Opposition showed itself to be ill-informed on the principles inherent in the Bill. The calculations of increases in rent, exaggerated as those were, bore no relation to the increases that were economically feasible given market conditions. Far more important, the Opposition's obsession with the provisions for slice decontrol caused them to overlook completely the role of decontrol by vacant possession. They, like the government, were deceived as to the significance of slice decontrol.

Parliamentary Opposition had many unresolved problems. Labour had a policy which was easy enough for the government to attack but hard for the Opposition to defend, or propound, even had they any real desire to do so. Labour lacked the intellectual or research resources which would have made Opposition more effectual – irrespective of strategy. Nor did the leadership settle upon a clear strategy of opposition. Did the party wish to stall the Bill, to obtain concessions, to obtain publicity in the country? The evidence seemed to be that the Labour leaders preferred to wage a parliamentary battle and leave the exploitation of the electoral consequences to the mass party.

Indeed, the only explanation of the strategy of Transport House and the local Labour parties was as an attempt to extract electoral advantage from the legislative process. For while all the techniques chosen were intended to reach out to the maximum number of voters, they could hardly have impact on the electoral process itself.

In January 1957 Mr Morgan Phillips, secretary of the Labour Party, instructed local parties 'to organise public meetings and

calculate "on a street-by-street basis" how much extra rent would
have to be paid by tenants in their constituencies. He hoped that these
calculations would then be passed on to the electorate. . . .'[70] The
call was repeated on 29 January. In February, Mr Morgan Phillips
commented: 'When we talk of a mass campaign we mean a universal
one that breaks away from vague, general resolutions. We are determined to visit every possible household in all areas affected by
government rents policy.'[71] So trivial were these efforts that they
went completely unmentioned in the Report of the NEC to the
NEC to the 1957 Annual Conference. If there were other efforts,
the secretariat at Transport House destroyed or concealed all
evidence.

Transport House did make some efforts at publicity. In a 'flyer'
published in 1956, a banner headline proclaimed that 'Millions Will
Help To Pay For. . . . A Present To The Landlords.' It said, in part,
that 'The Conservative government has arranged for a present to the
landlords. This present, which will total nearly £100 million, is to be
contributed by nearly every tenant in Britain. . . .'[72] Two other
'flyers' were issued during 1957. One, titled 'Help Labour to HALT
the Rent Bill' included such catch phrases as 'it's a Tory Gift to the
Landlords'. For use by local Labour parties on a ward basis it provided spaces where wards could write in the amount of the increase
likely to occur. It showed how to calculate the increase of controlled
rents, using Cmnd 17, and the schedules.[73] Another 'flyer' headed
'The Landlord's Charter, Higher Rents for All', contained such telling
subheadings as 'The Truth about the Rents Bill', '10 Blows for Landlord's Freedom', 10 Blows to your Budget'.[74] But *Talking Points*, the
principal brief for candidates and party officials, had remarkably
little on the Bill. Its 1956 issue contained a description of the Bill and
a special Scots supplement, but nothing more than the simplest
explanation. No case of any sort was constructed.[75] In 1957 *Talking
Points*[76] made clear that the Act would be an issue at local elections
but mapped out no special campaign. This, taken all together,
hardly constituted much effort to obtain political advantage from the
most controversial piece of domestic legislation of the 1955 Parliament.

Nor were the activities of the constituency parties more promising
of reward. The party most likely to take any interest was the London
Labour Party. In fact it took no interest at all. The executive committee gave little attention to what activities, if any, the party might

sponsor, beyond a conference at Caxton Hall. The party's newspaper, *London News*, carried less news, proportionate to its interest, than did the principal dailies. Indeed, all discussion in that paper was limited to an explanation of the Bill and reports of the L L P's annual conference. There was no publicity given to local parties' efforts to make the public aware of the problems attendant upon the Rent Act.

Certainly this was not for lack of party enthusiasm on housing questions. In 1954 the London Labour Party Conference had appointed a special committee, including some of the leading local experts, to study the question of differential rents.[77] While the 1956 Subsidies Bill was going through, the 1956 Annual Conference considered any number of resolutions condemning differential rents and demanding an increase in local authority subsidies.[78] But at the same time only Shoreditch and Finsbury urged that any public action be taken to protest the general trend of Tory policy.[79] In October 1957 the party co-sponsored a conference, addressed by Sir Richard Coppack and Mr Lindgren, to protest the government's housing policy.

But only two activities, the petition campaign and a meeting at Caxton Hall, were conducted by the party during the debate, labelled this 'momentous occasion'. The meeting was arranged by Mr Gibson and the executive committee at its meeting of 3 January 1957. They prepared a resolution, subsequently 'adopted' by the public meeting.[80] The meeting, addressed by Mr Mitchison and Mr Gibson, passed unnoticed in the national press, as did the resolution, which read:

That this special conference convened by the London Labour Party, representing many thousands of members of trade unions, cooperative societies and Labour parties in London and Middlesex, condemns in the strongest possible terms the government's Rent Bill.

The Bill proposes to impose grave additional burdens upon millions of tenants and particularly those in the fixed income group and old age pensioners. It provides no guarantees for security of tenure for the tenant and no practical enforcement of adequate repair and maintenance.

The Bill can only be described as a measure to extend landlords' profits without regard for the interests of tenants or the general housing needs of the nation. We applaud the magnificent fight now being waged by the Labour Party against the Bill in Parliament and urge all Labour supporters to do all in their power to make known to Tory MPs their detestation of this iniquitous measure.

The only hope for tenants is the Labour Party's Plan 'Homes of the Future' which would make housing a social service as opposed to the Tories' policy of housing merely as a source of private profit.[81]

The petition campaign, despite its parliamentary aspect, seems to have had little impact. In all, only some eighty thousand signatures were collected, a small fraction of the L L P membership. Apparently, despite the Church House meeting on 8 April 1957, the party did not place much confidence in, or take much interest in, extra-parliamentary efforts.[82]

On 30–1 March 1957 the London Labour Party held their annual conference, a perfect occasion for launching a spirited public campaign against the Rent Act. In fact, it was not. The conference went unreported in the national and local press.

The resolutions on rent at this conference can best be analysed by a study of their sponsors. Four resolutions came from constituency parties: Willesden, Norwood, Deptford and Brixton. Four were moved by trade unions: A E U, Plasterers, Draughtsmen and Vehicle Builders. The executive presented a composite and somewhat original resolution.

The Willesden and Norwood resolutions were of about equal intensity in protest. Both protested the increase of rents for 'millions' of tenants. They condemned the Rent Bill as 'vicious' and called for active campaigns against the Bill. Norwood, with the most detailed programme, demanded:

1. Immediately in conjunction with the London Trades Council to sponsor a series of protest demonstrations and meetings. . . . 2. To discuss with the London Trades Council and, if possible the various London and Middlesex District and Area Committees of Affiliated Trade Unions, future policy in the event of the government persisting in its plans.[83]

Brixton's resolution complemented the efforts of the P L P.[84]

Only one resolution, that of the Plasterers, mentioned the alternative Labour policy as an answer to the Rent Bill.[85] The resolutions of the A E U and Draughtsmen's made special mention of 'the weapon of intimidation which the landlord class will be quick to use'.[86]

The resolution offered by the executive was the mildest of the resolutions submitted to conference. It contained elements of the other resolutions, but proposed no definite action. It read:

This conference condemns the government's Rent Bill which will lower the control limits and allow rents to rise to levels which will reduce the standard of living of millions of working people in London and Middlesex, which will remove all security from the tenants of those houses subject to decontrol and which will provide an opportunity for landlords to increase rents . . . to a penal level and impose such conditions as they wish.

This conference pledges its unceasing opposition to this reactionary landlords' Charter and calls for the strongest protest from the millions of tenants affected.

Conference calls upon the government to withdraw this Bill.[87]

The activities of the local constituency parties in London were more extensive, if no more effective. The council in Erith was only one of many which sent protests.[88] Resolutions of protest were passed by the parties in Stepney, Croydon, Tooting and Fulham.[89] Public meetings were organised by the parties in Hackney, Croydon, Fulham, Clapham, Malden, Woolwich, Hornchurch, Dulwich, West Ham and Acton.[90] Other parties did more. Barking lobbied its MP.[91] Tottenham sent a protest to Middlesex County Council.[92] Clapham, Dulwich and Shoreditch distributed pamphlets. Not all these efforts were particularly successful. At Malden only twenty-four people were attracted to a meeting on the Act.[93] Nor, considering the number of London constituencies, was this a significant amount of activity.

There was some activity in the areas immediately around London. Resolutions were passed at meetings of Labour parties in Chiswick, Guildford, Chesham, Westerham, St Albans and Chislehurst. A petition was assembled at Chiswick; meetings were held at Dartford and information collected.[94]

Outside of the London area, in large towns and even rural areas, activity was evident. Birmingham, Sheffield, and Nottingham city councils passed resolutions attacking the Bill. Birmingham and Nottingham organised centralised campaigns. Meetings were convened in Sparkbrook, Oldham, Kircaldy, Corsham, Hastings and Birmingham Borough. Wolverhampton, Abertillery, East Flint, Brighton, Taunton, Bruton, Bedford, Stockport, Luth and Salisbury passed resolutions, Shrewsbury and Sunderland decided to establish advice bureaux as well as send petitions.[95] This was quite a lot of action. With the noticeable exception of Liverpool and Manchester, the principal towns affected agreed to act. But the public impact did not seem commensurate with effort.

One agent, in Reading, concluded that the anti-Rent Bill leaflets, some of which urged a switch to Labour in the upcoming local elections, were effective. At least, he contended, it was as effective as a lot of other expensive and less pointed material which the party distributed. But, he pointed out, it was not easy to fill in the blanks on the leaflets which estimated the amount of rent increases in each area. And it took a considerable force to handle the work. No matter how the forms were worked, considerable effort was required. Hence, few parties undertook the effort.[96] A sure avenue for Labour Party publicity was the pages of *The New Statesman*. But like most of the Labour left, the *Statesman* concluded that the repairs problem was serious and that something had to be done for the landlord. It disagreed with the government on the particular measures chosen. From its point of view, municipalisation would do the job 'just as effectively and without the risk of rack-renting'.[97] In an article published in January 1957, Mr N. MacKenzie put the case for social responsibility to provide housing for all. Though he made 'devastating' comments about the Bill and Mr Brooke's policy statements, there was little solid and constructive criticism.[98]

The day to day reports were covered by J. P. W. Mallalieu, then the parliamentary correspondent. He ridiculed the efforts of the Tory 'rebels' trying to obtain modifications. Except for an amusing tale of antimacassars, there was nothing of interest there either.[99] And, of course, A. Harvey constructed a post-Rent Act horror story to thrill the consciences of the liberal intellectuals.[100] There was little coverage of the Bill, or Labour Party activity upon it.

Labour ought to have had no trouble agreeing to a policy, and strategy, on rent control. Yet they proved no more able to agree on policy about rents than about nuclear weapons or nationalisation. The policy of municipalisation proved more effective as a stick to be used by Conservatives than as an alternative to be espoused by Labour. Indeed, Labourites were unable to agree on the meaning of the policy they had adopted. Disorganised thinking went hand in hand with inadequate research. Unable to present an alternative policy, unwilling to devise new ideas, Labour lapsed into the traditional forms of opposition. Nor was it even clear as to the reasons for opposition, other than the recognition that differences within the party need not be publicly displayed. Given the ease with which hack phrases could be used, Labour could claim it has played its role as the party of conscience. The campaign against the Bill, both in Parliament and in the country was completely unoriginal. The traditional phrases accompanied the traditional postures and led to traditional failure. For despite the great publicity given to the Bill, Labour got far less credit from Opposition than it might have expected. Its public campaign did not develop that spark that ignites electoral successes. Thus, the party neither opposed usefully in the Houses of Parliament nor capitalised on Conservative weakness in the country.

## NOTES

1 B. Crick, *The Reform of Parliament*, Weidenfeld and Nicolson, London, 1964, pp. 193 ff.
2 Disraeli, cited in W. Guttsman, *The British Political Elite*, MacGibbon and Kee, London, 1963, p. 195.
3 Cited in R. Rose, *Influencing Voters*, Faber, London, 1967, p. 51.
4 R. Maudling, *The Times*, 16 February 1967, p. 11; N. Lawson, *The Spectator*, No. 7234 (17 February 1967), p. 187.
5 S. H. Beer, *British Politics in the Collectivist Age*, Knopf, New York, 1965, p. 242.
6 J. Wheatley, 'Houses to Let' (The Labour Party, n.d.); G. D. H. Cole, *Building and Planning*, Cassell, London, 1945, p. 26.
7 D. L. Munby, *The Rent Problem*, Fabian Research Series, no. 151, London, 1952.
8 *Ibid.*, p. 3.
9 *Ibid.*, pp. 6–7.
10 *Ibid.*, p. 7.
11 *Ibid.*
12 *Ibid.*, p. 3.
13 *Ibid.*, pp. 4–6.
14 *Ibid.*, p. 4.
15 *Ibid.*, pp. 3–4, 12.
16 *Ibid.*, pp. 20–3.
17 *Ibid.*, p. 22.
18 Cooperative Party National Committee, *Rent Control, Special Report*, issued by the National Committee of the Cooperative Party, February 1953, p. 12.
19 *Ibid.*, p. 15.
20 *Ibid.*, p. 15.
21 *Ibid.*, p. 14.
22 Cooperative Party National Committee, *Special Reports, 2. Rent Control— A Supplementary Statement*, issued by the National Committee of the Co-operative Party, January 1954, p. 9.
23 *Ibid.*, p. 11.
24 *Ibid.*, p. 12.
25 *Ibid.*, p. 13.
26 *Ibid.*, p. 14.
27 *Ibid.*, p. 12.
28 *Ibid.* ,p .15
29 *Ibid*

30 D. Eversley, *Rents and Social Policy*, Fabian Research Series, no. 174, London, 1955. J. MacColl, *Plan for Housing*, Fabian Research Series, no. 164, London, 1954.
31 Eversley, *Op. Cit.*, p. 3.
32 *Ibid.*, pp. 16–18.
33 MacColl, *Op. Cit.*, pp. 11–12.
34 *Ibid.*, p. 12.
35 *Ibid.*
36 Labour Party, *Report of the Fifty-Sixth Annual Conference (1956)*, London, 1956, p. 28.
37 Comment of Mr W. Pickles.
38 Letters from Lady Gaitskell (dated 27 February 1966) and Mr A. Skeffington, M P (no date) to the author.
39 J. MacColl, *A Plan for Rented Houses*, Fabian Research Series no. 192, December 1957. Though published a good six months after the committee met, it presumably reflected his, and others', views at the time.
40 Labour Party, document number P5R, C.71.
41 *The Real Estate Journal*, vol. 6, no. 10 (March 1956), pp. 270–1.
42 Labour Party, *Homes of the Future*, London, 1956, pp. 9–20.
43 *Ibid.*, p. 12.
44 *Ibid.*, pp. 19–20.
45 *Ibid.*, p. 53.
46 *Ibid.*, p. 54.
47 S. Rose, 'Policy Decision in Opposition', *Political Studies*, June 1956, pp. 128–38. But see Professor R. T. McKenzie's rejoinder in *Political Studies*, June 1956, pp. 176–82.
48 Labour Party, *Agenda for the Fifty-Second Annual Conference of the Labour Party* . . ., London, 1953, pp. 66, 67. Labour Party, *Agenda for the Fifty-Third Annual Conference of the Labour Party* . . ., London, 1954, p. 74. Labour Party, *Agenda for the Fifty-Fifth Annual Conference of the Labour Party* . . ., London, 1956, res. 224.
49 Labour Party, *Agenda for the Fifty-Fourth Annual Conference of the Labour Party* . . ., London, 1955, res. nos 333–41. Labour Party, *Agenda* . . ., 1956, res. nos 234–53.
50 Labour Party, *Agenda* . . ., 1956, res. nos 254–6.
51 Labour Party, *Report of the Fifty-Fifth Annual Conference*, October 1956, p. 99.
52 *Ibid.*
53 *Ibid.*, pp. 99–100.
54 *Ibid.*, p. 107.
55 D. V. Donnison, *The Government of Housing*, Penguin, London, 1967, p. 165.
56 Labour Party, *Report* . . ., 1956, p. 107.
57 *Ibid.*
58 Labour Party, *Agenda* . . ., 1956, res. no. 220.
59 Labour Party, *Report* . . ., 1956, p. 107.
60 Letter from Mr Ashley Bramall to the author, dated 22 April 1966.
61 Interview with Mr J. MacColl, M P.
62 *Ibid.*

63 G. Mitchison, 'Fighting the Rent Bill', *Labour Press Service*, no. 9 (May 1957), pp. 3–4.
64 Viscount Kilmuir, *Political Adventure*, Weidenfeld and Nicolson, London, 1954.
65 20 October 1945.
66 6 May 1946.
67 560 H C Deb.5s., cols 158 ff.
68 Labour Party, *Report of the Fifty-Sixth Annual Conference*, 1957, p. 63; *Labour Press Service*, no. 9 (May 1957), pp. 3–4.
69 'Fighting the Rent Bill', *Labour Press Service*, no. 6 (February 1957).
70 *The Manchester Guardian*, 24 January 1957, p. 16.
71 *The Daily Worker*, 2 February 1957.
72 Labour Party MSS, *Labour Party Pamphlets and Leaflets Binder, 1956*.
73 Labour Party MSS, *Labour Party Pamphlets and Leaflets Binder, 1957*.
74 *Ibid.*
75 *Talking Points*, no. 23, and Scots. Supplement, pp. 185 ff.
76 Nos 7 and 8, pp. 50 ff.
77 London Labour Party, *Report of the London Labour Party*, 1954, p. 11.
78 L L P, *Report of the London Labour Party*, 1956, res. nos 4–17.
79 *Ibid.*, res. no. 2.
80 L L P, *Executive Committee Minutes*, doc. no. 113671.
81 L L P, *Report of the London Labour Party*, 1957, p. 11.
82 *Ibid.*
83 *Ibid.*, res. no. 5.
84 *Ibid.*, res. no. 10.
85 *Ibid.*, res. no. 4.
86 *Ibid.*, res. no. 2.
87 *Ibid.*, res. no. 7.
88 *The Kentish Independent*, 8 March 1957.
89 *The Daily Worker*, 30 January 1957; *The Croydon Times*, 8 February 1957; *The South Western Star*, 18 February 1957; *The Daily Worker*, 22 February 1957.
90 *The Daily Worker*, 30 January 1957; *The Croydon Advertiser*, 15 February 1957; *The Daily Worker*, 22 February 1957; *The South Western Star*, 8 March 1957; *The Kentish Independent*, 8 March 1957; *The Romford Times*, 13 March 1957; *The Surrey Cosit*, 18 March 1957; *The South London Observer*, 14 March 1957; *The Acton Gazette*, 15 March 1957; *The Stratford Express*, 22 February 1957.
91 *The Daily Worker*, 30 January 1957.
92 *Ibid.*, 1 January 1957.
93 *The Surrey Cosit*, 18 March 1957.
94 *The Sidcup and Kentish Times*, 1 March 1957; *The Herts. Advertiser*, 1 March 1957; *The Bucks. Examiner*, 15 February 1957; *The Kent Messenger*, 22 February 1957; *The Surrey Advertiser*, 23 February 1957; *The Chiswick Times*, 2 March 1957; *The Gravesend and Dartford Reporter*, 2 March 1957.
95 *The Shrewsbury Chronicle*, 1 February 1957; *The Manchester Guardian*, 29 January 1957; *The Flintshire Advertiser*, 2 March 1957; *The South Wales Argus*, 9 February 1957; *The Wiltshire News*, 15 February 1957; *The Notts.*

*News*, 16 February 1957; *The Chester Chronicle*, 16 February 1957; *The Somerset County Gazette*, 16 February 1957; *The Notts. Evening Post*, 15 February 1957; *The Bedford Record*, 19 February 1957; *The Salisbury Times*, 22 February 1957; *The Birmingham Mail*, 23 February 1957; *The Western Gazette*, 22 February 1957; *The Bedfordshire Times*, 19 May 1957; *The Birmingham Post*, 25 February 1957; *The Stockport Express*, 2 March 1957; *The Hants. and Sussex County Press*, 1 March 1957; *The Taunton Herald*, 2 March 1957; *The Lincolnshire Echo*, 4 March 1957; *The Guardian-Journal*, 15 March 1957; *The Hastings and St. Leonards Observer, Bolton Evening News*, 14 March 1957; *The Chatham Observer*, 8 March 1957; *The Sunderland Echo*, 20 March 1957; *The Evening Argus*, 21 March 1957.

96 L. H. Gibbs, 'Reading Rents Bill Campaign', *Labour Organizer*, vol. 36, no. 418 (March 1957), pp. 57 ff.

97 *The New Statesman*, 20 October 1956, p. 470; 17 November 1956, p. 611.

98 *Ibid.*, 5 January 1957, p. 5.

99 *The New Statesman*, 30 March 1957, p. 400: 'Rees-Davies and Mr Robert Jenkins applied their pressure – if pressure is not too vigorous a word – with the gentle good-natured insistence of parish ladies telling their bachelor vicar that his antimacassars need a wash; and Mr Henry Brooke replied in his puff-ball voice that he fully appreciated the good intentions of his visitors but that really, if they looked closely, they would see, wouldn't they, that the antimacassars were actually quite clean. Ten Tories eventually abstained from voting in the division which Mitchison was rude enough to force . . .'.

100 *Ibid.*, 16 March 1957, p. 332.

# 12
# Political Consequences

The political consequences directly attributable to the 1957 Rent Act were far from clear. Was the Act a cause, or merely a landmark in the withdrawal from ideology towards more empirical methods that characterised both parties in the 1960s? To what extent did the Bill, and the attendant publicity, affect the policies, methods, and personnell of the Ministry of Housing and Local Government? What new pressure groups arose? How did these affect the electoral scene? To what extent was the Act an issue at succeeding general elections? Was the Act politically harmful to the Conservatives? Was there a difference between the results in national and local elections? What impact did the Act have on the electoral fortunes of those members most involved, or those constituencies most affected? In short, was the Act politically relevant to the 1960s or did it become, like socialism and free enterprise, a mythical basis of party conflict.

The pursuit of the free market by Conservatives, and of nationalisation by Labour has not yet ended. That Mr Powell remained a power within his party and that the government has brought in a steel nationalisation bill were tribute to the continuing power of these formulations. But neither of these were part of the general consensus within which respective party policies were framed. Although both parties originally framed their rents policy within the framework of free market or nationalisation, it was in the field of rent control that both took the first steps towards abandoning these tenets (Tories in 1959, Labour in 1961).

Any causal connection between housing and general policy doctrines of the political parties was merely coincidental. However, the recognition by both parties that their respective positions were not *prima facie* bases for policy must be counted an important step in their respective policy transformations. Conservatives quickly became aware of the political difficulties which free market economics created. Whatever their philosophic assertions, after 1957 control became the dominant note of their policy in many fields. Similarly Labour, despite its rhetorical adherence to nationalisation, abandoned the policy over a wide range of concerns. Only in steel has the government of Mr Wilson acted. Whether this change was merely part of the growing acceptance of collectivism in the mid-to-late 1950s or not, the Rent Act ought to be viewed as at least a peripheral cause of the policy changes.

Like the alterations in party policy generally, the changes in the politicians' view of rent control took place for reasons which remain unclear. The failure of the 1957 Act, detailed in the next chapter, may have helped to draw Conservatives away from their former rigid anti-control position. The growth of new techniques for control made rent control an acceptable alternative to municipalisation for Labour. But probably the main reasons for the changes, like the reasons for the origins of the respective policies, lay in political exigencies. After 1959 the Conservatives were drawn by a series of politically motivated commitments back towards increased government commitment in the housing field. Labour was led away from municipalisation as part of the attempt to remove the 'red' image of the party, and also as the party became aware of the real opposition in Labour local authorities to the burdens which municipalisation would put upon them. Such was the state of the transformations within the parties.

But the impact on party policy was nothing compared with the impact on the Ministry of Housing, especially in the policy sector, though it followed seven years later and was more indirect. Here rent restriction as a major aspect of housing policy was replaced by a return to the more positive aspects of housing production. The information upon which this new policy was framed differed little in quality or quantity from the discredited stock used in 1956–7. A great change in policy was effected without the benefit of the administrative lessons cited in chapters 4 and 5. Sir Geoffrey Vickers contended in *The Art of Judgment*[1] that the most important aspect of policy-making is appreciation reached by the decision-makers, the factual and value judgments, even if the process by which they are reached remains unclear.

Previous judgments of fact by the Ministry of Housing's civil servants were slowly eroded by a series of White Papers on housing problems and the visible consequences of the legislation. Not only did these upset assumptions about the physical state of the stock but they also challenged the reasons for the consequences of particular policy approaches – such as decontrol in its various forms and repairs incentives. Far more important, there was a recognition of the growing importance of owner-occupation as against tenants wishing for accommodation to let, and that demographic and general economic problems of great magnitude had been either ignored or wrongly reported. In short, the Ministry discovered that its judgment of fact had been inadequate.

Nonetheless, the Ministry concluded that its value judgments remained, essentially, sound. The changed style of consultations and communications in the appreciation system resulted far more from a change in the character of the participants than from a recognition of the previous system's weakness. This was true despite the alteration in the interest and capacity of the political masters. In fact, the conclusion was drawn by the civil servants that if only there had been an adequate supply of information merely of the sort collected in preparation for the 1957 Act, correct instrumental (that is techniques which were appropriate to the situation) decisions would have followed from the appreciation that was achieved. The values attributed to the free market remained inviolate. The value of the private landlord was discounted only when Labour, broadly opposed to the breed, gained power. The point of this civil service appraisal was that an accurate factual basis for policy judgments was not essential for effective government activity.

This self-righteousness applied particularly to the instrumental decisions that were taken. Decontrol in its various forms was regarded as a means to be used by any government not opposed to the free market and in pursuit of a 'help the landlord' policy. Most of those who made the Ministry decisions in 1956–7 would still make the same sort of decisions today. Indeed, despite complaints about drafting in 1957, codification of the Rent Acts was not accomplished until 1968. And complaints about all subsequent legislation have remained of little concern. Old ways remained best ways.

The changes in judgment of fact, value and appropriate instruments which followed the 1957 Act took place incoherently. In fact there were never any significant changes in the appreciation of the situation held by the Ministry. They merely modified their view to meet the requirements of their political masters. Civil service continuity might be desirable, but in this case it seemed to frustrate policy and legislation.

The changes in party and Ministry following from the Bill occurred without much connection to the public, the titular legitimator of both. However trivial public opinion, and even election, in the practical operation of politics, its ritual place has commanded attention. The public has expressed itself most definitely in the electoral process. Not all the electoral surveys would discourage the British politician's faith in elections as a legitimation not merely of person or party but of policy. The individual politician has faith that his own policy will also be reaffirmed by the electorate. This has been his rationale, very often, for deviation. Thus to look at elections and the electoral trends should clarify whether these were causal or consequential of the particular policy on rent control.

Certainly the Conservatives feared that the Rent Act would have an impact upon the 1959 general election. To minimise this the party pleged that 'in the next Parliament we shall take no further action to decontrol rents'.[2] They contended that time was needed for more construction and the full effects of the 1957 Act to become apparent. Labour, however, pledged itself to return to the *status quo ante*. It pledged the repeal of the Rent Act and the reimposition of control. It warned that the Tory pledge not to decontrol further could not be trusted, citing a similar pledge in the course of the 1955 campaign.[3] But were these really anything more than traditional statements?

Both parties were notoriously anti-poll. But would their political sense have led them to the same conclusion as the Gallup poll, that as an electoral issue housing was trivial? Gallup reported that on only two issues, housing and pensions, did a majority of those replying suggest that Labour would be more competent than Tory. This, coupled with the fact that housing was, with education, one of the least important issues to the electorate indicated that the result said nothing about the public's reaction to the Rent Act.

The issues that did affect the election of 1959 were tabulated by Gallup. They were: cost of living and prices (28 per cent), pensions (25 per cent), foreign affairs (20 per cent), employment (20 per cent) production/expansion (10 per cent), housing and rents (9 per cent), education (7 per cent), other (5 per cent).[4] The general impression of the irrelevance of the policy to the election was further confirmed by the results.

The results of the 1959 general election were striking as much for what they did not reveal as for what they did. The swing to the Tories in the county of London averaged 2·1 per cent. Though the swing in the centre and West End was relatively small, only 0·9 per cent, this reflected as much the very large swing to the Conservatives in 1955. The total swing to the Conservatives over the 1951–9 period was just about equal in all parts of the county of London. The swing in the suburban boroughs was 2·2 per cent. Only Kent and Surrey showed very much less swing, without any justification similar to that offered above. Indeed, the London area and the midlands showed the largest swing to the Tories, with the south and east far behind (only 1·5 per cent) and the northern swing almost negligible (0·2 per cent). Thus London, which ought to have been most affected by the Act showed no electoral concern in aggregate.

But aggregates were, in this case, somewhat deceptive. The average swing in London boroughs was 2·2 per cent. But a remarkable number, almost half, showed swings of less than this. These borough seats were: Barons Court, Battersea South, Dulwich, Chelsea, London and Westminster, Fulham, Hackney Central, Hammersmith North, Hampstead, Lewisham North, Paddington North, St Marylebone, St Pancras North, Stoke Newington, Wandsworth Central, Putney, Streatham, Woolwich East and Woolwich West.[5] What these constituencies have in common is a strong Labour element; but, more important, they have a significant middle-class element. Both senior ministers (Mr Brooke at Hampstead with an 0·5 per cent swing and Mr Sandys at Streatham with an 0·6 per cent swing) did badly. Indeed, it was said that Mr Brooke would have done much worse were it not that the Labour Party candidate was a West Indian and subject to a certain amount of colour prejudice. Of course, not all of these constituencies' voting behaviour was explicable in terms of the Rent Act. But it seems probable that the Rent Act, or fears of it, resulted in greater Labour success and larger Conservative defection or abstention in the constituencies listed than in others.

The impact of the Rent Act as an electoral issue in the 1959 election was not studied with any great precision. It was obviously irrelevant in two of the four constituencies studied by the Nuffield Group (Tiverton and Newcastle-under-Lyme) but relevant to Kelvingrove and North Kensington. No conclusions could be drawn as to its electoral significance. One was a Scot's seat, subject to the special conditions that prevail in both housing and elections north of the Tweed; the other had race and fascism and a Liberal intervention as more relevant factors.

Thus, in the midst of a Conservative victory of massive proportions, any hints of the impact of rent control might have had in selected constituencies got buried. That politicians were able to ignore the warning, such as it was, seemed sufficient enough reason to discount the relevance of the Act in the election. Certainly the public was found either unable or unwilling to judge the Tories on rent control.

To develop the relationship of national policy to local elections is a dangerous attempt. Local variables weigh far more heavily in local elections than in the national contest. This has been especially true of local authority elections (as distinct from by-elections). Even the structure of politics, as Bealey, Blondel and McCann have pointed out,[6] is quite different when local positions are at stake than when an MP is elected. Another difficulty has been that local and national electoral swings cannot be treated as one. The swing in local authority elections is based on the triennial cycle of election. In part it reflects the national political scene. But in part it is merely a swing from the position three years previously which might, or might not, be parallel to a general election swing. Finally, the size of the poll at local authority elections has rendered it particularly suspect. But in a 'science' which possesses so few facts, every one must be pursued.

When one looks at the tables where the same councillor was up for election, i.e. 1955–8, 1956–9, the striking effect of the pendulum is evident. In both those cyles in the middle 1950s, despite the fact that the national pendulum was not working, the local pendulum worked almost exactly, in terms of numbers of seats won and lost. If one looks at the elections in this fashion, the losses of the Conservatives in 1958 and the gains in 1959 should not be at all surprising. Indeed, the figures would indicate that the Conservatives did rather well to lose so few seats – still remaining ahead of the pre-1955 position.

These impressions are reaffirmed by a study of the councils won and lost. It was noticeable that over the period 1955–9, despite the general trend of public opinion polls in favour of Labour (almost until the general election), the Labour Party lost steadily. Even in years when it captured councils, it tended to lose almost as many (with the exception of 1957). A closer examination of the councils involved might reveal some subtle pattern of gains and losses. But that pattern is not readily evident, and the conclusion must remain general.

Despite political sensibilities, the 1957 Rent Act seemed to have had remarkably little impact on the general run of local authority elections. In few of these constituencies, however, would the Rent Act have posed any major problem, certainly not for the activists who turned out to vote.

I

Table 19* indicates the overall returns in local authority elections between 1955 and 1959:

TABLE 19
*Summary of Local Authority Election Returns: 1955–9*

| 1955 | Gain | Loss | Net Change |
|---|---|---|---|
| Conservative | 344 | 35 | + 346 |
| Labour | 47 | 388 | − 357 |
| Liberal | 16 | 8 | + 81 |
| Independent | 75 | 49 | + 26 |
| 1956 | | | |
| Conservative | 58 | 15 | − 137 |
| Labour | 224 | 58 | + 186 |
| Liberal | 17 | 12 | + 5 |
| Independent | 41 | 95 | − 54 |
| 1957 | | | |
| Conservative | 55 | 233 | − 178 |
| Labour | 261 | 57 | + 204 |
| Liberal | 30 | 19 | + 11 |
| Independent | 45 | 81 | − 36 |
| 1958 | | | |
| Conservative | 28 | 320 | − 292 |
| Labour | 343 | 48 | + 295 |
| Liberal | 54 | 5 | + 49 |
| Independent | 33 | 84 | − 51 |
| 1959 | | | |
| Conservative | 213 | 55 | + 158 |
| Labour | 55 | 264 | − 209 |
| Liberal | 32 | 15 | + 17 |
| Independent | 71 | 37 | + 34 |

If there were any region which ought to have been concerned with the Rent Act, it was London. Here housing problems always attracted more interest and more political knowledgeability than elsewhere.[8] Here too the problems were far more evident and relationship between landlord and tenant far more acrimonious, or at best impersonal, than elsewhere. Labour's political organisation was, despite its limited efforts,[9] likely to achieve some impact with its anti-Rent Act campaign. In fact, the impact on local elections was remarkably slight.

As with other local authority election figures, many cautions must

* Tables 19 and 20 reveal full cycles for two years (i.e. 1955–8; 1956–9). They omit inner London which should be considered separately.

Table 20 reveals the gains and losses in terms of councils:

TABLE 20
*Local Authority Elections, 1955–9; Council Control Won or Lost*

| 1955 | 1956 | 1956 | 1957 |
|---|---|---|---|
| *Labour Loss* | *Labour Gain* | *Labour Loss* | *Labour Gain* |
| Landeloes | Blyth | Widnes | Widnes |
| Bolton | Peterborough | Lowestoft | Lowestoft |
| Northampton | Ellesmere Port | | Northampton |
| Nottingham | Nottingham | | Gloucester |
| Morley | Hemel Hempstead | | Dover |
| York | Morley | | Keighley |
| Reading | Widnes | | Brighouse |
| Ipswich | Darlington | | Watford |
| Dudley | Kidwelly | | Middleton |
| Daventry | | | Banbury |
| Goole | | | Bridgwater |
| Walsall | | | Chatham (Kent) |
| Darlington | | | Thetford |
| Kidwelly | | | Norfolk |
| Flint | | | Wallasey |
| | | | (Cheshire) |
| | | | High Wycombe |

| 1958 | 1958 | 1959 | 1959 |
|---|---|---|---|
| *Labour Gain* | *Labour Loss* | *Labour Gain* | *Labour Loss* |
| Stourbridge | York | Dagenham | Hereford |
| Wanstead | Brighouse | Newcastle- | King's Lynn |
| Luton | Kidwelly | under-Lyme | Keighley |
| Spenborough | Bridgwater | Burton-on-Trent | Stafford |
| Uxbridge | High Wycombe | | Lancaster |
| Dudley | Goole | | Macclesfield |
| Bolton | Banbury | | Shrewsbury |
| Daventry | Hartlepool | | Heywood |
| Walsall | West Hartlepool | | Walsall |
| Gillingham | Stafford | | Uxbridge |
| Brentford | Basingstoke | | Bradford |
| Chiswick | | | Lowestoft |
| Heston | | | |
| Isleworth | | | |
| Bradford | | | |
| Newcastle-upon-Tyne | | | |
| Shrewsbury | | | |
| Rochester | | | |
| Maidstone | | | |
| Cardiff | | | |
| King's Lynn | | | |

be indicated. The figures presented here represent only the consequences of elections. There is no computation of swing. Swings in such elections tended to be far more dramatic than the actual outcome of the election, especially with the increased intervention of third parties. Thus the 1961 LCC election saw swings of between 5 and 10 per cent against Labour.[10] Second, there were no LCC elections during the spring of 1957, when maximum political impact might have been expected. Metropolitan borough council elections were held in 1953, 1956 and 1959. LCC general elections were held in 1955, 1958, 1961. These cautions, taken with those previously indicated, form the background within which the London area elections will be considered.

No Metropolitan borough council changed hands at any of the elections between 1953 and 1959. Indeed, in none was the voting even close. There were some variations in the composition of the councils, but these never amounted to more than half a dozen seats. On this basis it would be impossible to determine the reasons for changes or to note any specific trend. To ascribe these changes to the Rent Act, though this might well have been a factor, would be foolish.[11]

The returns for the LCC elections deserve closer scrutiny. In these a pattern of changes which might be associated with housing could be drawn. Though changes occurred between 1955 and 1961 in several constituencies, and especially at the highly relevant 1958 election, many merely reflected the marginal nature of the seats. This was true at Battersea South, Dulwich, Lambeth (Norwood), Wandsworth Central and Clapham, Streatham and Woolwich West. Swings to Labour in 1958 were recorded also in Barons Court, Lambeth (Vauxhall), Lewisham North and Lewisham West. Islington East swung to Conservatives in 1961. Most of the 1958 changes were reversed in 1961. This was not true in Lambeth (Vauxhall) and Wandsworth Central.[12] The marginal nature of so large a proportion of the boroughs which changed hands in 1958 would make any definite conclusion suspect. But the general characteristics of these seats should not be overlooked.

All the boroughs in which there were switches from Tory to Labour were notably lower- and middle-middle class, as was the case in the reduced swings in the 1959 general election. It was generally thought that these were the occupants of houses most likely to be affected by the decontrol provisions of the new Acts. Though the operation of these provisions had been delayed, and though the fears proved, in the first instance, unjustified there was no question but that real concern existed. This was certainly the impression that the London Labour Party got from the 1957 by-election success for local authority seats within its area.[13] Thus, while in the case of the borough council elections conclusions must be indecisive, there was some reason to suggest that the Rent Act did have political impact on the 1958 L C C elections.

As in 1923, politicians were quick to see a by-election coming while the Bill was news as a 'Rent Bill by-election'.[14] Certainly many would concur with the B I P O statement, after the Ipswich by-election forecasts, that: 'Policies adopted by parties in Opposition play a minor role in by-elections. The voters are not electing a government, only registering approval or disapproval of it'.[15] The series of by-elections at Tonbridge, Chester-le-Street and Chester led to the conclusion that whatever else would happen, the Tories would not win the next general election, on current form.[16] Of the two elections held while the Bill was going through, one, Carmarthen, was clearly not relevant. But the other, Lewisham North, was as perfect a test for the Bill as East Fulham had been for rearmament in 1933. The outcome, in a much reduced poll, was a Labour victory. The people seemed to have spoken.

In fact, it would be impossible to be as conclusive as Labour and the bulk of the press were in their analysis. A Conservative majority of 3,236 became a Labour majority of 1,110. For Labour, Herbert Morrison, Mr Harold Wilson, Mr W. Griffith and Mrs B. Braddock all made speeches. For the Conservatives only Lords Hailsham and Hill did so. The Conservative candidate was a local man with only a grammar school education. By contrast, the Labour candidate, Mr Niall MacDermot, had been to Rugby and Oxford. Commenting on 31 January, *The Times* saw the issues as cost of living and rent, with Suez an unimportant third. Lady Summerskill's intervention on Suez, Leasehold and clause 9 (the decontrol clause) were seen by *The Observer* as the big issues.[17] But only *The Daily Worker* and *Daily Herald* thought that the Rent Bill was the only major issue.[18] By 8 February a bandwagon to Labour had begun. Both *The Times* and *The Manchester Guardian* concluded that Labour was right in believing it could win.

Was Labour's win the product of dissatisfaction with the Rent Bill? On reflection it would seem not. *The Times* pointed out, quite rightly, that one of the factors was certainly the failure of Mr Macmillan to establish his image in the short time between taking office and the by-election.[19] Mr Ian Trethowan in *The News Chronicle* pointed out that the Tories had a poor candidate, a split to the right, and a powerfully organised Labour Party as well as the Rent Bill to cope with. Against Labour were the Summerskill statement on Suez and the decision to fight on the old register – presumably favouring the Tory ability to get postal votes. Certainly, aside from not being in the Tory image, the failures of the Tory candidate on a platform were a contributory factor in the defeat.[20] And further, the Independent Loyalist's vote exceeded the Labour majority. All of this would probably have gone to the Tories. In sum, while Lewisham North may have been seen as an anti-Rent Bill gesture, even by the politicians, it ought to be viewed merely as the coincidence of pending legislation and a Tory defeat.

One tangible consequence of the Rent Act was the emergence of an intellectual pressure group, and the reinforcement of the tenant lobby. The academics, primarily those associated with the Rowntree Trust, but also others (especially economists) took an interest in housing that had not theretofore existed. The consequence was the emergence of politically significant data. It was significant because it was both public and in excess of that known to exist within the Ministry. It had to be taken into consideration when policy was being made and debates (both public and private) held. Such activity could not compel action. But once activity was determined it could alter the details of direction.

The other group to emerge stronger than it had begun was the tenant lobby. This survived, as it had not done after 1954, the completion of the legislative process. Perhaps the main reason was that the Act did have some impact on the tenants. Unlike in 1954, tenants were reminded that they had cause for complaint. Thus by 1964 there were seven large tenants' associations important enough to be consulted by the Milner Holland Committee, beyond the Communist-supported National Association of Tenants. This was a major change from the situation which had obtained in 1956–7. Never again could tenants as a political pressure be ignored.

The only general conclusion that could be drawn was that no one piece of legislation of the nature of the Rent Act could have a massive impact on the political structure. Its full import being understood by neither party nor public, the relevance of the Rent Act to everyday politics was often obscured. But the explanation for the seeming lack of political consequences cannot be seen merely from an examination of political events. Part of the explanation lay in the extent to which the Bill fulfilled the economic and social expectations of the government and Opposition. The connection between the economic and social consequences of the Act and the political consequences, could be seen once the distinction between expectations and realities became evident. This is presented in the next chapter. Whatever the long-term effect, by 1959 there was no indication of significant policy or public alignment transformations in consequence.

NOTES

1 Sir Geoffrey Vickers, *The Art of Judgment*, Chapman and Hall, London, 1965.
2 D. E. Butler and R. Rose, *The British General Election of 1959*, Macmillan, London, 1960, p. 262.
3 *Ibid.*, p. 270.
4 *Ibid.*, p. 71.
5 *Ibid.*, p. 219.
6 F. Bealey, J. Blondel and W. P. McCann, *Constituency Politics*, Faber, London, 1965.
7 *The Times*, 21, 25 April, 10, 11, 12 May 1955; 8, 9, 10, 11, 14 May 1956; 10, 12 May 1957; 6, 7, 8, 9, 13, 14, 22, 23 May 1958; 8, 9 May 1959.
8 L. J. Sharpe, *A Metropolis' Votes*, 'Greater London Papers', LSE, London, 1962, p. 73.
9 See above.
10 Sharpe, *A Metropolis Votes*, p. 31.
11 London County Council, 'Metropolitan Borough Elections', nos 3819, 3919, 4069.
12 LCC, 'Election of County Councillors (London County Council)', nos 3896, 4008, 4127.
13 London Labour Party, *Annual Report for 1957*, pp. 4–5.
14 *The Daily Mail*, 14 February 1957; see Introduction.
15 BIPO statement to press by Dr H. Durant, 28 October 1957 (mimeographed).
16 *The Manchester Guardian*, 14 February 1957.
17 *The Observer*, 10 February 1957.
18 *The Daily Herald*, 8 February 1957; *The Daily Worker*, 8 and 9 February 1957.
19 *The Times*, 15 February 1957.
20 *The Daily Mail*, 15 February 1957; *The News Chronicle*, 15 February 1957.

# 13
# The Economic and Social Consequences

Government and Opposition had been more or less agreed as to what would serve to improve the rented housing scene and as to the impact of the Rent Act (1957) towards that end. The government were to be proved mistaken in their estimate of the situation, and the solutions enacted were proved inappropriate to deal with the problems – both supposed and real. Though the failure of the Act was particularly noticeable in London, it was almost as apparent elsewhere. Some of the aftermath in the rented housing market could be traced to the Act, some of the new problems merely followed the Act in time. Some of the principal reasons for failure of the Act, and the situation which called for new legislation, are presented.

The intentions of the government in the 1957 Rent Act were fivefold:

A relaxation of rent restrictions—the government claimed—would increase the supply of rented housing by encouraging conversions and new building, and discouraging sales and prolonged vacancies; it would increase the mobility of labour and reduce overcrowding and under-occupation by getting people to move into housing more appropriate to their needs; it would improve the condition of rented property by making it possible and profitable for landlords to do repairs; and the injustices arising from more than forty years of rent restriction would gradually be eased.[1]

The first question to be answered is the extent to which these intentions became reality.

The government contended that the Act would increase the supply of rented housing. This was not the case. A total of about three hundred thousand dwellings were lost to the privately rented sector between 1958 and 1964. Of these half were sold and the other half were demolished.[2] The government had contended that the stock of rented housing would be increased by conversions and new construction while the drain of sales to tenants would be reduced.

Certainly some conversions took place. The London scene testifies to the construction of new private housing to let. But neither conversion nor new construction proved significant. The reasons for this failure were associated with the general problem of rented accommodation, and will be considered subsequently.

The government claimed that the new Act would redistribute the existing stock of housing on a more rational basis: tenants would hold units appropriate to their needs rather than take shelter in the security of tenure afforded by the Rent Acts. This depended first on the market having sufficient stock to make such mobility possible and second upon the particular circumstances in the market encouraging such a rational redistribution, so long as planned decanting (shifts to rational sized units) was eschewed.

In fact, the stock of housing did not permit such movements. In the first place there were insufficient additions to the stock. In the second, in many areas there were net shortages of accommodation. Indeed these shortages were quite visible on a national scale. The original proposal had been based on the assumption that during 1957 the supply and demand for housing would come into balance, that there would be dwelling units for each group which required separate accommodation. In fact, as Dr Cullingworth has pointed out, that assumption was mistaken:

Had there been no increase in headship rates between 1951 and 1957 there would have been 13,724,000 households at the latter date, i.e. an increase of 606,000. During the same period there was a net increase in dwellings of about 1,533,000 making a total for England and Wales of 13,922,000. This increase in dwellings was sufficient to house all the hypo-thetical 606,000 extra households together with all the census-enumerated sharing households and still leave an 'excess' of 198,000 dwellings. Assuming no significant increase in the number of vacant dwellings the conclusion must be that headship rates have, in fact, increased. It is not possible to measure how much headship rates for individual age, sex and marital-condition groups have increased, but an increase in the rate for married males aged 15–39 from 78·8 per cent to 83·6 per cent is consistent with the figures. Such a change would have increased the number of households to 13,919,000, and resulted in an excess of dwellings over households of only 3,000. Since it is unlikely that sharing . . . has been abolished the increase must, in fact, have been greater.[3]

In other words, households were splitting up into more numer-ous and smaller units. Their capacity for doing so had been underestimated – particularly among the young and single people and the aged – two groups most often found in private rented property.[4] Thus the stock proved insufficient to provide for much mobility.

Even had the stock of housing proved sufficient, there were other factors mitigating against much reorganisation of housing or increased labour mobility. The average Briton was, on the whole, unwilling to move far even in search of a more secure future. Most movements in Britain (three-quarters, according to one study) were very short, not sufficient to move from one employment area to another.[5] Indeed the older families, those which had dwellings suitable to house whole families but often housing only one or two adults, were unwilling to move. Partly this was a matter of attachment to a particular dwelling; partly it was the relative advantage and security of the controlled accommodation even at higher rent than a decontrolled accommodation. This was particularly true as the price of largish controlled accommodation (likely to be old and thence fairly low valued) was still cheaper than new accommodation or equivalent decontrolled accommodation of a smaller size.

In fact the system introduced by rent decontrol caused still greater distortions in occupation rates than had existed before. The controlled houses (mainly separate dwellings with gardens) were increasingly occupied by small, elderly, childless households – tenants of these dwellings well before July 1957. The decontrolled units consisted increasingly of subdivided multi-occupied dwellings and purpose-built tenement blocks (other housing being more likely to be sold for owner-occupation or demolished in clearance schemes). In this property, least suited for family occupation, were the larger households with young children – tenants moving in since July 1957. Private rented housing was dwindling; the portion of it that remained was distributed in the least efficient way.[6]

In fact far from reducing under-occupation the period between 1957 and 1959 saw an increase, as more units were occupied at a rate of one-half person or less per room, while fewer units were occupied at the rate of one-half to one person per room. The increase in under-occupation was at a significant level so far as the statisticians were concerned.[7] Thus the government failed both in its efforts to encourage labour movement and in its efforts to assure a more rational use of existing accommodation by encouraging families to live in units appropriate to their size.

The government claimed that the new Act would encourage landlords to do repairs and so prolong the life of much private rented housing at the same time making it more desirable. As privately rented housing tended to be older, it usually required more repair than other types of accommodation. The extent of the problem was indicated in a Rowntree Study which concluded that approximately one-third of the privately rented houses had some basic structural defect.[8] Of course responsibility for many of these repairs lay with the tenants. In the normal case, landlords in England and Wales assumed responsibility only for external repairs and fundamental internal repairs – leaving decorating to the tenant. It was often hard to determine who had responsibility for which repairs. Anything from 4–12 per cent of tenants of privately rented controlled dwellings (unfurnished) in 1963 in London did not know who was responsible for which repairs.[9] Mrs Cockburn reported that in London responsibility for repairs was being transferred increasingly to tenants.[10] The 1960 Social Survey Report indicated that anything from 40–50 per cent of repairs requested by tenants, either formally or informally, had not been done by the landlord in the nation as a whole.[11]

Finally, the government claimed that the injustices of rent control would be brought to an end. These were of two sorts: the injustices to landlords and those to tenants.

The injustices to landlords lay in the 'deprivation' of their complete control over their own property so far as possession was concerned and the limitation placed upon the rent that might be charged. Historical anomalies certainly existed which resulted in different rent for similar accommodation, and by comparison with other nations the amount paid by tenants as a proportion of income was quite low.[12] Indeed the principal injustice seemed to be the relatively low rent that the landlord received. In point of fact the landlord did not receive as much as the government proposed to give him. The government had supposed that most landlords would be able to claim the twice G R V given to landlords who did external repairs and major internal repairs. Either because fewer did such repairs than expected or because many landlords neglected to claim the full amount of the increase, the average ratio of new controlled rent to G R V ranged from 1·7 to 1·9 for tenancies where the occupier remained unchanged. On the other hand the ratio in decontrolled tenancies varied from 2·4 to 2·9 G R V.[13] A full 26 per cent of landlords were claiming more than twice G R V from controlled tenants.[14] The government had assumed an efficient and fairly prompt response from landlords;

they would fix rents at the prescribed multiples of gross rateable value, tenants would get security of tenure even if decontrolled, disrepair procedures would ensure that repairs were done. In fact the response from both landlord and tenant was patchy. The consequence was that the various inequities as to rentals did not alter very much so far as landlords were concerned.

The inequities so far as tenants were concerned lay in the inability of new households to obtain accommodation and the relatively higher price they had to pay for it. The first, as has been indicated, remained unaltered. The second became even more exaggerated. For new tenants were quite heavily penalised as compared to sitting tenants, as table 21 indicates:

TABLE 21

*1957 and 1959 Net Rents Paid by Unfurnished, Non-Service Tenants*[15]

|  |  | Increase per cent |
|---|---|---|
| *Metropolitan London* | | |
| Below control limit: | Occupier unchanged | 60 |
| | New occupier | 145 |
| Above control limit: | Occupier unchanged | 52 |
| | New occupier | 102 |
| | | |
| *Rest of England and Wales* | | |
| Below control limit: | Occupier unchanged | 40 |
| | New occupier | 58 |
| Above control limit: | Occupier unchanged | 33 |
| | New occupier | 74 |

(Source: Cmnd 1246, table 5)

A new inequity, so far as the tenant was concerned, lay in the revised disrepair procedure. This proved, perhaps intentionally, unworkable. Tenants simply could not understand or operate the procedure effectively. The consequences were many cases in which the landlord received rent in excess of what he ought to be paid given the state of the accommodation.[16]

The government's intentions in the 1957 Rent Act could not be fulfilled. The supply of privately rented accommodation was not increased, rationalisation of accommodation use was not achieved, repairs were not done, anomalies were not eliminated. The reasons for this failure lay in the inappropriate measures incorporated in the Act to achieve the desired ends, and the failure of the government to properly assess that which needed to be done.

The principal device employed by the government was decontrol. Events proved that the government's expectations as to the consequence of its own measures were quite inaccurate. The government had estimated that a total of 750,000 dwellings would be decontrolled immediately on the slice decontrol by rateable value. In fact, only 367,000–391,000 accommodation units were decontrolled in England and Wales.[17] On the other hand the government seriously underestimated the rate of decontrol by vacant possession. The rate of decontrol was one-twelfth of those units remaining under control. There were about 320,000–330,000 units *per annum* of this sort.[18] These mistakes originated in the poor information collected while drafting, and have been discussed in chapter 5.

The purpose of decontrol had been to create a free market. Even assuming such a market was possible (which will be disputed subsequently), would it have worked in practice? The success of the free market depended very much upon the private landlord. But these had been seen as impotent even before the first world war:

> The great obstacle to better housing was not the wickedness of the small landlord but his impotence. He belonged to another time and to different circumstances. He was already proving inadequate well before the first world war and his unsuitability in changed economic and social conditions became more evident as time passed.[19]

Professor Donnison has pointed out that the landlord could not respond to a free market even when he saw one.[20] Further, Professor Donnison pointed out, the new larger families of the middle 1950s were dependent upon rent control as the only alternative to council housing to secure living space.[21] The failure of the Act has been publicly attributed to its consequences. The true failure might well be seen as the inability to effectively transform the housing situation after the fashion of the government's intentions.

The failure of government activity could be explained in part by the inability of the government to gain an accurate impression of the physical and administrative setting in which rent control and privately rented accommodation were placed. These were not to become apparent until the middle 1960s, and are still not totally accepted by government and politicians.

Ever since 1915 the government had looked upon the regulation of privately rented housing as a national, and temporary, measure. Only with the Milner Holland Committee Report was there a recognition that in certain large metropolitan areas, such as London, the 'acute shortage and ... [the] difficulties and hardships are the product of social and economic trends which will continue for the foreseeable future; and they cannot be eliminated without a radical appraisal of present policies and procedures'.[22] The hardships in London, of which Rachmanism was an overpublicised part, and in other centres of shortage, were not duplicated throughout the country. Indeed, Dr Cullingworth showed that both the larger stock of houses and better landlord-tenant relations in the north made the operation of the Rent Act reasonably smooth and almost innocuous, if no more effectual.[23] Not only did the intentions of the government not become an actuality in London but a whole new series of problems came to the surface which were connected in the public mind with the Rent Act. The three most important were homelessness, insecurity of tenure and Rachmanism.

Homelessness was an ever-present problem in large cities. Mr J. Greve in his pamphlet *London's Homeless*[24] claimed that decontrol or more increases in controlled rent forced out tenants as the rent of private accommodation rose above their capacity to pay.[25] The evidence of this lay in the dominance of 'rent arrears' as the reason for a landlord's serving notice to quit. But in many cases it was simply that the landlord required the accommodation either for himself or for sale with vacant possession.[26] The extent of this problem was testified to by the C A B in a report on the problem.[27]

But more terrifying, as the Milner Holland Committee pointed out,[28] was the insecurity of tenure that the Rent Act made possible.[29] Anyone moving acquired a tenancy whose security was completely and solely dependent upon the terms of the lease. Unless the lease provided otherwise, his security ended with the termination of the lease, i.e. for the great majority who could be evicted with one month's notice. The old protection of statutory tenancy no longer applied. Nor did the provision for three-year leases improve the position.[30] The problem in London, the Milner Holland Committee reported, was particularly acute. In London, they pointed out, only 60 per cent of those houses to let on which owners acquired vacant possession were in fact re-let. And all were re-let free of control. The committee concluded that a movement rate of 16 per cent per annum in unfurnished lettings, and 45 per cent per annum in furnished lettings was sufficient 'to indicate discomfort and unsettled conditions'. But more important, it was discovered that 4 per cent of the households in unfurnished lettings and between 9 and 10 per cent of the households in furnished lettings 'found themselves obliged to move against their will'.[31] The committee concluded that many landlords acquired vacant possession to sell or to improve to an extent that the current tenants could not afford the rents, or to redevelop. The consequence of insecurity was that not only did many become homeless but also that tenants hesitated to claim their rights as regards repairs and legal rents.[32] Though the extent, both geographically and numerically, of dislocation was perhaps less than later press reports made it, for those involved, and for the community which had obligations to them, the problem was quite real.

For very many people the experience of losing their homes can be devastating in its effects. At least it is likely to involve a period of great anxiety while a search for other accommodation is being made, and it must follow that for those who have young children or other dependents to care for, the fear of being left without a home is immeasurably more serious than for those who have only themselves to consider. For some it can mean the disruption of their family life and the separation of husbands, wives and children, perhaps temporarily, perhaps for a considerable time.[33]

But the most public, and least significant, problem to emerge in the field of rented housing was the increase in slum landlords, now renamed Rachmanism. Though he gave the literature of vandal landlords yet another chapter, his fame rested mainly upon his involvement in the Profumo Affair. He was quite exceptional, say the Milner Holland Committee, to the extent to which he benefited from the abuse of the provisions of the Rent Act on vacant possession. The Milner Holland Committee and the CAB both reported extensive evidence of abuses. But the nature of these abuses varied widely and it would be difficult to attribute them to the 1957 Rent Act. In short, though Rachmanism brought the housing problem into the public eye, homelessness and insecurity were the major evils.

The social problems that have gained the public and official eye since the 1957 Rent Act were largely the result of shortages. Though migration into London may have been a contributory factor in certain sections of the area, it was not of great importance.[34] Indeed population within the LCC was falling at the time. A main factor, as the Milner Holland Committee pointed out was that:

The supply of privately rented accommodation in Greater London has diminished and is still diminishing fast. This trend will not be halted, still less reversed, unless investors can be assured that, provided their properties are properly maintained and managed they will be free from the hazards of political uncertainty and able to obtain an economic return.[36]

At the same time, as scholars have pointed out, the government must take a look at new factors not thought relevant in 1956. The council house and the owner-occupied house formed a much more important part of the market than was understood at the time. The role of the concealed and almost unintentional government subsidies had yet to be revealed.

In 1957 the government tried to abdicate responsibility for any of the sectors of the housing market to private enterprise and the mechanism of the free market. But, as Professor Donnison was afterwards to point out, this was impossible: 'The government cannot merely leave the decision to individuals for it has already assumed responsibility in this field as irrevocably, though not as comprehensively or deliberately, as in the fields of health and education'.[36] Rent control had concealed the 'true cost of housing and the cost of maintaining it'.[37] The Conservative government attempted to create a situation in which those who wanted particular sorts of accommodation would pay for it at free market rates; the 'laws of supply and demand' would sort out the priorities of quality, quantity, and purpose of house construction. Among the other factors this ignored was the time lag between construction or conversion and demand given the nature of housing. It also ignored the relatively small addition to the stock made by demand which could be affected by market considerations. Even more important was the false assumption that mere decontrol would establish a workable free market which would create a viable housing structure.

As was pointed out in the Introduction, the government and Opposition over-emphasised the importance of private rented housing as a part of the housing market. Owner-occupied and council houses between them were the keys to the market. Indeed, some academics were to argue that the Rent Acts themselves had encouraged the swing from private houses to let to owner-occupation.[38] One of the reasons for this, as the Milner Holland Committee pointed out, was that the private investor could hardly be expected to invest in something as unsure as privately rented housing. Freedom not from control but to make a fair return, was what landlords required. This could not be assured so long as controls came on or off as the social and political situation required. It was natural that investors turned to the Building Societies as an alternative to investment in houses to let.[39] Moreover, the position of the owner-occupier was strengthened by a series of tax subsidies that made housing to let at a given value relatively more expensive than equivalent accommodation obtained on a mortgage. The same was true of a council house dwelling, once the rate subsidy was taken into consideration. This is illustrated by table 22, taken from the Milner Holland Committee Report:

TABLE 22

*Illustration of the Weekly Cost of Accommodation under Various Types of Owner*[40]

| Area | Average Total Cost of Dwelling Including Land £ | Landlord (*Rent per week*) | | | Owner-Occupier | |
|---|---|---|---|---|---|---|
| | | Local Authority | Housing Association | Private Landlord | Before Tax Relief | After Tax Relief |
| | £ | £ s. d. | £ s. d. | £ s. d. | £ s. d. | £ s. d. |
| A | 5,500 | 3 3 8 | 7 14 1 | 10 1 8 | 8 13 1 | 6 7 6 |
| B | 3,750 | 2 7 0 | 5 9 0 | 7 1 6 | 5 18 4 | 4 7 0 |

Source: Milner Holland Committee

Since the landlord could not compete, it was quite natural that there should be little new investment in housing to let and that those with investments in that sector should make every effort to get out. To increase the supply of houses to let it would have been necessary to make major alterations in the whole of housing subsidy policy, as well as in the tax structure. In 1956–7 this was not seen, much less understood.

At the same time that the government overestimated the importance of private housing to let, it underestimated the importance of council housing. These charged a higher rent, a 'more economic rent' than equivalent accommodation could obtain under control. But it was not recognised that in a free market council housing would always be cheaper. More important, little account was taken of the extent to which higher council rents reflected superior amenities.

The movement away from new council house construction which accompanied the Rent Act (1957), meant that not merely would slum clearance programmes reduce the supply of private houses, but that both parts of the rental sector would be cut back simultaneously. Thus in places like London dislocation was almost bound to be serious, for there the cycle of movement was most evident. The newest families or units, and the oldest (the aged) were both dependent upon the private rented sector. They could not obtain places in the alternative source of accommodation, the council house, because of the prevalence of the list system in which they had relatively low, if any, priority. The young family, the large family, the aged, all suffered from the inadequacy of properly sized, reasonably priced accommodation. These were the groups who took substandard accommodation precisely because they were unable to pay 'market' rents for decontrolled dwellings. Yet it was these socially or economically inadequate groups that the 1957 Rent Act deprived of security of tenure, decontrolled dwellings, and for whom it raised controlled rents.

The vast bulk of the community, and probably a fair proportion of those in controlled dwellings larger than their needs, were unaffected. Most households lived in council housing or in owner-occupied housing. Many in the controlled sector found that they remained controlled after 1957 because their rateable value was below the level of decontrol. These only slowly moved out of the controlled sector. The middle classes probably hid behind their control or knowledge of procedure. Only the inadequate would suffer.

Inevitably, control was reimposed and the 1957 Act largely 'reversed'. Politics dictated recontrol though controlled rents have continued to rise. The combination of Labour's philosophy about private housing, and social welfare, coupled with the extensive publicity given to a broader view of housing by both social administrators and economists, made changes desirable. But the gains for government were not the changes themselves, but the comprehension that rent control had to be considered in the broader context of housing policy, the scope and nature of which had to be more clearly understood than was the case when the 1957 Rent Act was prepared and enacted. Legislation without information had proved ineffectual.

NOTES

1 D. V. Donnison, 'Aftermath of the Rent Act', Donnison *et al*, *Essays on Housing*, Occasional Papers in Social Administration, no. 9, Bell, London, p. 7.
2 D. V. Donnison, *The Government of Housing*, Penguin, London, 1967, p. 194.
3 J. B. Cullingworth, *Housing Needs and Planning Policy*, Routledge, London, 1960, pp. 40–1.
4 See J. B. Cullingworth, *English Housing Trends*, O P S A No. 13, Bell, London, 1965, pp. 24–5.
5 Donnison *et al*, *Essays on Housing*, pp. 51–2.
6 *Report of the Committee on Housing in Greater London*, Cmnd 2605, 1965, pp. 69 ff.
7 P. C. Gray and E. Parr, 'Some Effects of the 1957 Rent Act', Ministry of Housing and Local Government, *Rent Act, 1957: Report of Inquiry*, Cmnd 1246, 1960.
8 D. V. Donnison, C. Cockburn, T. Corlett, *Housing Since the Rent Act*, O P S A no. 3, Condicote Press, Welwyn, 1961, table 23, p. 54.
9 Milner Holland Report, Cmnd 2605, 1965.
10 C. Cockburn, 'Rented Housing in Central London', Donnison *et al*, *Essays on Housing*, p. 20.
11 Gray and Parr, *Rent Act*, 1957, table 9B, p. 30.
12 P. F. Wendt, *Housing Policy – The Search for Solutions*, University of California Press, Berkeley, 1963.
13 Gray and Parr, *Rent Act, 1957*, p. 26.
14 *Ibid.*
15 *Ibid.*, p. 25.
16 *Ibid.*, pp. 31–2,
17 *Ibid.*, p. 21.
18 *Ibid.*, pp. 21–2, and Donnison, *The Government of Housing*, p. 74.
19 J Greve, *Private Landlords in England*, O P S A no. 16, Bell, London, 1965, p. 10.
20 D. V. Donnison, *Housing Policy Since the War*, O P S A no. 1, Condicote Press, Welwyn, 1960, p. 32.
21 Donnison, *Government of Housing*, p. 172.
22 Milner Holland Report.
23 J. B. Cullingworth, *Housing in Transition*, Heinemann, London, 1963.
24 J. Greve, *London's Homeless*, O P S A no. 10, Bell, London, 1964.
25 *Ibid.*, p. 41.
26 *Ibid.*, p. 17.
27 Citizens' Advice Bureaux, *Finding Accommodation. A Citizens' Advice Bureaux Report on Greater London*, n.d., 1963?, p. 2.
28 Milner Holland Report, p. 227, para. 4.
29 *Ibid.*, chapter 10.
30 Donnison, Cockburn and Corlett, O P S A no. 3, p. 44.
31 Milner Holland Report, pp. 180 ff.
32 *Ibid.*, pp. 180–3.
33 *Ibid.*, p. 183.
34 *Ibid.*, p. 311.

35 *Ibid.*, p. 227.
36 Donnison, *Housing Policy Since the War*, p. 31.
37 Milner Holland Report, p. 227.
38 Cullingworth, *English Housing Trends*, p. 98.
39 *Ibid.*, and Milner Holland Report, p. 227.
40 Milner Holland Report, table 38, p. 42.

# 14

# Appendix: The Legislative Process

In a lecture at the London School of Economics, Sir Geoffrey Vickers directed attention to the significance of regulation in political systems. He saw as a threat the 'breakdown in the conditions which make possible the regulation of political systems such as support us now....' He pointed to the ecological trap into which the political system seemed to be slipping and the communications failure which seemed to be both cause and consequence of the trap.[1] Sir Geoffrey's thesis can be used as a model within which the legislative process on the 1957 Rent Act can be examined. The obvious breakdown of the legislative process in the case of the 1957 Rent Act demonstrated the extent to which the legislative process contributed to the polity's approach to an ecological trap. If this failure of the legislative process can be attributed to the failure of communication, the legislative process may be observed as only one aspect of a failing political system.

For these conclusions, a political system must bear the following definition, originally proposed by Sir Geoffrey:

I will distinguish a political system as constituted by those relations which society seeks to regulate by the exercise of public power. This definition would be too narrow for some purposes but it distinguishes one group of relations which deserves a name. The departmental organisation of central and local government distinguishes a host of relations which it is the function of these departments to regulate—the relation of roads and road users, houses and home seekers, schools and school children, sickness and hospitals; the level of employment, the balance of trade, the balance of payments, the balance of international power, and so on. Every political activity is directed to the regulation of some set of ongoing relations, whether internal to the system controlled by the regulator or external, between that system and other systems.

As rent control dealt precisely with such relations (between landlord, tenant, and accommodation) this definition is applicable to a discussion of this example of the legislative process. Of equal importance were the relationships internal to the regulating system, the legislative process itself. Sir Geoffrey explained why both these relations can be distinguished from others as examples of political regulation:

Regulation operates by manipulating one or other term of the relationship or both. We may build roads or restrict traffic, build schools or abstain from raising the school leaving age, increase the armed forces or cut our international commitments. Equally, of course, we may fail, partly or even wholly, in our regulative efforts. But even where we fail, I regard the relations in question as having been brought within the political system by the decision to treat them as regulable by acts of public power and thus to separate them from the host of other relations which are left to the regulation of the market or the family or of other determinants.

This was precisely the intention of the government in dealing with rent restriction. It proposed to increase the supply of accommodation to let on the one hand, and rearrange the demand on the other. The result, it was hoped, would establish balance.

The balance was not necessarily the legal balance of equality as between landlord and tenant. Rather, the purpose was to restore or create the desired state of affairs as regards rented housing. Three separate factors necessitated activity. There had been physical changes which called for action, especially the state of housing. The institutions by which collective living had been carried on, government and Parliament in their various aspects, seemed inadequate. There were changes in the appreciative aspect: the government chose to notice conditions different from those that had previously been considered: the priorities had been revised.

Circumstances in 1956 were quite different from those of 1915 when rent control was first introduced. In 1915 the scarcity appeared to be temporary, the consequence of wartime mobility and building restrictions. In 1956 the problem was seen in part as a supply and demand dilemma rapidly being put right. More important seemed the need to assure for the future that the balance could be maintained. More houses were visibly necessary to supply the increasing population. The stock had to be increased, the still usable stock had to be kept in good repair, and the unusable stock replaced. Rent control, which originally served as an emergency measure, had become a major instrument of the relations between landlord and tenant. And the light in which rent control was viewed had altered. A necessary measure in 1919 and a necessary evil in 1939, by 1956 rent control had become a positive hindrance to a suitable policy for rented housing. These transformations reflected, in part, the necessary role of human valuation as the basis of standards which regulation was to maintain.

Sir Geoffrey described the process of regulation thus:

> The engineer watches dials, each of which displays the course of some important variable, showing how closely it approximates to some desired standard or how dangerously it strays toward some critical threshold. These standards and thresholds are the settings of his system; and these signals of match and mis-match alert him to the need for regulative action. The picture serves equally well for the political governor. He too watches the course of a limited number of variables – limited by his own interests in them and further limited by the number which he can usefully attempt to watch and regulate; and he too depends on signals of match and mismatch for his guidance.
>
> The indices which the political governor watches are for the most part not mere observations of the present state of critical variables but estimates of their future course, based on his latest knowledge of them (which is usually imperfect) and worked up by a process of mental simulation. A more important difference is that half his skills consists in setting up the standards which he shall try to attain. For unlike the engineer who controls a system designed to be controllable, the politician intervenes in a system not designed by him, with the limited object of making its course even slightly more acceptable or less repugnant to his human values than it would otherwise be.

The regulator is caught in a dilemma. On the one hand 'the size and scope of things to be regulated has grown' but the capacity of political society to regulate has been eroded. The limited bases for decision-making, the numbers who must participate in the consultative process, and the speed now needed for effective action, make regulation almost impossible.

Government, Parliament and People, are always the three principal pieces of the political system's regulator. The extent to which these harmonise or dominate one another has always been a fruitful source of dispute for political scientists. There was no indication, in the debates on the 1957 Rent Act, that any reappraisal of the currently accepted notion that government was the principal regulator was called for. The Rent Act was very much a Ministry product. The combined thought of civil servants and political ministers had sorted out the priorities, the appropriate techniques, the relevance, of rent control to housing to general public policy. Under the umbrella of 'The cabinet' or 'The government' the measure ultimately produced was virtually guaranteed enactment. The pressures of Parliament, in its several parts – the two houses, the two parties, the factions within the majority party – and the people, through pressure groups, could only force alterations in the measure. As regards the 1957 Rent Act, the action and interactions of the principals in the legislative process seemed largely 'constitutional'. The study of the 1957 Rent Act revealed that many of the difficulties which political scientists had noted in a general way about the capacity and relationship between the various parts of the Government-Parliament-People regulator could be demonstrated from the operation of the parts to the legislative process on the Rent Act.

By 1956 many questions had been raised about the role of Parliament. Few then contended that Parliament could itself legislate. But Parliament was still seen as checking and revising legislation committed to it. The processes were both formal and informal. The formal processes – second reading, committee, report, third reading – both in Commons and Lords had a significance for the publicity they gave to efforts at amendment.[2] But more important, perhaps, were the government backbench pressures, both individually and through party committees, upon the government.[3] For only desertion by government MPs could, in the normal course, compel changes. But as the business of Parliament increased, and the capacity to act either formally or informally seemed to decline, the very role of Parliament as an effective part of the legislative process seemed to be called into question. Was Parliament, still, a significant institution?*

But the seeming decline of the role of Parliament produced only a relative rise in the capacity of government. Although the cabinet was seen to gain an overwhelmingly powerful position to legislate, the capacity of government to act seemed not to increase. Instead, as the concerns of government became more complex, the capacity of government to oversee its affairs reduced.[4] Successively, the chief executive (be he king or prime minister), the cabinet, the ministers, and finally the Ministries themselves, were found unable to keep control or more than a very general oversight upon their business. Government in post-second world war Britain, has been seen, like Parliament before, hampered in its decision-making efforts by a surfeit of situations which called for decisions, and a shortage of the time and knowledge necessary to make decisions with reasonable insight.[5] The regulator received many signals, but he often lacked the

* Every book which mentions Parliament or parliamentary democracy has something to say on this splendid topic.

knowledge to sort out the signals into a meaningful pattern and could seldom settle the standards upon which action was to be taken.

Sir Geoffrey pointed out that there was

> no reason to assume that political society will prove to be regulable at any level which we would regard as acceptable. If our kind exterminates itself and leaves an earth habitable only by creatures tolerant of a high degree of radiation – cockroaches are, I believe, favoured for the succession – only a judgment which values man and his works will notice any serious discontinuity.

That man, like other species, could create institutions in one era which would prove insufficient to control the innovations of that era in the next was quite possible.

> ... We now seem to be approaching a point at which the changes generated within a single generation may render inept for the future the skills, the institutions and the images which form that generation's main legacy to posterity – and to the next generation's principal heritage.

This was the ecological trap into which political man seemed to have fallen.

Could regulation persist under these conditions? What indeed were the conditions for regulation? Sir Geoffrey suggested that these were four in number. The regulator had to be able to determine the relevant variables and have some knowledge of the patterns they would form in the future. The regulator must preserve 'sufficient constancy among its standards and priority to make a coherent response possible'. It had to have some effective tool for regulation and must be able to operate the tool as quickly as need required. Sir Geoffrey argued that aptness was not a necessary condition, or at least one that in practice could be dispensed with. But the requirements for successful regulation remained formidable.

The need to discriminate the relevant variables for regulation ought to have been simple. The main topic of rent control was privately rented housing. The providers of this form of accommodation, the stock of accommodation, and those who used it formed the groups and objects of regulation. But the regulators, be they government or Parliament, knew remarkably little about that which they proposed to regulate. Nor did this seem to be of great concern to the participants. Neither government, front or backbench, or Opposition seemed much concerned about the extent of their own ignorance. The civil service distrusted information because it tended to force conclusions on the direction in which action should be focused. The ministers distrusted the extra data demanded by social scientists because it seemed to lack relevance to their limited appreciation of the variables. Even Opposition politicians took remarkably little interest in information. They had little concrete data to support their claims of social injustice. Nor were pressure groups more helpful. Assistance, even from the professional associations, was given on matters of drafting rather than on rent control. Only the N F P O in its paper on the under-£10-valued dwellings provided any specific information on the problems to be dealt with. Indeed, it was not always evident at various stages in the debate that any of the participants had a clear conception of which variables were relevant. Certainly, there was little agreement on this. But even within each group there were different emphases. Some emphasised repairs, some capital. Some were concerned about the landlord-tenant relation, others with the landlord-property relation. Thus some thought in terms of reducing the under-occupation, while others thought of providing more accommodation to let. This was evident in the mixed bag of solutions which were finally embodied in the Rent Act (1957).

Primary responsibility for this state of ignorance lay with the government, for, in the contemporary setting, it had primary access to the relevant data. But during the planning for the Rent Act the Ministry of Housing failed to collect accurate data. There were many explanations for this failure. But at least one was the organisation for the collection of information within the Ministry. It might seem to the critical observer that failure was built into the information gathering network. Governmental failure might have been remedied, in some measure, by the activity of the party research organisations. But neither of these made any major effort to provide the data. The landlords' pressure groups and the professional associations had no reason to supply the deficiency, the first because their interest in silence coincided with the government's, the second because they would not provide information unasked outside of the technical matters of direct interest to them. All of these deficiencies would have been lessened and perhaps prevented, had the mass media – press, magazines, radio, and television – taken an interest. They neither supplied the want of information through their own efforts, nor ensured an informed public capable of asking the critical questions, of both government and Opposition, that would have elicited research efforts.

Certainly neither House of Parliament was able to supply itself with information. Whatever merits have been ascribed to the House of Lords for its expertise, housing was not a field where their lordships had any great supply of information.[6] The Commons was dependent upon independent effort. There was no committee which could balance the data from the government against information of its own devising. The parties did not supply their members with much information. Nor, interestingly enough, did the pressure groups. While these all provided suggestions, they had remarkably little new data to present. In any case, even had Parliament been provided with data, how could the material be evaluated? The inability of the Opposition to provide an effective answer to the limited data provided by the government in Cmnd 17 was merely illustrative of the incapacity of legislators to have more than a passing acquaintance with the problem they were attempting by legislation to regulate.

Sir Geoffrey suggested consistency as a necessary criterion for the evolution of standards and priorities in regulation. But was this possible in the political world? In a period of frequent alternations in power between parties with substantially different conceptions and perceptions this might, indeed, be impossible. But such was hardly the case in 1957. A single party had been in power continuously through more than one Parliament, and indeed had held the dominant position in the country since 1915 (if not earlier). Nor were the priorities of either party different in essentials. The social, economic and international position placed limits on the evolution of new patterns or priorities by any governing party. But despite these permissive conditions there was no coherence of standards and priorities either within the government or between the principal rivals for power. Housing standards had never been set on anything other than the most pragmatic basis. What the regulators – be they civil servants, government, or Opposition – had regarded as the basic standards for quality and quantity of accommodation had never been fixed separately from the economic and social problems then current. It was impossible to predict the future course of variables, for the standards upon which these would be judged were sure to require modification in the future. Nor indeed were priorities particularly clear. Was the debate between free market and control, the provision of private or public housing, or between the participation or withdrawal of government? There was never any clear perception by the participants as to priorities among these. Even Labour, with its stronger predisposition to ideology seemed, in the last analysis, unsure as to the priorities which would govern their housing policy and the place of housing policy in the overall strategy of government.

But primary responsibility for the failure to achieve consistency lay with the government and its parliamentary party. When the Conservatives returned to power in 1951 the achievement of decontrol seemed a sufficient end in itself, over a wide area of political concern. Yet coupled with it were many political commitments of a more specific nature, the products of campaign exigencies. Ministers of Housing came to office during the period prior to 1957 with only the vaguest of priorities, or with specific pledges (such as the construction of three hundred thousand houses per annum) to fulfil. No effort was made by the mass party, the parliamentary party, or the leadership to further define Conservative intentions. Thus, the initiation of policy and priorities was left to the civil service. There was some indication that the civil servants in the Housing Division did have an overall strategy, of which the 1957 Rent Act was a part. But the coherence of this strategy was limited by the civil servants themselves and by their masters. The changes in personnel within the Ministry and the shifts in responsibility meant that originally established priorities were bound to be altered to suit the personalities of those charged with implementation. Further, the priorities developed by the civil servants had to be modified in practice to meet the political requirements and limitations set down by different ministers at different times. These in turn were influenced by electoral considerations and the general state of opinion in the party and country, so that neither was a coherent set of policies and priorities in housing and rent restriction imposed by the government nor could a coherent set of policies emerge from the civil service.

The confusion over what was being regulated and by what standards it was to be regulated made the actual task all the more difficult. How then, in the absence of a clear perspective, could regulations be devised?

By 1956 Britain had had forty years of experience with rent control. Yet none of the policies devised, either for rent control in particular or housing in general, had proved totally successful. Indeed, in the matter of rent control, policies of the past seemed merely to have exacerbated current difficulties. The various forms of control and decontrol, disrepair procedures and special grants, even tax reforms, never seemed to be effective instruments to direct the supply and demand for rented accommodation. Was there ever any prospect that something could have been devised that would have proved successful to cope with the problem? Even more recent academic observers have been unable to devise any potential solution. The devices embodied in the 1965 Rent Act have yet to prove much more efficient than those of 1957.

There were many considerations, mostly political, that mitigated against any successful response to the problems of rented housing. After all, there were limits upon the range of solutions available to the government. These limits were partly party-political. The government was committed to a particular kind of decision – along lines embodied in contemporary Tory beliefs – that would restore the free market, or at least reduce government participation in the market. But the government, as it indicated during the amending process, felt unable to alienate some of those most likley to be affected (especially as these were thought to be Tory voters), merely in defence of a principle. The government felt unable to propose new techniques for control or decontrol. They proposed to rely on those devices which past experience had shown to achieve the decontrol that was sought. Yet, in the course of implementing these old techniques, modifications had to be introduced to correct the failures that past experience had revealed, such as that over disrepair procedures.

Further limitations were imposed by the political and legislative process. The government was unable to use the radical proposal of total abolition of control which would have avoided the need for parliamentary action. This was impossible because such drastic curtailment of parliamentary activity by non-parliamentary means would have excited the wrath of many parliamentarians, including Conservatives, who approved of the intentions.[7] The civil service objected on the more practical grounds that some elements of rent restriction had to be preserved. Once committed to parliamentary legislation, the government had to tailor its proposals to permit consideration within the limited time available in a parliamentary timetable. At the same time, the sensitivities of MPs had to be allowed for – despite an assured majority for the ultimate decision. Only a limited amount of parliamentary time could be spared for debate on the floor. Yet in addition the work of Standing Committee had to be limited by the timetable of the House itself.[8] When, as in the case of the Rent Act, the Opposition wished to seem obstructionist, a timetable resolution was required. Yet even the most generous government could hardly allow the Opposition to do more than seem obstructionist. There was not the time available given the press of parliamentary business, for the Opposition to carefully consider the new proposals. The forms of drafting and amending had their inevitable impact upon the original Bill and its final form in an Act. The techniques of consideration almost necessarily led to an obscure set of conclusions rather than the cohesive solution which policy seemed to demand. In short, there was no evident solution to such of the policy problems that were propounded. Even had such solutions emerged, there was some doubt whether they would have emerged in the coherent pattern which was required. The problem of rented housing had been long in emerging, but it seemed equally long in solution.

Even had it been possible to devise an effective response, could the response have been implemented in reasonable time? The history of the Passenger Acts* indicated that sixty years passed by the time all aspects of regulation had been dealt with. By that time the flood of immigrants who had precipitated the problem had largely passed. Rent control had been dealt with almost as long, with equal lack of success. But in the case of rented accommodation the nature of the problem had simply been transformed rather than passed by. Two primary questions emerged. Could effective policy have been devised and implemented in good time? Were the limits on policy such that it could not possibly be effective?

Time was particularly necessary, and lacking, for effective regulation of rented accommodation. Decisions taken had to be based on accurate estimates for ten to twenty years in advance. Yet this sort of data was lacking. The reasons were to be found in the failures of the Ministry to do research and collect data in advance of real need. The legislative process itself, once begun, was relatively rapid, lasting approximately one year from commitment to act to the introduction of the Bill for first reading. Decisions were taken too fast and too unpredictably to permit *ad hoc* research. Hence quality of thought and aptness of response depended upon past research and public discussion. If the apparatus of relevant concepts and an educated public opinion, for at least the sophisticated and knowledgeable journalists and politicians, was not available, trouble was inevitable. Only by suspending the commitment to act could the necessary information be gathered. While swift decisions could have, *per se*, no immediate impact upon the housing situation, the longer decisions

* 1800–1860.

were delayed the greater the problems to be dealt with. Very often the absence of sufficient data was seen as inevitable. In any case, there were so many problems requiring immediate regulation that the inclusion of long-term regulation in the solution of short-term problems came to be natural. By the same token, there was insufficient time to see the effect of any particular new device. Problems emerged which needed to be dealt with and time had to be taken to correct mechanical mistakes of a new solution before progressing to alternative solutions. It was always easier, both from the policy decision and legislative priority point of view, to patch than to start again. The 1957 Act was as much an attempt to correct the mistakes of 1954, the previous legislation, as an exercise in regulation. Not only did the time factors of the subject for regulation limit effective action, but time limits upon the regulator made action more difficult. These and the other factors mentioned made the task of effective legislation virtually impossible.

The legislative process upon the 1957 Rent Act was a clear example of political society in the ecological trap Sir Geoffrey described. The regulator, that is the government and Parliament, proved unable to distinguish the important variables or to correctly foresee their future course. They did not possess a coherent strategy of standards and priorities. There was no effective strategy. Circumstance and political judgment combined to deprive the regulator of time to devise a new strategy or put it into practice.

Sir Geoffrey Vickers suggested that the long time-lag between the dawn at which a problem becomes visible and the achievement of effective regulation can be accounted for, partly, as a failure of communication. The failure, he suggested, is a 'failure to maintain, within and between political societies, appropriate shared ways of distinguishing the situations in which we act, the regulations we want to regulate, the standards we need to apply and the repertory of actions which are available to us. This fabric, on which communication depends, is itself largely the product of communication'. Three aspects of communication need analysis: 1. Who defines problems? 2. Does everyone concur in the definitions and appreciations? 3. Have the problems been correctly evaluated? In sum, why were the institutions and individuals who participated in the legislative process unable to reach a working agreement?

Could there have been agreement among the participants as to the scope and nature of the problem of rented accommodation? There would have been no difficulty in a static society where the problems were familiar and visible to all. But in a complex society the relationships must be subtle. To what extent was the privately rented house considered in the context of the broader housing scene, by any of the participants? There were some hints that certain civil servants* had this overview. But certainly the particular civil servants responsible for the preparation of the Rent Act did not. Politicians, even the ministers directly responsible, looked at the Rent Bill only in part as a housing measure. Their concern was with general decontrol and an increased role for non-governmental providers of housing. They imposed the burden upon private enterprise without ever asking whether private enterprise, even with assistance, would be able to take responsibility. Nor could the pressure groups be of much assistance. First, they were not given an opportunity to participate at an early stage. But even had they been given such opportunity, their interests and skills were necessarily specialised. Each pressure group was primarily concerned with rented housing rather than with housing as a whole. The landlords and the tenants were concerned with the direct impact of the proposals upon them. The professional groups were concerned with the impact upon them as mediators between regulator and subjects of regulation. None had expertise with the whole range of housing. None had solutions for the general problem of provision of housing (except that they had a generally Tory outlook in favour of private enterprise). The more subtle relationships that affected rented accommodation were never revealed. Even ten years later new aspects of the whole problem were being revealed which placed totally different complexions upon the setting for regulation.

The legislative process and attitudes towards it were ill-designed to bring these problems into perspective. Government proved unable to sort out the problems of rent control. But whatever solutions government produced were not subject to effective review by either pressure group or Parliament, party or private member. Parliament, so long as it was prepared to maintain the government in power, could apply only moral pressure in policy questions.[9] In matters such as rent control there were no pre-existing limits beyond which the government could not hope to carry the House of Commons. For in the absence of a settled national opinion, the House had no basis for

---

* Messrs Wilkinson and Symon. Both left the Ministry before detailed preparation of the Bill began.

judgment. None of the formal stages of parliamentary consideration aided the House as a whole or any of its members in an evaluation of the relevance of government activity. For most of these stages were taken up with a dispute whose real significance was often seen as either procedural or electoral. The Opposition intended to 'play the game' by making passage difficult. They also hoped to reap electoral profit from their opposition. They saw their opposition as only marginally constructive, and their arguments, even the valid ones, were seen in the same light by government. So long as the Opposition could not persuade the government, and the requirements of the constitution made force impossible, the government's majority was assured. Nor did the parliamentary process give more weight to individual opinion, even that of government supporters. Party policy was necessarily either very general, in favour of free enterprise, or very specific, demanding the construction of three hundred thousand houses per annum. The mass party did not attempt to deal with the problem of rent control as such, as part of the general policy about housing. The research departments could provide such information, and often had ideas about housing policy, but were given little opportunity to participate. The individual member might make representations on particular points, especially where a constituency interest was involved. But these necessarily came too late to affect general policy. Nor indeed, however hard they pressed, could individual members persuade their own government to abandon an announced policy because of the electoral consequences. These had been discounted, however inadequately, in the decision-making process. Pressure groups were in much the same position as the private member. Unless they were consulted in the preliminary decision-making process, they could not hope to influence the principles of legislation. They too could affect only the details. The legislative process buried policy questions in the formalism of debate and party competition. Simplicity of problem and ease of solution were necessary to allow Parliament to appear to give consideration to legislation. The legislative process could not cope with the complex problems which legislation was designed to regulate.

Even about the most fundamental details there was no agreed appreciation. Sir Geoffrey Vickers pointed out how difficult this is, of necessity: 'the situation to which the policy-maker attends is not a datum but a construct. It has to be simplified or it becomes unmanageable. ... It has to reflect present and future reality. ...'

K

Especially in the field of rent control, where the basic material for the construct was itself vague, different constructs were likely to emerge. In fact, as was indicated, not merely did these follow party lines but group lines as well. Two successive ministers had quite different impressions of the causes and consequences of the Bill for which they both claimed responsibility. Their impressions coincided with but were not identical to the view held by their civil servants, and backbench members of their party. An alternative construct, though similar in some details, was presented by the Labour Party. This too was presented in many variations. What was lacking was any agreement on how the situation to be dealt with could be most usefully regarded. There was no agreement on which of the complex relations were the most significant.

The consequence of confusion was that there could be no opportunity to evaluate programmes. 'Action now,' Sir Geoffrey pointed out, 'may not serve any policy at all. It may be historically caused, it may be self-perpetuating, it may serve some long-abandoned purpose. . . .' What indeed was the purpose of the Rent Act? The evidence on its consequences showed that it was very much the product of the past. It failed to deal with the contemporary realities, the pockets of scarcity – both geographical and housing type. These resulted from the extensive commitment of the government to housing through policies not directly classed as housing policies, and the Conservative Party's commitment to disengage government as much as possible in spheres where private enterprise had traditionally played the dominant part – ignoring the fact that the role of private enterprise or its capacity to act might have been severely curtailed. But the Labour response was no better. Once the government had succeeded in mobilising support, internally, and with pressure groups, press, and public, to take action on rent control there was no escape. Political sense dictated action in the first half of the Parliament to avoid any possible electoral repercussions. Once the decision was taken to act, there was remarkably little time to plan precisely the form action should take. First decisions generated subsequent decisions. Except for the pre-planning, however little, that had gone on within the Ministry by civil servants, decisions had to be taken in the shortest possible time. The future was not the life of the relations being regulated but the political events leading to the next general election. It was not housing considerations that mattered but rather parliamentary procedural considerations, however irrelevant those might be to the facts of government, the position of the majority party and the dominant role of the cabinet. The relevant relations were those between Conservative and Labour Party.

Parties are necessarily concerned with public opinion and elections. Bagehot feared that universal suffrage would mean that the ignorant masses would dictate the direction of legislation.[10] In fact, experience seems to show that parties are not dictated to by public opinion. Rather, the parties make electoral gestures in order to sway public opinion.[11] Concessions to government backbenchers, especially the delay in transition to decontrol, could be viewed in this light. Similarly, Professor Crick suggests that debates in Parliament should be viewed as electoral efforts.[12] Certainly the government can be assured of its majority in all but the most abnormal circumstances. Having obtained some concessions that seemed electorally desirable, the backbenchers rightly allowed the government to justify the Bill to the country. The Opposition was in a more difficult position. It was hard to make opposition to details comprehensible to the public. The failure of the Labour Party to devise an effective alternative policy, i.e. the failure of municipalisation as a generally acceptable alternative, made effective opposition difficult. In the short run at the least, the government was able to make the public believe in the efficacy of action while the Opposition was unable to prove its superior capacity if given power.

No longer do students of British politics assign the function of legislation to Parliament, or to any mystical formulation including Parliament. Primary responsibility is now normally seen as residing within the executive, political and civil service. Almost all the theories on the current role of Parliament are variations on communications theories. Only gradually are the essential communications nets – those within the executive and those between the executive and its parliamentary party – being opened to view. But it is already evident that it is the process of communication, of which decision-making is a part, that can provide clues for the philosopher concerned with the nature and stability of British politics. In the absence of greater detail, conclusions must necessarily be limited.

It was evident that at least as regards the 1957 Rent Act the legislative process led Britain into an ecological trap. The institution and the participants proved unable to cope with the requirements of the situation which needed regulation. The government did not have enough information even about the limited range of problems and relations with which the politicians proposed to concern themselves. They certainly never appreciated the range of problems with which they ought to have dealt if an effective solution was to be achieved. There was never any single clear-cut standard by which housing policies should be judged. More important, there was never any evaluation of the priorities of housing and the various pieces of housing policy. The alternation of time-worn techniques of control and decontrol served as the dominant theme of privately rented housing. A hope and a prayer were too often the substitutes (admitted) for a regulation whose need was accepted. The legislative process made possible no clear perception of the future and discouraged any effort to deal with more than the most immediate of present problems. This was largely a matter of an existing pattern of legislation and legislators no longer able to cope with the rapidly changing world and the far-reaching decisions required of it. This applied as much to the executive as to Parliament.

The failure of the political system was both a cause and consequence of inadequate communications. Institutions and participants in the legislative process geared to contemporary requirements *might* have made possible better communication. But communication had obviously failed when no clear and generally acceptable concept of the problems and solutions possible had emerged. In part, the communications difficulty was the continuity of conventional wisdom. The condition had not yet arrived when, as Sir Geoffrey desired: '. . . we have reached the end of ideology . . . it is not because we can do without ideologies but because we should now know enough about them to show a proper respect for our neighbour's [ideology] and a proper sense of responsibility for our own'. Neither of the alternatives which passed for ideologies in the two major parties provided the basis for effective communication. In the absence of direction, decision-makers at all levels wandered aimlessly, unable to choose definitively between alternate solutions or to demand still further possible solutions. Effective regulation became, for that moment at least, impossible.

NOTES

1 Sir Geoffrey Vickers, 'The Regulation of Political Systems' (a public lecture at the London School of Economics and Political Science on 22 November 1966). The quotations and ideas attributed to Sir Geoffrey in this chapter were

drawn from a typescript copy of the lecture supplied to the Politics Department of the L S E by Sir Geoffrey. This essay has now been published as chapter 4, 'Limits of Regulation', in Sir Geoffrey Vickers', *Value Systems and Social Processes*, Tavistock, London, 1968.

2 Jennings, *Parliament*, Cambridge University Press, Cambridge, 1961, pp. 235 ff.

3 Crick, *The Reform of Parliament*, Weidenfeld and Nicolson, London, 1964, pp. 96 ff.; J. P. Mackintosh, *The British Cabinet*, Stevens, London, 1962, pp. 491 ff.

4 Crick, *The Reform of Parliament*, pp. 37 ff.

5 *Ibid.*, pp. 76 ff.

6 *Ibid.*, pp. 100 ff. H. Burrows, 'House of Lords—Change or Decay', *Crisis in British Government*, ed. by W. J. Stankiewicz, Collier-Macmillan, London, 1967, pp. 100 ff.

7 G. Marshall and G. Moodie, *Some Problems of the Constitution*, Hutchison, London, 1964, pp. 110 ff.

8 See Lord Morrison of Lambeth, *Government and Parliament*, Oxford Paperbacks, London, 1964, pp. 244 ff.

9 Mackintosh, *The British Cabinet*, pp. 489 ff.

10 W. Bagehot, *The English Constitution*, Doubleday, New York, n.d., pp. 10 ff.

11 See R. Rose, *Studies in British Politics*, Macmillan, London, 1966, pp. 314 ff.

12 Crick, *The Reform of Parliament*, p. 193.

# Bibliography

## Papers

British Institute of Public Opinion
Chartered Auctioneers' and Estate Agents' Institute
Citizens' Advice Bureaux
Conservative Research Department
Conservative and Unionist Central Office
The Labour Party
The London Labour Party
Ministry of Housing and Local Government
National Federation of Property Owners
Royal Institution of Chartered Surveyors

## Official Publications

### Parliamentary Proceedings

*Parliamentary Debates* (Hansard), 5th Series
House of Commons Debates, vols 560–7
House of Lords Debates, vols 203–4
House of Commons Standing Committee Debates, vol. I, 1956–7
    session
*Minutes of Proceedings, Standing Committee A* (*The Rent Bill*)
    H C 109 (1956–7), House of Commons Papers
*Supplement to the Vote*, 1956–7 Session (Sessional Order Papers)

### Departmental Annual Reports

Ministry of Housing and Local Government,
*Report of the Ministry of Housing and Local Government for the Period
    1950/51 to 1954*, Cmd 9559 (1955)
*Report of the Ministry of Housing and Local Government for the Year
    1955*, Cmd 9876 (1956)

*Report of the Ministry of Housing and Local Government for the Year
1956,* Cmnd 193 (1957)
*Report of the Ministry of Housing and Local Government 1957,* Cmnd
419 (1958)

## *Parliamentary Papers*

Scotland,
*Departmental Committee Report, 1914–16,* Cd 8111, xxv, I (Hunter,
ch.)
Committee,
*Report (Rent and Mortgage Interest (War Restrictions) Acts), 1918,*
Cd 9235, xii, 73 (Hunter, ch.)
Committee,
*Report (Rent and Mortgage Interest (War Restrictions) Acts), 1920,*
Cmd 958, xviii, 315 (Ld Salisbury, ch.)
Departmental Committee,
*Report (Increase of Rent and Mortgage Interest (Restrictions) Act,
1920), 1923,* Cmd 1803, xii, pt II, 517 (Ld Onslow, ch.)
Committee,
*Report (Rent Restriction Acts) 1924–35,* Cmd 2423, xv, 517 (Constable, ch.)
Ministry of Health, Inter-Departmental Committee,
*Report (Rent Restriction Acts), 1930–31,* Cmd 3911, xvii, 281 (Ld
Marley, ch.)
Inter-Departmental Committee,
*Report (Rent Restriction Acts), 1937–38,* Cmd 5621, xv, 217 (Ld
Ridley, ch.)
*Government Policy on Rent Restriction, 1937–38,* Cmd 5667, xxi,
1017
Inter-Departmental Committee,
*Report (Rent Control), 1944–45,* Cmd 6621, v, 499 (Ld Ridley, ch.)
*Houses: The Next Step, 1953–4,* Cmd 8996, xxvi, I
*Rent Control: Statistical Information,* Cmnd 17 (1956)
*Report of the Committee on Housing in Greater London,* Cmd 2605
(1965) (Milner Holland, ch.)
P. C. Gray and E. Parr,
*Ministry of Housing and Local Government, The Rent Act, 1957,
Report of Inquiry,* Cmnd 1246 (1960)

## Other Publications

Ministry of Labour,
*1953–54 Household Expenditure: Report of an Enquiry into Household Expenditure*, Non-Parliamentary Papers, 1957

Louis Moss,
*The Social Survey in the Government Process*, Unpublished evidence submitted by the Social Survey to the Heyworth Committee

## Contemporary Pamphlets

Block, G. D. M.,
*Developments in Rent Control Between 1915 and 1955*, Conservative Research Department (Doc. P H C 55C2) (mimeo.), London, 1955

Chartered Auctioneers' and Estate Agents' Institute,
*Memorandum on the Amendment of the Rent Restriction Acts*, C A E A I, London, 1952

Conservative Research Department,
*Notes on Current Politics*
*Rent Control, Housing Policy and the New Rent Bill*, C R D, London, 9 November 1956 (Doc. P H C 56 (4), mimeo.)
*The Campaign Guide*, C U C O, London, 1959

Cooperative Party National Committee,
*Rent Control, Special Report*, 'Issued by the National Committee of the Cooperative Party, February 1953'
*Special Reports, 2. Rent Control – A Supplementary Statement*, 'Issued by the National Committee of the Cooperative Party', January 1954

Eversley, D.,
*Rents and Social Policy*, 'Fabian Research Series', no. 174, Fabian Society, London, 1955

Howe, G. and Jones C.,
*Houses to Let*, Conservative Political Centre (for Bow Group), London, 1956

The Labour Party,
*Agenda for the Fifty-Second Annual Conference of the Labour Party ...*, The Labour Party, London, 1953
*Agenda for the Fifty-Third Annual Conference of the Labour Party ...*, The Labour Party, London, 1954

*Agenda for the Fifty-Fourth Annual Conference of the Labour Party . . .,*
   The Labour Party, London, 1955
*Agenda for the Fifty-Fifth Annual Conference of the Labour Party . . .,*
   The Labour Party, London, 1956
*Agenda for the Fifty-Sixth Annual Conference of the Labour Party . . .,*
   The Labour Party, London, 1957.
*Homes of the Future,* The Labour Party, London, 1956
*Report of the Fifty-Fifth Annual Conference of the Labour Party . . .,*
   The Labour Party, London, 1956.

London County Council,
*Metropolitan Borough Elections* (Returns), L C C, nos 3819, 3939,
   4069
*General Election of County Councillors,* L C C, nos 3896, 4008, 4127

London Labour Party,
*Report of the London Labour Party, 1954* (and also 1955, 1956, 1957),
   London Labour Party, years as above

London Trades Council (1952),
*Annual Report for the Year 1956,* L T C, 1956
*Annual Report for the Year 1957,* L T C, 1957

MacColl, J.,
*A Plan for Rented Houses,* 'Fabian Research Series', no. 192, The
   Fabian Society, London, 1957
*Plan for Housing,* 'Fabian Research Series', no. 164, The Fabian
   Society, London, 1954

Munby, D. L.,
*The Rent Problem,* 'Fabian Research Series', no. 151, The Fabian
   Society, London, 1952

National Union of Conservative and Unionist Associations,
*Seventy-Third Annual Conference, Programme of Proceedings,*
   N U C U A, London, 1953
*Seventy-Fourth Annual Conference, Programme of Proceedings,*
   N U C U A, London, 1954.
*Seventy-Fifth Annual Conference, Programme of Proceedings,*
   N U C U A, London, 1955
*Seventy-Sixth Annual Conference, Programme of Proceedings,*
   N U C U A, London, 1956
*Seventy-Seventh Annual Conference, Programme of Proceedings,*
   N U C U A, London, 1957
*Seventy-Sixth Annual Conference, Report,* N U C U A, London, 1956.

Joseph Rowntree Voluntary Trust,
*Memorandum on the 'Housing and Rents' Study* (Dated 10 March 1958) (mimeo.)

The Royal Institution of Chartered Surveyors,
*A Memorandum on Rent Restriction and the Repairs Problem*, R I C S, London, 1951

Trade Union Congress,
*Report of Proceedings at the Eighty-Sixth Annual Trade Union Congress*, T U C, London, 1954
*Report of Proceedings at the Eighty-Seventh Annual Trade Union Congress*, T U C, London, 1955
*Report of Proceedings at the Eighty-Eighth Annual Trade Union Congress*, T U C, London, 1956
*Report of Proceedings at the Eighty-Ninth Annual Trade Union Congress*, T U C, London, 1957

## Newspapers
### National

The *Daily Express*  
The *Daily Herald*  
The *Daily Mail*  
The *Daily Mirror*  
The *Daily Telegraph*  
The *Daily Worker*  

The *Manchester Guardian*  
The *News Chronicle*  
The *Observer*  
The *Sunday Pictorial*  
The *Sunday Times*  
The *Times*  

### Local

The *Aberdare Leader*  
The *Acton Gazette and West London Post*  
The *Aldershot News*  
The *Bedford Record*  
The *Bedfordshire Times*  
The *Birmingham Mail*  
The *Birmingham Post*  
The *Bolton Evening News*  
The *Brighton Gazette*  
The *Bristol Evening Post*  
The *Bucks. Examiner*  
The *Cardigan and Tivy-Side Advertiser*

The *Chatham Observer*
The *Chester Chronicle*
The *Citizen*
The *Clapham Observer*
The *Clitheroe Advertiser and Times*
The *Croydon Advertiser*
The *Croydon Times*
The *Daily Record* (Glasgow)
The *Derbyshire Times*
The *Dorset Daily Echo*
The *East Anglian Daily Times* (Ipswich)
The *East Grinstead Observer*
The *Evening Argus*
The *Express and Star* (Wolverhampton)
The *Flintshire Advertiser*
The *Gravesend and Dartford Reporter*
The *Guardian-Journal*
The *Hackney Gazette*
The *Hampstead and Highgate Express*
The *Hants. and Sussex Times*
The *Harwich and Dovercourt Standard*
The *Hastings and St Leonard's Observer*
The *Hendon and Finchley Times*
The *Henley Standard*
The *Herts. Advertiser*
The *Islington Gazette*
The *Kent Messenger*
The *Kentish Independent*
The *Kentish Mercury*
The *Leicester Evening Mail*
The *Lincolnshire Echo*
The *Morecambe and Heysham Times*
The *Manchester Evening News*
The *Newcastle Journal*
The *Northamptonshire Evening Telegraph*
The *Nottingham Evening Post*
The *Nottingham News*
The *Oldham Chronicle*
The *Romford Times*
The *Salisbury Times*

The *Scotsman*
The *Sheffield Telegraph*
The *Shrewsbury Chronicle*
The *Sidcup and Kentish Times*
The *Somerset County Gazette*
The *South London Observer*
The *South London Press*
The *South Wales Argus*
The *South-Wales Echo-Evening Express*
The *South Western Star*
The *Stratford Express*
The *Streatham News*
The *Stockport Express*
The *Sunderland Echo*
The *Surrey Advertiser*
The *Surrey Cosit*
The *Surrey Times*
The *Taunton Herald*
The *Telegraph and Argus* (Bradford)
The *Walsall Observer*
The *Waterloo and Crosby Times*
The *Western Evening Herald*
The *Western Gazette*
The *West London Observer*
The *Wiltshire News*
The *Wood Green, Southgate and Palmers Green Weekly Herald*

## Magazines

*The Chartered Surveyor*
*The Economist*
*The Estates Gazette*
*The Journal of the Chartered Auctioneers' and Estate Agents' Institute*
*Labour Organizer*
*The Listener*
*Londoner*
*The Municipal Journal*
*The Municipal Review*
*The New Statesman and Nation*
*Planning*

*The Primrose League Gazette*
*Property*
*The Real Estate Journal*
*Talking Points*
*The Spectator*

## Secondary Sources

### Books

Allen, C. K., *Law and Orders*, Stevens, London, 1956.

Bagehot, W., *The English Constitution*, Doubleday, New York, no date.

Bailey, S. D., *British Parliamentary Democracy*, Harrap, London, 1962.

Bealey, F., Blondel, J. and McCann, W. P., *Constituency Politics*, Faber, 1966.

Beer, S. H., *British Politics in the Collectivist Age*, Knopf, New York, 1965. (US edition of *Modern British Politics*.)

Bevins, R., *The Greasy Pole*, Hodder and Stoughton, London, 1965.

Brittan, S., *The Treasury Under the Tories, 1951–1964*, Penguin, London, 1964.

Butler, D. E., *The British General Election of 1955*, Macmillan, London, 1956.

Butler, D. E. and Rose, R., *The British General Election of 1959*, Macmillan, London, 1960.

Butt, Ronald, *Power of Parliament*, Constable, London, 1968.

Campion, ed., *Parliament: A Survey*, Allen and Unwin, London, 1947.

Chih-Mai Chen, *Parliamentary Opinion of Delegated Legislation*, Columbia University Press, New York, 1933.

Cole, G. D. H., *Building and Planning*, Cassell, London, 1945.

Crick, B., *The Reform of Parliament*, Weidenfeld and Nicolson, London, 1964.

Cullingworth, J. B., *Housing in Transition*, Heinemann, London, 1963.

—— *Housing Needs and Planning Policy*, Routledge and Kegan Paul, London, 1961.

Dicey, A. V., *Introduction to the Study of the Law of the Constitution*, St Martin's Press, New York, 1961.

Donnison, D. V., *The Government of Housing*, Penguin, London, 1967.

Dowse, R. E., *The Left in the Centre*, Longmans, London, 1966.

Eckstein, H., *Pressure Group Politics: The Case of the British Medical Association*, Allen and Unwin, London, 1960.

Epstein, L. D., *British Politics in the Suez Crisis*, Pall Mall, London, 1964.

Finer, S. E., Berrington, H. B. and Bartholomew, D. J., *Backbench Opinion in the House of Commons*, Pergamon, London, 1962.

Griffith, J. A. G., *Central Departments and Local Authorities*, Allen and Unwin, London, 1966.

Guttsman, W., *The British Political Elite*, MacGibbon and Kee, London, 1963.

Herbert, A. P., *Independent Member*, Methuen, London, 1950.

Jennings, W. I., *Cabinet Government*, Cambridge University Press, Cambridge, 1961.

—— *Parliament*, Cambridge University Press, Cambridge, 1961.

Kersell, J. E., *Parliamentary Supervision of Delegated Legislation*, Stevens, London, 1960.

Viscount Kilmuir, *Political Adventure*, Weidenfeld and Nicolson, London, 1954.

MacDonagh, O., *A Pattern of Government Growth, 1800–1860*, MacGibbon and Kee, London, 1961.

McKenzie, R. T., *British Political Parties*, Mercury Books, London, 1964.

Mackintosh, J. P., *The British Cabinet*, Stevens, London, 1962.

Marshall, G. and Moodie, G., *Some Problems of the Constitution*, Hutchison, London, 1964.

Lord Morrison of Lambeth, *Government and Parliament*, Oxford Paperbacks, London, 1964.

Mowat, C. L., *Britain Between the Wars*, Methuen, London, 1955.

Needleman, L., *The Economics of Housing*, Staples Press, London, 1965.

Nevitt, A. A. *Housing, Taxation and Subsidies*, Nelson, London, 1966.

Rose, R., *Influencing Voters*, Faber, London, 1967.

—— *Studies in British Politics*, Macmillan, London, 1966.

Sampson, A., *Anatomy of Britain*, Hodder and Stoughton, London, 1962.

Sisson, C. H., *The Spirit of British Public Administration*, Faber, London, 1959.

Stankiewicz, W. J. ed., *Crisis in British Government*, Collier-Macmillan, London, 1967.

Taylor, A. J. P., *English History: 1914–1945*, Oxford University Press, London, 1966.
Vickers, C. G., *The Art of Judgment*, Chapman and Hall, London, 1965.
de Visscher, P., *Democratie Anglaise* . . . Casterman, Paris, 1947.
Wendt, P. F., *Housing Policy – The Search for Solutions*, University of California Press, Berkeley, 1963.
Wilson, H. H., *Pressure Group: The Campaign for Commercial Television*, Secker and Warburg, London, 1961.
Wood, J., *A Nation Not Afraid, The Thinking of Enoch Powell*, Batsford, London, 1965.

## Pamphlets

Block, G. D. M., *Rents in Perspective*, Conservative Political Centre, London, 1961.
Cullingworth, J. B., *English Housing Trends*, 'Occasional Papers in Social Administration', no. 13, Bell, London, 1965.
Donnison, D. V., *Housing Policy Since the War*, OPSA no. 1, Condicote Press, Welwyn, 1960.
Donnison, D, V., Cockburn, C. and Corlett T., *Housing Since the Rent Act*, OPSA no. 3, Condicote Press, Welwyn, 1961.
Donnison, D. V. *et al.*, *Essays on Housing*, OPSA no. 9, Bell, London, 1964.
Greve, J., *London's Homeless*, OPSA no. 10, Bell, London, 1964.
—— *The Private Landlord in England*, OPSA no. 16, Bell, London, 1965.
Sharpe, L. J., *A Metropolis Votes*, Greater London Papers, LSE, London, 1962.
Wheatley, J., *Houses to Let*, The Labour Party, London, no date.

## Journal Articles and Addresses

Beer, S. H., 'Treasury Control: The Coordination of Financial Policy in Great Britain', *American Political Science Review*, XLIX, pp. 144–60.
Howard, A. 'Behind the Bureaucratic Curtain', *The New York Times Magazine*, 23 October 1966.
Neustadt, R. E., 'White House and Whitehall', 'Prepared for Delivery at the 1965 Meeting of the American Political Science Association . . .' (Washington: APSA, 1965, mimeo.).

Rose, S., 'Policy Decision in Opposition', *Political Studies*, June 1956, pp. 128–38, and rejoinder by R. T. McKenzie, pp. 176–82.

Sharp, E., 'Housing: The Past Ten Years', *The Chartered Surveyor*, December 1956, pp. 295 ff.

Vickers, C. G., 'The Regulation of Political Systems', A Public Lecture at the London School of Economics and Political Science on 22 November 1966, typescript.

# Index